D0065252

CHARLES H. PERCY

A Political Perspective

CHARLES H.
PERCY
A Political Perspective

by Robert E. Hartley

Rand McNally & Company   Chicago · New York · San Francisco

Library of Congress Cataloging in Publication Data

Hartley, Robert E.
    Charles H. Percy: a political perspective.

    Bibliography: p.
    Includes index.
    1. Percy, Charles H., 1919–
E840.8.P4H37   328.73'092'4 [B]   75-22320
ISBN 0-528-81018-9

First printing, 1975

B
PERCY
H

CONTENTS

To Mary,
who knew it could be done

FOREWORD

If any U.S. senator is to be remembered beyond his days of service, it will be because he has been significantly involved with the events of his time. Many will be raised to prominence by this interaction; others will be ruined by it.

History has recognized some senators more than others. Lyndon B. Johnson would have been remembered just for his achievement in the Senate. But John F. Kennedy and Harry S. Truman have a place in history that is due to their rise to the presidency rather than to their Senate careers.

Charles H. Percy is looking for the opportunities that could make a special place for him in history. From the beginning of his political career, he seemed to be aiming for a try at the presidency. His comments on the great issues of the day—such as Indochina, Watergate, the Middle East, and the domestic economy—have gained him nationwide recognition. And his aborted foray into the presidential arena in 1973-74 may be indicative of his future ambitions. It is important to understand a man who has moved into the forefront of national affairs.

This biography attempts to give the reader an insight into Charles Percy's politics. It is a modern-day story that recognizes Percy as a person of achievement and attempts to analyze the merits of the work of a man who has sought a national constituency rather than restricting his service or interest to Illinois. This comprehensive approach to his Senate job creates problems for him with his electorate, and this dilemma is a major part of his story.

The book also discusses the events that have surrounded Percy during his political career and shows how he was shaped by them. Without this perspective the story would be little more than an exercise in probing the Percy veneer. Through Percy we gain a glimpse of how the leaders of the Republican party react to fears, threats, major events, crises, and challenges. This is particularly important at a time when the national Republican party has again fallen on hard times. We see the jealousies that direct relationships. We witness the Illinois Republican party struggling with its identity and fighting a continual war with its senior senator. The situation is not unique; similar battles rage in many states.

The writing of this book presented one problem that is worth discussing

7

—defining the political terms that describe philosophy or ideology. A conscious effort was made to use the words "liberal" or "conservative" or "moderate" only within an established framework. If another more-descriptive word better suited the purpose, it was used. In the chapter on Percy's involvement with the Illinois Republican party, for example, the word "traditionalist" seemed more appropriate because so much of the state party heritage is built on tradition rather than on any definable and durable political philosophy. But on the national level, the situation is different. Here the liberalism and conservatism of many politicians are more obvious, and these terms were used to reflect their positions on national issues and theories of government.

The most illusive aspect of analyzing Percy's political life was to determine his position on the philosophical spectrum. Is he a liberal or a moderate or a conservative? Perhaps the chapter that reveals the most about his approach to issues and the depth of his thinking is the one that explores his association with Richard M. Nixon. Theirs was a relationship that grew, faded, and eventually died in their various confrontations on national issues. However, Percy's political philosophy is also revealed throughout the book in the discussions of his loyalty to the party, his sincerity on issues, and his relationships with other public officials. The Charles Percy of this book is a man easily admired by some and quickly condemned by others. When a final chapter is written on the public life of Charles H. Percy—and that promises to be well in the future—it may be, as this book reveals, more a tale of how he saw events and reacted to them rather than how he directly altered them.

Many people have contributed immeasurably to this book. Paul Simon, now a U.S. representative from Illinois, was especially kind and encouraging to a first-time author. His early counsel was vital.

My gratitude goes to Hal B. Neitzel for his comfort and suggestions. Our brainstorming sessions, week after week, were important to the development of the material. Many colleagues with expertise in Illinois and national politics unselfishly provided observations, criticism, recollections, clippings from personal files, and even sympathy when needed. Of this group, my special thanks go to Robert Reid and Robert W. Sink.

I am indebted to archivist Ralph McCann for his assistance in researching the files of the Dwight D. Eisenhower Library. Joseph A. Farrell and Calvin Fentress of the Percy staff answered dozens of nuts-and-bolts questions. The accommodating workers in the *Decatur Herald and Review* newspaper library deserve special thanks.

Someday I will think of words to express my appreciation to Mary Hartley.

Robert E. Hartley

CHAPTER I

THE YOUNG MAN FROM BELL & HOWELL

Throughout his political career Charles Percy seldom has worried about obscurity. Percy's national visibility undoubtedly has something to do with his storybook rise to the top of the business world before reaching the age of 30. Some observers ascribe his success to his good looks. Others say it is a combination of a too-good-to-be-true personal life, handsome children, an ability to rebound from tragedy, and the aura of mystery surrounding a moderate politician trying to make it big in the party of conservatism.

There are also other factors, such as the people with whom a public official is acquainted, the issues on which he carefully chooses to speak, and the degree to which he is willing to chase the media without appearing overly aggressive. Call it timing or planning or orchestration. Don't call it luck. A senator who courts a national image cannot leave much to chance.

But these are cosmetics, and few persons rise to national prominence and stay there without something else going for them. In Percy's case the drive has been there, the determination to pursue the opportunities. Those attempting to defame Percy have labeled him an opportunist, with all the negative connotations of the word they can muster. Without question Percy is an opportunist, and his career is dotted with situations in which he saw an opportunity and took it.

Charles Harting Percy is not everyone's ideal average American. His business career successes at an early age propelled him into the world of high finance and brought him in contact with the top-level executives of domestic and international commerce. He acquired a family—two, in fact—through all of that and more than a normal share of tragedy. Instead of laboring in the vineyards of politics by running for a series of minor offices and finally reaching the top, Percy started at the pinnacle.

His life is the dream of social climbers. He lived among the cream of Chicago society and then moved to the headwaters of national and international society in Washington, D.C. There he and his wife, Loraine, sit down to dinner with people who are familiar around the world from headlines, gossip columns, and television screens. He knows Rockefellers and Eisenhowers and Kissingers intimately. He is friendly with other important people whose names are unknown to most citizens but whose influence is legend. He enjoys the friendship of Indira Gandhi of India and is acquainted with other heads of state.

To the public the most interesting aspects of the senator's life are his family and his money. This is because of the obvious interest of people in the children and background of those in public life and the focus in recent years on the personal finances of officials and the sources of their money. Percy has a large and visible family, some of whom have become public persons in their own right. His millionaire status and his wife's substantial financial holdings enable them to obtain the trappings of wealth and make them vulnerable to the fears and concerns of the wealthy.

Loraine Percy has said frequently that her husband's life story "sounds like a soap opera." Stories of his early life, chronicled in books and magazine articles, do not vary in retelling. In 1964, Time magazine, having "discovered" Percy when he was a candidate for governor of Illinois, used its characteristically breathless prose to picture the dashing young man for its readers:

"Chuck Percy really looks and acts the part of the Algeresque hero.... He has frank brown eyes, a frank, open face, a trim, exercise-toned body. ...He is hard-working, fun-loving, self-disciplined and perfectly organized. He reads deep-think books, takes religion, politics and self-improvement seriously.... He neither smokes nor drinks."

Although some more-recent accounts have been less effusive, the same conclusions often are reached. But as writers have grown more cynical and readers more suspicious of overly righteous public officials, the basic background story often is sprinkled with adjectives that attempt to describe his less-flattering characteristics. He is occasionally viewed as a phony, an opportunist, a "Mr. Prissy." Dozens of descriptive terms—such as too stuffy, indifferent to the problems of constituents, wishy-washy, naive, too rich, insincere—have been purposely used to put a wink in the Percy story. There have been some minor changes in his personality, but Percy's character remains essentially the same. Thus, it is possible for those who know him to make an accurate assessment. One person who has done just that is Mrs. Vivian Jacobson of Chicago, a longtime volunteer worker for Percy and confidante of the family. In her analysis Percy is "not a believable man for our times. People don't want someone in public life who holds to basic Christian ethics and has a totally positive viewpoint about life. They think something is wrong with him."

Charles Harting Percy was born on September 27, 1919, in Pensacola, Florida. When he was an infant, the family moved to Rogers Park on the North Side of Chicago. From that point on, Chicago was "home." His parents, Edward H. and Elisabeth Harting Percy, had two other children. A daughter, Doris, was born in 1920, and a son, Howard, in 1921. (Doris is married and lives with her husband, Robert Strauss, and their four children in Perrysburg, Ohio, near Toledo. A self-employed municipal bond salesman, Howard, with his wife, Rowena, and their three children, resides in Ladue, Missouri.)

Until the Depression, Percy's father worked as a cashier in the Rogers Park National Bank in Chicago. The job provided nicely for the middle-class family, but in the thick of the Depression, Edward Percy lost his job when the bank failed. Charles Percy was 15 years old at the time. Because of a state law that made stockholders in a bank liable for the depositors' money, Edward Percy eventually was forced into bankruptcy. He had a small amount of bank stock and became personally liable for a part of the bank's debt.

After that, life turned increasingly difficult for the Percys. Edward Percy worked at a variety of jobs, including selling cars and insurance. The family moved to Wilmette, a suburb of Chicago, in 1935, where Mr. Percy worked as manager of a paint store, until he lost his job to a younger man who was willing to work for half of Percy's pay. For a time the family lived on Edward Percy's relief checks, and young Charles contributed to the support of the family by working at odd jobs when not attending school. The work did not interfere with young Percy's schooling. He attended Sullivan High School, in Rogers Park, for his first two years of high school and New Trier High School for his last two years. Meanwhile, Edward Percy found a job as a night clerk in a cheap hotel. Charles Percy recalls that his father worked seven days a week and 12 hours a day for $35 a week. He has always felt that the long hours were "injurious to his [father's] health," and the recollection of the family's life during this period is an emotional experience for Senator Percy today.

With the family continuing to have financial problems, young Percy asked Joseph McNabb, his Sunday-school teacher at the Wilmette First Church of Christ Scientist, if he could find a daytime job for his father. McNabb—then president of Bell & Howell, a Chicago-based camera-equipment firm—hired the elder Percy as an accountant for $35 a week, the same pay he had earned in the hotel. Edward Percy worked at Bell & Howell until he retired as office manager in 1957. He died two years later when he was 75.

In his book about the problems of the elderly, *Growing Old in the Country of the Young* (published in 1974), Senator Percy talks about the difficulty his father had finding work during the Depression. Percy recalls his father writing to more than 50 companies for employment, only to be repeatedly told that he was too old. Mr. Percy was in his 40s at the time. In Percy's early campaigns for public office, he often referred to his family life and the Depression difficulties. He has remarked frequently that he was greatly affected by the experience of seeing his father out of work or working at menial and exhausting jobs. A lengthy interview with Percy can hardly pass without his recalling some experience from his teenage years during the Depression. As traumatic as this time may have been for the Percys, millions of Americans survived those years under much worse circumstances.

The Percys were far from being down and out. They were proud and fairly comfortable, considering the times. Percy remembers his father's southern heritage and points out that he came from "landed gentry." He believes that his father's background plus his mother's appreciation of culture and the arts helped the family get through the difficult years.

Mrs. Elisabeth Percy is an accomplished violinist, and she saw to it that music was a part of the lives of her children. Percy learned to play the piano and the clarinet. In her 81st year Mrs. Percy was playing in the Evanston Symphony Orchestra.

Early in life Percy displayed the initiative that has become such an important part of his story. Even as a child he seemed driven to achieve. Percy was motivated by a desire to earn money, help his family, and be considered dependable. If there was time left, he played with other children. His mother does not believe this pattern of behavior hurt her son one bit.

His early years are filled with examples of his initiative. Percy's mother confirms that her eldest son sold subscriptions to *Country Gentleman* magazine at the age of five and won an award from the publisher for selling more copies than any other urban salesman in the United States. During the Depression Percy sold his mother's cookies door-to-door to help earn money to meet the family's needs.

In 1937 Percy entered the University of Chicago on a scholarship that paid half his tuition. He worked his way through college by engaging in a variety of activities, some of which earned him large sums of money for those times. One of his schemes while in college involved obtaining the names of high school students who might be interested in attending small colleges, some of which were hard-hit by the Depression. The colleges paid Percy 5¢ a name and $10 if the student actually enrolled. As other activities took more of his time, Percy found others to do the recruiting work, and he paid them 3¢ per name and $5 if the students enrolled. The remainder was profit.

Another Percy enterprise was a campus cooperative agency to provide services to students. He sold food, coal, furniture, and linen to fraternity houses and residence halls. By his senior year his business grossed $150,000 a year, and Percy's take-home pay amounted to $10,000. He used the money to begin other enterprises and help the family.

Percy does not regret the long hours he spent on business ventures, but he feels that his preoccupation with work kept him from obtaining a more complete education, and it made a full social life difficult. His grades in school were average. He served as captain of the university water-polo team and was president of his fraternity, Alpha Delta Phi. Various investigations into his background by writers and officials have failed to turn up anything that could be considered a blemish on his youthful record. Percy hardly had time to get into trouble.

One of the more fateful relationships of Percy's life was the friendship begun during his teenage years with Joseph McNabb, president of Bell & Howell, a camera-equipment company. The firm's major lines were a 16-mm. movie camera and large equipment for the movie industry. The company then was far from being the giant in its field, with a full range of mass-market cameras, that it would later become under the guidance of McNabb's young protégé.

McNabb took a liking to Percy and put him to work during summer vacations. One summer Percy's job was to handle customer complaints. He noted improvements that could be made in the operation and passed them along to management, thus drawing attention to what otherwise would have been routine and unnoticed summer work. One of his innovations was to devise as many as 60 different form letters to be sent to complaining customers. On another occasion Percy called attention to his skills by writing McNabb a report that recommended doing away with the summer job he had just held. Percy continued to work at Bell & Howell on a part-time basis during his college years.

At one point McNabb and his wife invited Percy to their home for dinner. Despite his many business experiences and contacts up to that time, Percy recalls being nervous: "He said come on over to the house and let's talk about your life and what you plan to do with it and have dinner with me. I went up to this house—I guess on my bicycle—it was a huge house.... It doesn't look so big to me now, but then it looked sort of like the place Queen Elizabeth would live in." Percy's next surprise came when the three of them—Mr. and Mrs. McNabb and Percy—sat down to dinner. He recalls, "I'll never forget my feeling when they brought a platter with three or four squabs on it. I didn't know whether to carve off a leg or what. They fortunately served her first, and she took a whole one, and I took a whole one. I'd never seen anyone eat a whole bird before." Percy remembers that dinner as one of the few times he felt uncomfortable in a social situation.

After graduation from the University of Chicago in 1941 with a bachelor's degree in economics, Percy remembers being offered several opportunities for employment. He accepted a permanent job with Bell & Howell as manager of the company's war-coordinating department, which manufactured gunsights, radar devices, lenses, and other items used in warfare. By the time Percy joined the armed forces, he seemed on his way to positions of greater responsibility with the company. McNabb, recognizing Percy's ability, made him a director of the company and also named him assistant secretary of the firm.

In 1943 Percy enlisted in the navy as an apprentice seaman. He earned a commission as ensign and was discharged in 1945 a lieutenant. He was stationed in New Hampshire, Florida, California, and Washington, D.C. Much of his time was spent in a training capacity. He did not go overseas. Only one incident during this period would have any future effect on him. At some point, noise apparently caused a hearing impairment in his right ear. Although this hearing problem bothered him immediately, he did not start wearing a hearing aid until he entered the Senate.

After the service he became corporate secretary of Bell & Howell and held the title of assistant to McNabb. He became involved with the company's attempts to resume its camera business after the war. During World War II, Bell & Howell had converted completely to the production of war materials. As the company diversified its product line, Percy took greater control of production and marketing. His style of management differed from his mentor's. McNabb's style was to be personally involved in all aspects of the company. Percy, on the other hand, deferred to managers on matters of operations.

Many unfounded rumors have surfaced to explain Percy's rapid climb to corporate leadership in the years after the war. One rumor attributed his business success to his marriage to the boss's daughter. This story apparently started because his first wife's father, George Dickerson, was part owner of a pipe-manufacturing firm called Bell & Gossett, which had no connection with Bell & Howell. The similarity in the names of the firms gave rise to the rumor, but Percy never worked for Bell & Gossett.

No family ties helped Percy at Bell & Howell. His success was the result of the executive ability that had been recognized early by McNabb, who finally decided that Percy should succeed him as company president. A longtime employee of the firm remembers that McNabb's decision angered some other employees who thought they should have received the consideration given Percy. Though they recognized that Percy would some day become head of the company, no one was too concerned about it happening immediately because Joseph McNabb was still a relatively young man.

When McNabb died unexpectedly, a letter he had written to the directors was opened. Percy remembers McNabb telling him about such a letter, in which McNabb stipulated that Percy was to become company president. In accordance with McNabb's wishes, Percy became president of Bell & Howell on January 12, 1949. At that time Percy was the youngest man ever to lead a major U.S. corporation. At just 29 years of age he was the "Whiz Kid of U.S. business."

That Percy was successful as the corporate head of Bell & Howell is evident from the company's records in terms of sales growth, earnings, and share of the world market for camera equipment. When Percy ended his association with Bell & Howell in 1966, the figures showed that during Percy's 17-year leadership sales had increased from $13 million to $160 million and profits had climbed as well, resulting in substantial increases in the price of the company's stock.

While at Bell & Howell, Percy looked for young people to bring along in the business. One protégé of his was Peter G. ("Pete") Peterson, who followed Percy as president. Peterson later served as secretary of commerce in the Nixon administration and is now involved in New York investment circles. Another young person Percy encouraged was Herman Stein, Jr., a Bell & Howell executive who became Percy's assistant, financial adviser, and political aide, serving in these capacities until a plane crash ended his life. Percy and Stein were not only business associates, but also friends who lived only six blocks from each other when Percy had a home in Kenilworth, on Chicago's North Shore.

During his Bell & Howell years, Percy earned the reputation as a leader who was intensely interested in the ideas, thoughts, and morale of his employees. He instituted a program of profit sharing when the concept was not widespread in business and industry. At Christmastime he spent the better part of three weeks calling on every employee in the company to offer greetings to each of them personally. From these visits he obtained a sense of company morale and the minor stresses that sometimes irritate employees. Percy attended all of the brief ceremonies at which employees were presented pens for years of service.

In the 25 years Percy worked full-time at Bell & Howell, he served in a variety of management capacities. As president, beginning in 1949, he literally ran the business until 1961, at which time he became chairman of the board as well as chief executive officer. Percy moved up to chairman so that Peterson could be elevated to the position of president. However, because Peterson still needed to learn the corporate ropes, Percy continued to run the business. Peterson assumed full control of the company in 1963 when Percy made the decision to run for governor of Illinois. From that time until just before the U.S. Senate race in 1966, Percy's sole responsibility at Bell & Howell was his job as chairman of the board. In 1966 Percy ended his association with the company. At that time he said he would not seek any position with the firm, including a seat on the board of directors.

In his first years as president of Bell & Howell, there were only occasional indications of his future interest in politics. He had previously worked as a Republican precinct captain in Kenilworth. Later on he had been involved in some party fund-raising affairs, but this kind of involvement was just about what could be expected from any businessman of his stature. According to acquaintances of Percy's at the time he began thinking of seeking public office, his political interest was slow in manifesting itself. Initially his familiarity with politics resulted from the need to develop overseas markets for Bell & Howell equipment. He learned quickly that companies dealing in foreign markets needed to keep abreast of the political situation.

CHAPTER II

THE NOT-SO-PRIVATE LIFE OF THE PERCYS

Charles Percy met Jeanne Dickerson when they were both students at New Trier High School. Later, while he was attending the University of Chicago, she went to Northwestern University. They were married on June 23, 1943, shortly after Percy had been commissioned an ensign in the navy. The newlyweds lived in Washington, D.C., where Percy was stationed, for about a year and then in Oakland, California, when he was transferred there. On December 10, 1944, in Oakland, Mrs. Percy gave birth to twins named Valerie Jeanne and Sharon. After Percy was discharged from the navy in 1945, the family returned to Wilmette so that Percy could resume his career with Bell & Howell. A third child, Roger, was born on November 22, 1946. Before Roger was a year old, Jeanne underwent two operations for ulcerative colitis. After the second operation she died of a reaction to penicillin. Jeanne Dickerson Percy was not a Christian Scientist.

The young executive was left with three small children; the twins were three years old and Roger was a year old when their mother was buried. During the next three years Percy took care of his family with the help of housekeepers. When he could, Percy attended school meetings and took the children with him on business trips and vacations. Sharon, now grown and with a family of her own, believes that the present closeness of the family is an outgrowth of the days after her mother's death when Percy had the delicate job of balancing the care of his young family with the demands of his work.

One of Percy's favorite pastimes is skiing, and on a vacation trip to Sun Valley, Idaho, in 1949, he met a young Californian named Loraine Guyer, the daughter of a West Coast investment banker. Percy immediately began courting her and followed her when she returned to California. Percy even pursued her to Europe, where he finally proposed. They were married in 1950 and went to Hawaii on their honeymoon.

The new Mrs. Percy had attended Principia College, near St. Louis, and so she was familiar with the Middle West, where she and her family would make their home until early 1967. The Percys had three children: Their first son, Jay, who was born in 1951, lived only one week; Gail was born July 24, 1953; and Mark was born July 26, 1955. Home for the Percys and their five children was a 17-room Tudor mansion called Windward in Kenilworth. The house is adjacent to Lake Michigan, and this location, besides offering picturesque living the year round, enabled the family to engage in many of their favorite water-sport activities. After the Percys moved to Washington, D.C., the Kenilworth home was sold to William B. Graham, an old friend and political helpmate.

All the Percy children have been involved in Percy's political campaigns. The three eldest—the twins, Sharon and Valerie, and Roger—were most visible during the 1964 gubernatorial contest in Illinois, and they all did their part in the 1966 Senate contest until the night of September 17.

On that particular night Mrs. Percy, Sharon, and Valerie talked after dinner before the girls went to bed in their Kenilworth home. Although they were Mrs. Percy's stepdaughters, the three were close. The two younger children, Mark and Gail, were also at home. Roger was in college in California. Percy was out campaigning during the evening and did not return home until around midnight. By then the girls were in bed, and Mrs. Percy was watching television. After he arrived, Percy and his wife stayed up until about 1:30 A.M.

About five in the morning, Mrs. Percy was aroused by a noise. She made her way in the dark to Valerie's room where she was shocked to find a male intruder. The room was dark. The intruder, surprised by Mrs. Percy, fled, and Mrs. Percy screamed. In the next few minutes the family learned that Valerie had been beaten and stabbed to death. Although Mrs. Percy could have seen the murderer for only a few seconds, and then in a darkened room, she later sketched the features of the man. The drawings that were made from Mrs. Percy's impressions have been used in the ensuing investigations.

Many notable and sometimes confusing events occurred in the aftermath of the murder. The Senate campaign came to a halt in the Percy camp, and Paul Douglas called a hiatus to his. Investigations of the crime were begun that continue to this day, although not as intensely as during the first few years. By 1974, Percy said, there had been more than 1,400 investigations made by authorities. No arrests have been made. But police officials and the Percys now feel they have the scenario and know most of the circumstances surrounding the crime. "We'll never be satisfied until it is cleared up once and for all," Percy has said. "We're satisfied they've narrowed it down...as far as the motive is concerned. As far as the principals involved we're not exactly sure in our minds which one it was."

For several years after the murder, speculation persisted that the crime was somehow connected with Percy's political career or was directed at him personally. However, authorities and the Percys are convinced that a gang of thieves committed the murder and that it was not in any way related to Percy's political activity. Housebreaking was the motive, Percy believes. The suspected gang often used insurance records to get a line on homes of the wealthy that could be burglarized. Percy does not know why they chose his home, but he suspects it was because of insurance policies the Percys had on artwork or jewelry. The Percys are satisfied that they know the motive for the crime and what apparently happened in the home that night, and they believe the murderer "must have been drugged." But positive proof is not there to erase all doubts. There is not enough evidence to prosecute anyone, and the investigations probably will continue as long as there is an interested public official in Illinois.

The *Chicago Sun-Times* reported that investigators believe Francis L. ("Frank") Hohimer, a convict in an Iowa prison, may have done the killing. At least he is linked with three others—Fred Malchow, Harold L. Evans, and William Jackson—who are believed to have formed a burglary ring which plundered the homes of wealthy persons. Evans and Jackson have denied involvement in the crime, and Malchow was killed in 1968, when he plunged from a railroad trestle in Pennsylvania during a jailbreak attempt with Evans. *Sun-Times* reporters Arthur M. Petacque and Hugh F. Hough won a Pulitzer Prize in 1974 for their revelations in the Percy murder case.

The Percys are not as convinced of the identification of the killer as the newspaper reporters appeared to be. They believe Hohimer might have been the person Mrs. Percy remembers seeing "casing" the house sometime before the murder. In her mind the man in Valerie's room was thinner, and the sketch she drew of him after the crime shows that he had a thin neck. "It is Loraine's feeling that the man she saw did not have such a heavy neck," Percy said. Hohimer has a "heavy" neck. The Percys believe Malchow, now dead, might have been the murderer because his features resemble Mrs. Percy's sketch more closely than Hohimer's.

Percy sees no lasting political implications from the murder. He asked the Illinois State Police to tell him if they found any evidence that could be used politically. Percy does not recall any of his opponents trying to use rumor or innuendo against him. Rumors that members of the Percy staff or close friends were somehow involved in the crime have surfaced in Illinois for years. The state police did check out the possible involvement of those close to the family—its standard operating procedure—and there is no evidence that anyone but strangers committed the crime. Percy does not believe any part of the case could be used against him in a future political campaign. The final footnote on the Valerie Percy case may be nothing more than the personal satisfaction of the police and the Percys that all possible angles have been explored and an acceptable scenario constructed.

Occasionally the subject of the murder will receive renewed public attention. In March, 1974, for example, the Senate debated and approved the reinstatement of capital punishment in the federal court system. (The House took no action in 1974.) Percy took the floor for his comments and noted that no arguments had been made that would persuade him to vote for capital punishment. Then he put himself to the ultimate test: "What if I were called upon to decide what sentence should be imposed upon the vicious murderer of my own daughter?" Percy said he would not impose the death penalty:

"I would want that person hopefully someday to realize the gravity of the crime against God and one of His children that he had committed. I would hopefully want this person to be convinced that he had committed a sin against God as well as against society and ask for God's forgiveness for that act." Percy said it would be too easy to kill the murderer and added, "I would not want to be guilty of committing another crime in the name of society."

No family completely sheds the traumatic effects of such an ordeal as the murder of a loved one, but the Percy family has learned to live with it, though Mark, according to Percy, may have adjusted less well than the others. There were early concerns about the psychological impact on Loraine and Gail. Percy says that Roger, because of his maturity at the time of the murder and the fact that he was the only family member not in the house, seemed to have managed the best of any of the children. As a gesture in Valerie's memory Percy gave $10,000 to an East St. Louis, Illinois, community center for the needy. The gift was matched by Percy's friend James S. McDonnell, chairman of the board of McDonnell Douglas Corporation in St. Louis. A reward of $50,000 was offered for Valerie's murderer, but it was canceled on September 8, 1970, on the advice of investigators and a special committee.

Evidence of the indelible imprint the murder has left on the lives of all the Percys is that each year on September 18, the anniversary of the murder, the family members are in touch with one another in person or by telephone. Sharon, Valerie's twin, says the episode brought the family closer together and made them more sensitive to one another's feelings.

Family members take pride in the closeness of the children and parents despite great geographical distances and Percy's political career. There are few signs of the cracks in the family fabric that often occur in the lives of those close to political figures. Sharon acknowledges some difficult moments: "I won't say we haven't faced some of those same pressures, but particularly since Valerie's death we have tried harder to maintain closeness." The children feel their father has placed them first in his life. "That's particularly difficult for men in important positions," Sharon said. When his first wife died, the three oldest children were still small, and Percy was on the threshold of becoming president of Bell & Howell. Sharon says he did an especially good job of raising his motherless children until he remarried. Even now Percy shows special attention to the children. "He'll always come to the airport to pick me up, and he's always making that extra effort on a personal basis," Sharon said.

Sharon was the first Percy child to marry. After graduating from Stanford University and working with the Peace Corps in Africa, Sharon married John D. ("Jay") Rockefeller IV on April 1, 1967. The couple presented Percy with his first three grandchildren, whose names tell significant family stories. They are John ("Jaimie"), Valerie, and Charles Percy Rockefeller.

The marriage has not lessened Sharon's interest in her father's political career. She contributed to his campaign in 1972 and was one of a handful of persons to donate money to an exploratory committee which looked into Percy's chance at the presidential nomination in 1976. Sharon believes having a father in one party and a husband in the other is actually helpful. "Jay has never been accused of riding coattails, and each has retained his professional integrity," she said. In 1972 Rockefeller sought the West Virginia governorship and lost.

Not since Percy's 1966 contest for the Senate has Sharon worked steadily in politics for her father. Her appearances have been limited to large fund-raising dinners. She is not so sure her working more frequently in Illinois politics would be helpful for her father or Jay. "Daddy has enough appeal to independent votes without us campaigning for him," she says.

The next Percy child to marry was Roger. On August 8, 1970, he wed Penelope Chambers in Atherton, California. He and his wife live in London, where Roger is employed by the McCann-Erickson advertising firm. Roger attended junior college in Menlo Park, California, and then Stanford University. He received a master's degree in business from the University of Washington.

The remaining Percy children, Gail and Mark, are both single and are frequent visitors at the Percy home in Washington. Gail attended college at the University of California's Santa Cruz campus, and Mark attended Stanford.

Public figures have a difficult time keeping their private lives private, and the Percys are no exception. They fight to preserve their privacy but at the same time do not forget that public attention is important to a senator. However, on questions of personal finances the Percys hold fast to as much secrecy as possible. This is particularly true of Percy's wife, Loraine, who has been the more tenacious of the two about not divulging such information. On one occasion in her husband's first Senate term, Mrs. Percy said that interest in the financial affairs of public officials amounted to little more than unprincipled nosiness by the media. She felt that such curiosity constituted an unwarranted questioning of her husband's integrity and honesty by suggesting that disclosure might reveal a conflict of interest. She also worried about the political impact, remembering the troubles encountered by Senator Joseph Tydings of Maryland. His wealth became an issue in the reelection contest of 1970, and he lost. Mrs. Percy feared that something similar might happen to her husband if his wealth were made an issue. Percy never expressed that exact concern, although he realized what happened in Tydings's case might happen to him.

Mrs. Percy expressed her feelings with emphasis. "When the whole Senate has to make public disclosure, then we'll do it," she said at a time prior to Percy's 18-month pursuit of the 1976 presidential nomination. Senate rules do demand that a senator file copies of federal income-tax returns and statements of debts, financial interests, and sources of income with the Senate Ethics Committee, but the information is confidential. Only under the most extreme conditions would the information be revealed.

The Percy concern for privacy is not limited to financial disclosure. Percy has argued that there must be a separation between a senator's public and private lives. In asking for some discretion on the part of the media, he said, "What I do in my bedroom is my business."

Some of Percy's desire for privacy has roots in his past associations and activities in the business world. Although in his business dealings he had a reputation for openness and a distaste for corporate secrecy, he was very closemouthed about his life outside Bell & Howell. When he was an industrial leader, public views of his private life were more easily controlled. He spent much less time in the limelight than he did as a senator.

Most of Percy's wealth came from large salaries, stock options, and bonuses. When he left Bell & Howell in 1966, he said his holdings in Bell & Howell common stock would "continue to constitute my principal personal investment."

After his election to the U.S. Senate in 1966, Percy estimated his personal fortune at $6 million, which he said was a "conservative" figure. That included 82,017 shares of Bell & Howell stock worth close to $5 million on the 1966 stock market. Percy turned his holdings over to Stein, Roe & Farnham, a Chicago investment firm, with instructions not to invest in companies which could cause a conflict of interest. The holdings remained with the firm until 1970.

Late in 1969 the first of several pressures occurred to bring Percy toward further disclosure. Percy voted against confirming Judge Clement F. Haynsworth, Jr., for the U.S. Supreme Court. During debate on the question of fitness, Percy criticized Haynsworth's personal holdings, which some felt constituted a potential conflict of interest with his court work. That may have helped convince Percy to establish a blind trust, which he did on April 6, 1970, with the Harris Trust & Savings Bank of Chicago.

Mrs. Percy has accumulated personal wealth in her own right. Her money came from interests in her family's Los Angeles investment banking business and through inheritances. The Percys own Illinois farmland, which has been in Mrs. Percy's family for decades. No estimate of the holdings has been made public. On January 1, 1971, Mrs. Percy established a blind trust with the Fiduciary Trust Company of New York, giving the trustees full authority to make investments on her behalf. Mrs. Percy once said that the blind trusts "cost Chuck and me money" every year. She was referring to the cost of professional management for the funds and the fact that neither principal can direct his own investments. Percy says the management situation of the funds is one of the "frustrations" of having the money in trust.

In 1972, before his campaign for reelection to the Senate got under way, Percy complied with the Senate rules on disclosure of all honoraria over $300 received for speaking engagements and appearances. His statement showed that he had received $9,600 in 1971 for honoraria. Then he took a step toward revealing more information about his holdings. With his statement he enclosed a letter addressed to him from Arthur Anderson & Company, an accounting firm in Washington. The letter traced the establishment of the Percys' blind trusts and said, "Both you and Mrs. Percy receive regular financial reports indicating only the aggregate portions of the respective investment portfolios that are invested in stocks, bonds, and other assets, but not disclosing individual investment or industry holdings." The firm said it understood that Percy advised the investment firm of his Senate assignments "as a further precaution to avoid investments that might have the appearance of a conflict of interest." The Anderson firm also said that all salary, honoraria, and writing fees received by Percy since he became a senator were used to supplement public money available for staff salaries and other office expenses. Percy can use his salary for operating expenses because of the income he receives each year from his trust. Information about the amount he receives is not available, but it is possible to make a guess. If Percy's total trust is valued at $5 million and the net return annually is 5 percent, his income would be $250,000.

In 1967, his first year as a senator, Percy reportedly spent nearly $70,000 of his own funds on staff expenses. Percy estimated in 1974 that since 1966 he had used his Senate salaries of more than $200,000 for office expenses.

The letter from the Anderson firm supported at least part of Mrs. Percy's complaint about losing management control of the funds. The firm noted that between December 31, 1966, and December 31, 1971, Percy's individual estate dropped in value. Mrs. Percy's estate did not, but the company said the appreciation was due to an inheritance from her mother's estate and market investments. Percy said his net worth totaled "about $5 million" in mid-1974 and that it had not changed much from totals announced in earlier years. Common stocks make up a large portion of the trust, and they were worth less on the stock exchange in 1974 than in previous years.

Percy's wealth is viewed by his associates as a strength in resisting the temptations of easy money in Washington. One longtime friend observed, "It's amazing what a few thousand dollars can do in Washington." Percy has kept his distance from special interests and has avoided using large campaign contributors as close advisers.

Pressures changed Percy's mind about disclosure when he began his quest of the presidential nomination. The revelations of Watergate and the misuse of campaign funds in 1972 by Richard M. Nixon's Committee to Reelect the President created pressures on public figures to disclose their finances. Also the public became increasingly curious about the financial affairs of politicians after Nixon made his income-tax payments public. In February, 1974, at a Washington conference on the influence of money in politics, Percy announced he had changed his mind about disclosure. He said that if he were to become a "full-fledged" candidate for the 1976 presidential nomination, he would disclose the value of his assets and would release tax statements for the years he has held public office. "The public trust has been so frequently and flagrantly abused that I am forced to conclude that some form of significant disclosure is in the public interest," said Percy. Percy's making this disclosure always remained contingent upon his candidacy for the presidency, and that he would do so reluctantly was reflected in the words he spoke.

Percy cited the loss of privacy that goes with financial disclosure. At the time no mention was made of Mrs. Percy's holdings and whether the pledge involved her too. Subsequently Percy said, "Though we still have personal reservations, reinforced recently by the Hearst case and other incidents, both Loraine and I will make full disclosure should I become a full-fledged candidate." The "Hearst case" to which Percy referred was the kidnapping of Patricia Hearst, daughter of San Francisco publisher Randolph Hearst. The Hearsts paid large sums of money in fruitless attempts to gain their daughter's freedom, and Hearst's personal financial matters, including details of his holdings, became the subject of extensive publicity. The Percy family has had enough of its own personal tragedy to know that public persons are vulnerable. For these reasons it is doubtful that Percy would see any value in releasing data on his personal finances as long as he remains a senator.

Still, pressure on all public officials to make some kind of disclosure, whether voluntary or compulsory, has been building since the late 1960s and is not likely to subside. Many senators who have large fortunes have begun making disclosures. The congressional committees' investigation into President Gerald R. Ford's and Vice-President Nelson Rockefeller's financial affairs—especially the latter's—as part of the confirmation process under the 25th Amendment to the Constitution resulted in greater public demand for details about other government officials. In 1974 the possibility of his entering the 1976 presidential contest—later declined by him—led Senator Edward Kennedy of Massachusetts, one of the Senate's wealthiest members, to make his 1973 income-tax forms public. Kennedy's returns showed a total income of $461,444, most of which came from trust funds established by his father but did not disclose the senator's net worth or the family's total holdings. This financial disclosure was the first that Senator Kennedy had ever made. More senators are likely to begin to follow suit.

Money, whether in trust or in hand, gives the Percys an opportunity to enjoy the good life, although Percy is quick to remind people that "we don't live ostentatiously." While the Percys do not have many of the expensive material goods that other wealthy persons accumulate, they live most comfortably. "Loraine isn't slaving away in the kitchen, and I'm not doing the dishes," Percy reminded a visitor. "I did enough of those when I was home and working my way through school. If I never have to wash another dish, it will be fine with me." Though the Percys prefer a low-key life-style, they are nevertheless considered to be among some of Washington's "right people." They make the society columns of the Washington newspapers with some regularity. Writers make much of their home and its decor and also of their cars—especially the big ones (although after the energy shortage of 1974 Percy began driving a Mustang). Women's Wear Daily featured them as "juicy people," and enough tongues wag about them for people to observe for publication that the Percys are "not exactly a Middle American couple." They often are invited to dinner parties given by the capital's most successful hostesses. They are patrons of cultural events in Washington, D.C., as they were in Chicago. Mrs. Percy has been a member of the Women's Committee of the Smithsonian Associates. Percy has been instrumental in getting federal support for the Kennedy Center for the Performing Arts in Washington. Leaders of cultural activities also are contributors to Percy election campaigns. Being an integral part of the Washington social circuit keeps the senator in touch with vital political contacts.

The Percys own no condominiums, resort homes, estates, boats, or other items frequently accumulated by the wealthy. They do own two houses. Their home in Wilmette is the Percys' official Illinois residence. In Washington, D.C., the Percys enjoy the elegance of a tastefully decorated Georgetown home, although the neighborhood is by no means the most exclusive in the capital area. Vine-covered brick houses line the narrow streets of Georgetown, and a modest neighborhood grocery is located less than a block away from the Percy home. There is no sign, real or imagined, telling visitors that a U.S. senator lives nearby.

The Percy brick home is not excessively large by most standards of wealth and is picturesque in a Georgetown way. Percy tells of the reaction of visiting Russian officials who were entertained at the Percy home in Georgetown: "They were surprised at such a modest house that a United States senator they felt was a wealthy man and industrialist lives in."

The Georgetown property has a swimming pool in an attractive backyard setting and a guest house, which is used by visiting Percy children and their families. A distinctive feature, not apparent to the eye, is a security system, one of which has been installed in each of Percy's homes. Their former home in Kenilworth had security devices before Valerie's death, but since the tragedy the family has been even more aware of the need for security. In their Washington home, alarm devices are placed throughout the grounds, and police will arrive in a moment's notice if one of the alarms is triggered. The Percys are aware of their vulnerability, and they try to guard against it.

The distance from home of Mark and Gail during their college years caused some anguish for the Percys. As a precaution, they consulted the FBI for guidelines on avoiding circumstances that could encourage kidnappers. As a result, the children never left their residences unless there was someone with them. They had telephones put in their rooms and were instructed to call their parents every few days. If the Percys did not hear from the children on schedule, they called California. Information as to the exact location of their children was closely guarded.

When threats are made against Percy or the family, there is never any reluctance to accept protection from authorities. Percy calls it an unpleasant aspect of public life, "but you can't shirk doing what you feel is right. There is probably a risk every time you step out on the street."

In May, 1969, Percy and Governor Richard B. Ogilvie of Illinois camped out at Lake Glendale in southern Illinois during a day and night of well-publicized communing with nature. They traveled more than 100 miles through the rugged southern Illinois countryside. Percy and Ogilvie seemed unconcerned about other business despite the fact that Percy's life had been threatened. Actually, Percy had state police protection for most of the trip.

Because of their sensitivity to the need for vigilance, the Percys, particularly Mrs. Percy, can recall several incidents at their Georgetown home that have made them suspicious. Mrs. Percy believes the residential telephone has been tapped on occasion, and "bugging" has been a special concern of the family since 1970. Percy tells of the time during the 1972 election campaign when Mrs. Percy noticed a telephone truck outside their home. She saw men apparently cutting into the telephone lines and questioned them as to their activities. They refused to give her any information. She called the senator's office, and the telephone company was informed immediately. Percy says the telephone company knew of no truck in the vicinity nor of any service calls scheduled in that part of town. When one of the "telephone" men came to the door and entered the house after showing identification, Mrs. Percy thought she recognized him as a Watergate burglar. After being shown pictures of the seven Watergate burglars, she decided she had been mistaken. Nothing further came of the incident.

The Percys' concern for security has not stopped them from continuing to travel abroad extensively, sometimes at public expense through his work on Senate committees. However, most of their overseas travel is at their personal expense. Percy notes that "the few thousand dollars" of public money allotted to a senator for travel is far short of the amount he personally has put back into staff expenses from his own funds.

Percy occasionally asks for official credentials, especially if it appears he might encounter some difficulty abroad. He claims to travel less than many other senators on the Foreign Relations Committee. However, there have been complaints about the extent of Percy's foreign travel, but so far these have not been used effectively against him by any of his political opponents.

Occasionally, Percy files a report on his travels. From November 26 through December 23, 1972, Percy toured the Far East during one of the most controversial periods of the Vietnam conflict. The trip came close to the end of the Vietnam war when the United States was engaged in the intensive bombing of North Vietnam. After his return Percy filed with the Foreign Relations Committee a report entitled "Economic and Political Developments in the Far East." The report discussed some of the U.S. policies toward other nations, including the problems of continued support of these nations in the future. In 1973, when the Senate recessed for the summer, Percy traveled to India, Pakistan, and neighboring countries. He reported to President Nixon on the domestic affairs of the nations he visited and the impact of Watergate revelations on U.S. stature in those countries.

The entire Percy family enjoys overseas travel. Percy's interest in foreign travel began when he became personally involved in developing overseas markets for Bell & Howell. Mrs. Percy, a world traveler before she married, usually accompanies the senator on the official trips as well as the pleasure jaunts. All the children have been abroad on several occasions, sometimes for education and work, sometimes for fun. Percy says they usually return from a trip enthusiastic about the countries they have just visited "but far more appreciative of our own culture." To the Percys travel is more than an escape from life and work in Washington or Illinois: It is a "lifetime interest."

CHAPTER III

THE MAN AND HIS IMAGE

The characteristics of Percy's personality have their roots in his religion, his devotion to keeping busy, and his work experience. Percy's life-style has caused derisive comments by politicians, businessmen, and the media. Richard Nixon is supposed to have called Percy a "Boy Scout." During the early months of Percy's push for the 1976 presidential nomination, a magazine quoted a *National Observer* article which said that when Percy faced Illinois Governor Otto Kerner in 1964, "he quickly got the reputation of 'Chuckie Goodboy,' the gee-whiz wonder boy who went through life looking for widows in distress." More than one publication has used and reused the statement that "Mr. Percy . . . affects an elaborate piety, like a figure in stained glass." These descriptions betray a lack of knowledge of Percy but are accurate reflections of the reaction many people have to him.

Percy is a product of his environment, and while he may have altered certain characteristics through the years, his basic habits and personality are unchanged. The experience Percy gained running a big corporation and working with many persons older and more experienced than he has refined his ability to deal with other people and to judge their abilities. His seriousness often makes him appear humorless, stiff, formal, and uneasy. This was particularly true in his early political campaigns, but his self-discipline has helped him to overcome some of those faults and to rebound from political defeat and personal tragedy.

Percy's parents were Christian Scientists, and he and his wife are members of the church. The Charles Percys reared their children in that faith. None of their children has pursued it with as much dedication as their mother and father. But the Percys believe the upbringing in a religious atmosphere will never be lost on the children even if they are not active participants in their church. Some of the children are subscribers to the *Christian Science Monitor*, which Percy believes helps them keep in touch with some of the teachings and beliefs of their faith.

In recent years the Percys have kept in touch with their religion through personal study, reading, and thought but do not attend church. The Christian Science religion is based on the teachings of Jesus Christ as interpreted by Mary Baker Eddy. Members use love, prayer, faith, and understanding to overcome disease, death, and evil. Instead of ministers the churches have readers who use the Eddy material and the Scriptures. Other members of the church are called practitioners, and they often serve in counseling roles similar to that of ministers in other denominations. Perhaps the best-known aspect of Christian Science is that its members do not believe in seeking medical assistance but prefer to use the beliefs of the church and its interpretations of the Scriptures to fight ill health.

The tenets of Percy's religion when applied to his political activity provide a humbling quality as well as a source of personal strength. "Politics tends to almost corrupt an individual," Percy explains. "The focus of attention is on the individual, but I like to think in terms of how quick that attention leaves if you're defeated or leave office; how quick the invitations will drop off, how quick the autograph seekers stop asking." His religious background, Percy says, helps him depersonalize his role—or focus less attention on himself as the end all. Part of this depersonalization is "feeling I am a part of something." That "something" for Percy is a "family of supporters," which started as a handful in his early years and has grown to hundreds since. He sees them as his "counselors." "I like to think of my playing a role, but each of them is terribly important in it. My role is a different role than theirs, but it would be impossible without them." His religion helps Percy see himself "as an instrument, as a child of God in a sense, carrying out one's work." As Percy talks more about religion in his life, he takes on an evangelistic quality. He feels that his actions in performing the work he does should reflect a sense of values, many of which he has learned through his religious study.

Another tenet of Christian Science is that one should feel there are no limitations on what an individual can accomplish. However, a person must "be happy with the level of achievement" he has attained. Percy thinks it is foolish to risk happiness and success in one's job by always "aspiring to something else."

Percy believes it is important to seek help with human problems. For him this means consulting a Christian Science practitioner. He has said that if he were elected president he would follow the custom of having a White House physician but that he also would consult a practitioner if he felt the need to do so. Upon finding his daughter Valerie murdered in 1966, Percy immediately summoned a medical doctor and a practitioner to the scene.

Another of Percy's beliefs is that persons should recognize "we are not wise enough to know what's best for us; we must be part of some overall plan that goes beyond our abilities to perceive, and when something happens, it is not always within our power to know whether it's good or bad."

Percy cites his defeat in the 1964 Illinois gubernatorial campaign to illustrate his ability to accept loss without any outward excessive emotion.

"Maybe in defeat there was a lesson I had to learn," he says. If he believed that at the time, he also recognizes that other members of the family could not understand his attitude: "It was a great deal harder on my children than me. They might have been annoyed with me after I had worked so hard." He says those around him were "astounded" when he did not take a vacation immediately after election day but instead started work to privately implement some of the programs he had proposed during the campaign.

Displaying emotion in politics, especially during a campaign, is foolhardy, Percy believes, mainly because it may be necessary to work with someone again. He recalled some differences of opinion in 1964 with William J. Scott who contested him in the primary election. "I know Loraine was emotionally angry at some of the things in that campaign," Percy says. "But I never permitted myself to be angry. Anger is an emotion you can't afford to have. A politician can't afford to have feelings. Bill Scott and I would have to work together again, and we have worked well together through the years."

It might even have been providential that he was not elected governor, Percy feels, and he rejects the possibility that he only rationalizes the loss. Because he did not have the background as a lawyer or legislator, Percy now sees the Senate experience as rounding him out politically and individually. As a senator he no longer had a large staff or an executive position, with the opportunity to order things done. "I needed to sit in the more frustrating position of a legislator," Percy says, "and accomplish things through patience and persuasion and means other than direct orders."

Percy does not believe his religion has helped or hurt him politically. Public comment by letter and in conversation during his campaigns in Illinois has been negligible. He recognizes that many persons do not understand Christian Science, but those who disagree with its concepts have not made a political issue of his religion. Interviewers frequently ask him if there would be any conflicts between his religion and the questions of national health-insurance programs that have come up in the Senate or that could arise if he were president. The answers have been the same each time: no problem. He has often stated that his position on a national health-care law would reflect his feeling on what is best for the public and not how he might feel personally about medical care. Percy believes that if a person wants to follow a certain religious doctrine, it is strictly his own business and should not be binding on others.

Percy admits to having had some disagreements but no serious breaks with the church on health matters. He argued for the fluoridation of water and believes he may have convinced the church to soften its hard line on the subject. The hearing aid and glasses he wears are not in violation of any church doctrine. He does not believe the church should deny membership to persons because they smoke or drink.

Writers probably have made more than is justified of the fact that Percy does not smoke or drink. However, Percy does serve alcoholic beverages to guests in his home. The point was made by Theodore H. White in *The Making of the President, 1960* when he quoted a Percy aide as saying, "When Percy takes a drink of Dubonnet on the rocks, he thinks he's being one hell of a fellow and dissipating like mad." Percy's attitude toward smoking and drinking, while having religious roots, also fits in with his effort to remain in excellent physical condition.

Percy does not have a specific and regular program of exercise. "I feel better when I exercise," he says, "and I exercise when I feel the need for it." With a pool in his backyard, he swims frequently in good weather. He does not jog. He plays an occasional tennis game with a Senate colleague or some other personage. Skiing is a sport that Percy and Mrs. Percy particularly enjoy but seldom have time for. When he was a business executive, the Percys managed to get in 25 days of skiing a year, on the average; but in his Senate years the most time he has found for skiing was in 1973 when he and Loraine got away for a total of eight days. Percy's concern for his physical condition and appearance is supposed to have elicited this comparison from an envious observer: "He's got a body like a moose."

Peter G. Peterson is one friend and admirer who has a long list of stories about Percy's energy. "Chuck's energy level is incredible," he says. "I remember once when I was president of Bell & Howell and he was campaigning for office. He'd been up till 2 A.M. or some such time, and I had to meet him at 6 A.M. so he could sign something. He had to start his campaign again early. When I got over to see him, he was swimming several lengths of the pool, and he gave me an enthusiastic, cheery 'good morning' as if he'd been on a four-week vacation."

While Percy's physical regimen may be of interest to some people, lasting impressions are made by a man's personality. Does he look straight into the eyes of a visitor or glance at his shoe tops? Is he attentive or bored? Is his handshake firm or weak? People often remember Percy's handshake and his greeting: "So nice to see you" or "Gee, it's good to see you. I'm so glad you could make it." The good looks and cordial welcome are not always enough to dispel preconceived misgivings and even suspicions about him. A. A. Smyser, editor of the *Honolulu Star-Bulletin* saw Percy in action for the first time in 1974 during his presidential campaign swing into the islands and noted Percy's success with businessmen and other politicians. "Still, he seemed formal and stiff to me," the editor admitted.

Percy is aware of the accusations of stiffness, excessive formality, and unfriendliness. He believes his hearing problem contributes to feelings by others that he intentionally snubbed them: "Someone will walk past me and say 'good morning,' and I don't say 'good morning,' and they think, 'The guy doesn't care.' I just didn't hear them." Percy forces himself to be more conscious of conversation and often turns his right ear toward the person to make sure he hears what is being said. His experience with a hearing aid led to his criticism in 1974 of the hearing-aid industry for what he called gimmicky advertising, overselling, and overpricing. In letters to the Federal Trade Commission and the Food and Drug Administration, Percy maintained that hearing aids were being dispensed without prior medical diagnosis or doctors' prescriptions. He proposed regulations affecting such sales. The charges were refuted by critics such as Marvin H. Pigg of Detroit, president of the National Hearing Aid Society, who said Percy made "wild-swinging, inaccurate, and exaggerated claims ... which obviously are politically motivated."

Percy attributes some of his reputation for being an "automated industrialist" to incidents during the 1964 Illinois gubernatorial campaign against Otto Kerner. The contest marked Percy's entry into politics. Many of his mistakes on the 1964 campaign trail were corrected before he ran for the Senate in 1966, and there were greater improvements in the 1972 contest. In 1964 Percy's approach reflected his somewhat sequestered business background; in subsequent campaigns his approach reflected a growing awareness of campaign politics.

Going into the 1964 gubernatorial campaign, Percy says he wanted to learn as much as possible about the state. "I didn't know from my background much about, let's say, Douglas and Moultrie counties and Arthur [a town] in the center of the state," Percy said. So the candidate and his staff drew a social and economic profile of every county in Illinois, describing its migration patterns, ethnic background, urban-suburban relationships, and major crops and businesses. As a result, Percy recalls, many of the citizens would say, "You know more about us than we do." As flattering as that may have been, Percy also remembers that it angered local politicians for him to "know" more about their area than they did. Consequently Percy earned a reputation as a "walking IBM machine." When he wanted to talk with the voters about their problems, they often "looked at me as if I were the census taker coming in," Percy said later.

From his days as the heir apparent at Bell & Howell to his work in the U.S. Senate, a consistent trait of Percy's has been his ability to "quick study" almost any subject or situation. His election campaigns have reflected an adroitness in sizing up a situation and a thorough grasp of the appropriate facts and figures, giving the impression of a man who has done his homework. Those associated with Percy through the years agree that he learns quickly and is willing to seek the opinions of others. One former aide who worked with Percy before he ran for governor of Illinois in 1964 said, "He's a helluva learner, and much of it comes from talking with other people." When issues arose in the Senate on subjects unfamiliar to him, such as in the field of law or national defense, Percy frequently consulted experts to gain their perspective. On military affairs, for example, he often talked with retired Admiral Elmo R. Zumwalt. Percy has maintained close contact with business associates in Chicago, including William B. Graham of Baxter Laboratories and Robert Galvin of the Motorola Company. Percy seeks their opinions on business matters.

In an attempt to project a more casual and informal image, Percy, in the 1964 contest and in each successive election effort since, has run as "Chuck." The nickname did not surface just for political purposes. Friends and associates used it during his years as an executive with Bell & Howell. Correspondence involving Percy and the White House in Dwight Eisenhower's administrations often began "Dear Chuck." But to some critics, the use of the nickname appeared to be studied informality for a person who, in 1964 at least, did not come across genuinely as someone named "Chuck."

William C. Groninger, a Downstate reporter who worked for many years in the political environment of Champaign County in the central part of Illinois, recalls his first meeting with Percy: "I was calling him Mr. Percy. 'Call me Chuck,' he said with that grin that carries so much calculated charm." During the primary and general election, Groninger interviewed Percy a number of times, and always on a "Chuck-to-Bill" basis. He remembered that the first time he had occasion to interview Percy after his election as senator was at a press conference: "I asked a couple of questions, beginning, 'Say, Chuck,' or something of the sort. An aide sneaked up behind me and whispered, 'Senator Percy prefers to be called Senator Percy,' which when you look at it, makes sense."

Those who have watched Percy campaign believe he has mellowed since he first ran for public office. One says: "He's much more sagacious than in 1963. He's learned a lot about politicians and politics and strategies. He's more relaxed and less intense than previously. He has a better sense of humor." The same people can see other changes in Percy's approach. In the beginning his interest in people often manifested itself in concern for the masses and not individuals. Percy has expanded his interest to individuals so that, as one observer puts it, "he's a more attractive human being now."

Projecting a folksy, down-home style is not Percy's forte, although some people can remember that in 1972 he campaigned on Illinois farms in shirt sleeves, without a tie, and with a windbreaker tossed "recklessly" over his shoulder. The official 1966 campaign picture was an informal shot of Percy in a shirt open at the collar. Television ads showed him, in studied casualness, talking to farmers in the fields, with tractors and other farm equipment forming the background. He told an interviewer: "I don't consciously work on image; I am what I am. You don't change dramatically when you've reached the age of 54 and are the grandfather of three. I am not a cracker-barrel type." All Percy's individual traits, personality quirks, and personal habits and his life-style indicate that he is not the kind to sit around a potbellied stove or lean back in a chair and prop up his feet. When he has occasionally tried to leave such an impression, he has given strength to charges of phoniness. Friends insist that in private Percy's sense of humor and informality come easily, and they are hard put to explain why he does not project these characteristics well in public.

On occasion Percy has tried to inject some humor into his presentations, but he is guided by the realization that "to try to be something you're not is a mistake." When Percy does use humor in a speech, it usually is carefully programmed in advance. At a dinner for Senator Jacob Javits of New York, Percy realized that nothing he would say in competition with 21 other speakers would be remembered for its great impact. His remarks were informal and almost entirely humorous. He and his staff members were pleased when the feedback they received indicated the talk had been well received. They reflected almost a boyish sense of pride in the achievement. Percy does not encourage his staff to write one-line jokes or pay others to do it for him. "I'm not a Bob Hope.... My work is more to inform and in a sense to educate and to learn myself from the audiences, not to have them rolling in the aisles."

Occasionally an offhand remark will leave his listeners chuckling, perhaps in surprise. Michael Howlett, a longtime Democratic state officeholder in Illinois, remembers an episode involving Percy that made the jovial Howlett comment, "You know, I never thought of Percy as having a sense of humor before, and I was astounded." At a dinner Percy was presented with a special license plate from Secretary of State Howlett. When Percy turned away from the microphone, he said to the director of the motor vehicles department, "I never got anything like this from a Republican secretary of state." Howlett immediately handed Percy the microphone and asked him if he wanted to repeat his statement. Percy declined.

The exact level of Percy's humor has not always been easy for even his speech writers to fathom. One who wrote for Percy in the early 1970s admitted defeat: "I never could figure out his brand of humor. He'll never be known for his humor, but I think he's better able to see the humorous side of himself than he used to be." It may be easier for Percy to see his humorous side, but he has not been able to communicate it to others as well as John F. Kennedy, for example, who had a self-deprecating kind of humor that made him appear down to earth despite his wealth and position.

Although Percy denies any conscious effort to improve on his image, concern for his physical appearance in public is on the minds of staff members. "Chuck has a real problem with his shiny forehead," a former Percy staff member recalls. "That's not nearly as much of a problem, though, as his bruised ego if it makes him look older. He wants to remember how youthful he looks. He's really not as young as he used to be, although he still puts most senators in his age group in the shade." He fights having his face touched up for the cameras, but staff members believe he needs it to improve on nature. In preparation for filming a 15-minute television show in a Washington studio with Senator Adlai E. Stevenson and an interviewer, a new young staff member of Percy's approached him with a dab of pancake makeup. The senator pulled back, looked painfully at the young woman, and said curtly, "I don't need that." The woman fled. No one offered to work on Stevenson's features. "Well, she'll learn to hang in there," a Percy staff member said later. "If someone doesn't, the combination of glare off Chuck's forehead and Adlai's bald head will blind the viewers."

There is reason to believe that Percy is sensitive about his height. Many women and most men stand taller than Percy's 5 feet 8 inches. Illinois political reporter William C. Groninger remembers an incident during an interview with the senator. The reporter took along an attractive young woman who had asked to meet Percy. "Unfortunately, as the senator approached," the reporter recalled, "she stood up. Percy promptly sat down since she had him by a good six inches. He didn't rise again when we left." Many women are surprised at his short stature; somehow they expect him to tower over them. The rich baritone voice doesn't seem to fit his frame.

Percy's staff is concerned not only with the senator's appearance but also with his public statements. Even with the protection of the staff and the wealth of advice available, Percy cannot be programmed completely. He makes a normal number of gaffes in public, all of which make staff members cringe, some of which provide fodder for members of the press. Some of these remarks have become part of the Percy "bonehead comments" legend.

Percy's Washington staff, which controls access to the senator and budgets his time, is often casual about the Percy image, especially when the effort is to make him appear human and informal. At the same time those on the staff who do not deal directly with the media are cautious about releasing inside information, such as his thinking on issues or his political strategy, unless the reporter has established a close relationship with the staff.

Reports vary as to the extent of Loraine Percy's involvement in her husband's political affairs. Percy refers to her as a source of strength. Her participation in campaigning has been limited, although she meets people easily and conversation comes naturally to her. She did not do much campaigning in 1964 and only slightly more in 1966 until the murder of Valerie, after which she stopped. By 1972 Mrs. Percy had grown more confident, and she frequently accompanied her husband, although her appearances consisted mostly of being at Percy's elbow in a reception line.

Whether or not she participates in campaigning is up to her. She is always scheduled to accompany Percy unless she tells someone she does not want to go. Percy says, "She is never requested to do anything."

Loraine Percy is respected for her firmly voiced opinions about the couple's private life, their finances, the security of their home, and the privacy of their children; and she is not reluctant to express her views on national issues and personalities. Known as "Lonny" by close friends and associates, she became impatient and finally disgusted with Percy's 1972 opponent, U.S. Representative Roman Pucinski of Chicago, because of what she felt were Pucinski's misrepresentations—she called them lies—of Percy's positions. At one point late in the campaign, Percy declined an invitation by the Associated Press editors' organization in Illinois to appear on the same program with Pucinski. An aide to the senator told AP officials that Percy did not want to appear on the same program with the congressman. Mrs. Percy, in particular, felt strongly about giving Pucinski another chance to "twist the record" in face-to-face combat.

There is little evidence to indicate that Mrs. Percy is the strength behind the throne on policy questions, but her thoughts are known to Percy. "Loraine likes Washington and the Senate and social life. She is not a pusher and doesn't attempt to speak for Percy," a former aide said. "In fact not many persons speak for him. We always felt he tested some waters with her and asked her advice on personal questions, but there is no indication that she had influence on positions Chuck took."

Percy's own description of his wife's role clashes mildly with the former aide's observation: "She thinks things through with me. We discuss issues a tremendous amount, and she influences me very much." Percy tells of their joint study of the court record of G. Harrold Carswell, who was nominated by President Nixon for the Supreme Court in 1970. "We were disturbed when [Senator] John Sherman Cooper, who I admired, decided to vote for him [Carswell]. That caused us to go back to our books. . . . We sat up the final night before the vote still reading cases." The Percys were particularly interested in the number of times Carswell's decisions had been reversed. Percy's study reaffirmed his original decision to vote against Carswell.

Mrs. Percy has been outspoken on no single issue more than the Vietnam war. Some writers have reported that during the war years she put pressure on her husband to become more of a dove. Percy's recollections confirm this report. "She had a very strong feeling about Vietnam," Percy says. He described her attitude as "more vocal, more demonstrative" than his own sentiments. "She would march, but I didn't feel as a United States senator I should march," Percy recalls with a laugh. "Don't underestimate her convictions."

At one time Mrs. Percy was stronger for Richard Nixon than her husband was, particularly in 1968 before the party nominated Nixon. "At the time I endorsed [Nelson] Rockefeller, I think she would have preferred staying right with Nixon," Percy remembers. After that Mrs. Percy took increasing exception to the Nixon viewpoint. "Then she became on certain issues much stronger against Nixon than I did, particularly the Vietnam war."

Other members of the Percy family freely express their feelings about issues too. Visitors and friends who have been with the Percys' when all or most of the family is present report that issues often dominate discussions. One longtime friend observes that Percy has been willing to listen to all members of his family, his wife no more than the others. The most vocal family members are Sharon, the oldest, and Mark, the youngest. The views of most family members are categorized as "liberal to moderate, certainly more reasonable than most persons in the Republican party." Family members also exchange views through correspondence and frequent telephone conversations, some initiated by Percy and some by one of the others. It is not unusual for Percy to have correspondence, clippings, and memos circulating among his children.

Mrs. Percy finds ways to assert herself in the political picture. One staff member recalls the difficult decision before the 1972 reelection campaign over the selection of official campaign pictures. After the staff had selected the ones it felt would be most effective, the candidate asked for his wife's opinion. It differed markedly from that of the staff. Percy finally chose his wife's selection. It irked the staff, although most of them felt Percy had followed her advice because he wanted her to feel a part of the reelection effort. Mrs. Percy does occasionally sit in on political strategy sessions, and "we don't always agree," one strategist said. "But then the staff doesn't always agree either."

Mrs. Percy's attitude toward seeing her husband as president of the United States or as a candidate for president has changed. In the year or so after the murder of Valerie, she preferred not to talk of the presidential rumors that started. Not only were the memories of the murder fresh, but also the assassination of John F. Kennedy was only a few years past. The dangers that confront presidential candidates were clearly on her mind. Even as late as 1972, Percy indicated that a major consideration in his decision on a 1976 presidential bid was the attitude of Mrs. Percy and whether the family was up to it. When the presidential effort began in 1973, he inferred that some of the fears of a few years earlier remained. However, on the occasions of her appearances in public, Mrs. Percy appeared to have put all those concerns behind her.

A wife's role in a political campaign is important to a candidate, but in the long run he is on his own. It is not enough to have views on major political issues; the candidate must still sell himself to the individual voter. This is a fact of political life that Percy learned early in his public career. Above all, he must appear human. Survival in state and national politics may often depend on projecting the proper image in every situation. But the danger is that in trying to be all things to all people, a distorted picture of the man may emerge. Friends and associates agree that Percy is at his best when he appears to be himself and that the inconsistencies in the image he presents result from his being pushed into acting or speaking unnaturally. Despite his efforts to resist that drift in programming his image, there are those even among his friends who have asked, "Will the real Chuck Percy please stand up?"

CHAPTER IV

INTRODUCTION TO POLITICS

Percy got his introduction to the heady business of politics at the national level only a few years after he had taken over as president of Bell & Howell. The opportunity that permitted him to enter politics on a grand scale was his close relationship with President Dwight D. Eisenhower, the popular military hero. When the general became president, he was 62 years old, the fourth oldest man ever to be elected to the job. Percy was 33. The friendship, once established in the 1950s, lasted until the general's death in 1969. In the years after his presidency, Eisenhower took an interest in the political career of Percy by urging him to seek an elective office and campaigning for him in 1964. In a 1961 letter to Percy, the former president said, "I look forward at some future date to supporting you for political office—and should it be the highest office in the land my satisfaction will be all the greater."

Percy expressed his admiration of Eisenhower in 1970 in an oral history project conducted by Columbia University: "General Eisenhower was the controlling influence that caused me to come into public life. He was the only man who could have caused me to seek elective office."

Percy's statements about Eisenhower and the correspondence between them do not reveal that a close personal bond developed. Percy is not the subject of lengthy passages in Eisenhower's memoirs or reminiscences.

Percy admired the general's ability to survive in a political world without benefit of a partisan political background. Percy also respected Eisenhower's interest in foreign affairs, a subject of concern to the Bell & Howell executive who was seeking foreign markets for his products.

In the first couple of years of the Eisenhower administration, the president may have been aware of the young industrialist, but there is no evidence that a friendship was developing. Percy was one among thousands who showed an interest in Eisenhower's programs.

During this period Percy began learning more about Eisenhower through a third party. Early in the 1950s Percy made the acquaintance of Milton S. Eisenhower, the president's youngest brother. The friendship grew while the two served as trustees of the Ford Foundation's Fund for Adult Education, which ultimately started educational television. Serving as trustees for 10 years, they got together at board meetings and often at other times. Milton Eisenhower later encouraged Richard M. Nixon to choose Percy as his vice-presidential nominee in 1968. Milton also talked to his brother about Percy. At a meeting with Percy early in 1960, the president mentioned that his brother had recommended Percy on several occasions and he always respected Milton's opinions.

Percy visited the White House in 1954 as a member of a delegation of businessmen, and this visit resulted in an exchange of correspondence with Eisenhower that was released to the public. Eisenhower was battling Congress for trade reforms, and the correspondence fit nicely into the presidential strategy. In his letter Percy told of the delegation's interest in Eisenhower's foreign economic policy proposals: "We are persuaded that your sound and moderate program represents an essential step toward the achievement of a higher level of trade and investment." Percy later worked on behalf of legislation to implement Eisenhower's trade policies.

It was not until 1955 that the personal relationship began to develop. Percy recalls the first time he had a personal meeting with Eisenhower. The occasion was the swearing-in of Marion Folsom as secretary of Health, Education, and Welfare in 1955. Percy's invitation to the Folsom ceremony surprised him. Folsom had been connected with Eastman Kodak, a competitor of Bell & Howell. When Percy arrived for the ceremony, he realized the only other guests were the Folsom family and White House personnel. He was the only "outsider." His suspicions aroused, Percy was further puzzled by cryptic remarks from aides urging him to "do it." The "it," as it turned out, was the job of finance chairman for the Republican party in Illinois. Percy said later, "That began my life in politics."

Late in 1955 Percy delivered a speech entitled "The Price of Protection" to the Farm Bureau Federation convention. This speech brought Percy's interest in foreign trade to the attention of White House aides. In his speech Percy made a firm defense of free trade and no tariffs: "For our own part, to refuse to trade with the world . . . in no way seems in our own self-interest. Ultimately our refusal will isolate us from the free world and the friendship of free nations, as it will surely aid the cause of communism." Two decades later Percy still uses that theme, minus the reference to communism. In another part of the speech, Percy referred to consumer interest in free trade and the opportunity for Americans to purchase a full range of products from abroad. That, too, is often mentioned by Percy in present-day arguments against protectionist interests.

Prior to the Farm Bureau speech, Dr. Gabriel Hauge, a financial adviser to President Eisenhower, wrote Percy and suggested that he mention one of Eisenhower's favorite projects, the Organization for Trade Cooperation. Percy acknowledged the suggestion, and the text of the speech contained a reference to the organization. This international trade group was one of Eisenhower's pet projects. During the years from 1954 through 1957,

Eisenhower sought congressional approval of U.S. membership in the international group, which hoped to further expansion of world trade, but Congress never acted on the request. Eisenhower feared that failure of the United States to participate would lead to foreign restrictions against U.S. exports and injure military alliances.

After the Farm Bureau speech, the relationship between Percy and the White House warmed but still remained formal and was limited mostly to staff-level contact. Through 1955 Percy remained "Mr. Percy" in such correspondence as the acknowledgment by the president of the receipt of some gifts of photographic equipment. In 1956, after an exhaustive selection process, Eisenhower and his aides chose Percy, among others, to represent the president at the inaugurations of the presidents of Peru and Bolivia. Percy survived the screening and became the official representative to Peru and a member of the official party to Bolivia. Secretary of State John Foster Dulles, making one of his infrequent trips to Latin America, accompanied the two parties.

Percy contends that during the Eisenhower years he turned down several opportunities to join the administration. One job offered him, Percy recalls, was first assistant secretary of Health, Education, and Welfare under Oveta Culp Hobby. Another was assistant secretary of Commerce, and still another was head of the foreign aid program. Percy declined all offers. When he was interviewed in the Columbia University oral history project, Percy remembered Eisenhower telling him, "If you promise me that when you come into government you'll run for office...I will do everything I can to help you, no matter what the office is you're seeking."

The next shift in the relationship occurred from late 1956 to early 1957. In October, 1956, a special birthday party—called Ike Day—was held for Eisenhower. Percy helped organize the celebration. In a note addressed "Dear Mr. Percy," Eisenhower said, "Last evening you gave me the warm feeling that I was among good and true friends." In a PS the president added, "I know that you masterminded the whole affair, and I particularly appreciate your kindness in adding this to your already heavy burdens." Percy's reply a few days later called the Ike Day activity "one of the most thrilling experiences I have had." The language reflected the still formal relationship, the age difference, and the awe Percy held for President Eisenhower, even over something as minor as a birthday party.

In 1956 Percy and his wife were invited to Eisenhower's second inaugural. The invitation included a personal note addressed "Dear Chuck and Mrs. Percy." The Percys had not been to an inaugural in Washington, so it was an exciting event in their lives. From that point the correspondence between Percy and Eisenhower and between Percy and Sherman Adams, Eisenhower's chief of staff, became less formal and began to touch on important issues. For Christmas, 1958, Percy received a reproduction of Eisenhower's painting *Deserted Barn*. This gift signaled an ever-increasing warmth between the two men.

Overseas travel by Percy and his family, some trips for pleasure and a great many for expansion of Bell & Howell's business, gave Percy an opportunity to discuss foreign affairs in his correspondence with Eisenhower's staff. In March, 1958, while on a trip to Europe, Percy wrote Adams about European fears over the lagging American economy. Writing from Switzerland, Percy referred to the recession of 1958 and urged drastic action to allay the fears of Europeans.

Americans were also concerned about the economy, an attitude that was reflected in the 1958 congressional elections, which marked the low point of Eisenhower's influence. As the 1958 campaign progressed, Percy worked hard to raise funds for Illinois candidates. Late in October, Eisenhower visited Chicago to bolster candidates, and later the president wrote Percy: "You are making one of the real contributions to the campaign effort this year. I particularly appreciate your help because this year, as you know, the apathy has been astonishing and to me inexplicable." Republicans lost 48 seats in the U.S. House of Representatives. Not since 1937 had there been fewer Republicans in the lower chamber.

Nothing could have prevented the Republican congressional losses in 1958. With the party sagging, Percy and a handful of others received invitations from Eisenhower to a meeting in Washington shortly after the turn of the new year to discuss the off-year election results.

Eisenhower wanted Vice-President Nixon to become better acquainted with the young industrialist and urged the two to know each other better. Percy recalls that in those days the role Nixon played was a necessary counter to that of Eisenhower, who disdained political matters. Percy remembers that the president "literally never talked politics with me." But even then Percy saw that Nixon had a feel for politics: "I've always had the impression that he [Nixon] was totally and completely the political animal and I say that in terms not disparaging at all; but someone who is totally consumed with politics, who loves the political aspects of government and was forever thinking of the political connotation." Percy thought the Republican party needed someone close to the White House to worry about politics since the president eschewed political involvements to whatever extent he could.

A day before its session with the president, the group that had been invited to Washington to discuss the 1958 election disaster met with Nixon. Percy told that group, which included such party officials as Meade Alcorn and Leonard Hall, that the party seemed to lack goals and a program for the future. The next day, with Eisenhower in attendance, Nixon asked Percy to explain his concept of goals for the nation. Percy remembers Eisenhower being impressed with his statements and asking him to stay another day. Percy did, and the two fleshed out the idea of national goals. Eisenhower's State of the Union address mentioned national goals, and a few days later Percy remembers Eisenhower saying, "I think this will be the only thing that will ever be remembered in the presidential message to

Congress of 1959." Eisenhower appointed a presidential commission on national goals, which was to report to him.

From Percy's idea and the discussions that followed came the idea for a Republican party committee to discuss future directions. Before long, the Republican National Committee established the Republican Committee on Program and Progress. It was purely advisory and had no official authority to establish a party philosophy. Charles Percy was named chairman. The committee's goal was to record the philosophy of the modern Republican party and to establish principles for party action that would last for 25 years.

For Percy the chairmanship was an important step in his still-embryonic political career. Thirty-nine at the time of his appointment, he had little front-line political experience with factions of the party. As chairman he was thrown together with representatives of all wings of the party. The committee included such hardy Republicans as U.S. Senator Everett McKinley Dirksen; U.S. Representative Charles A. Halleck of Indiana; Harry Darby, former U.S. senator from Kansas; and John A. Volpe of Massachusetts, who later would be a member of Richard Nixon's cabinet. Regional party officials were also part of the group. Those from Illinois were Cook County State's Attorney Benjamin S. Adamowski and William H. Rentschler, who worked at various party jobs and often ran for public office. Professors such as Dr. Malcolm C. Moos and Dr. Gabriel Hauge, advisers to Eisenhower, and familiar political personages such as Robert A. Taft, Jr., of Ohio were on the committee.

The committee was organized into four sections—human rights and need, impact of science and technology, economic opportunity and progress, and national security and peace—partially to minimize the possibility of any clique dominating the proceedings. Each subcommittee reported individually, and the final document was edited by Percy and his staff. Percy presided over the four meetings of the full committee, and he also attended many subcommittee meetings.

A variety of influences were felt by the group. Eisenhower, perhaps not realizing how dangerous it was to organize a committee to decide principles that supposedly had already been established by the actions and thoughts of the president, worked mainly through the members of his staff who were on the committee. There were some attempts to enlist the support of cabinet officers and high-ranking government officials to persuade the committee that the party position should be the administration position, but the efforts were resisted. Vice-President Nixon followed the proceedings closely through his staff members, and he met with the group. His obvious interest was in the potential impact on the 1960 election campaign.

After a cursory meeting, attempts were made to disband the committee. Senator Barry M. Goldwater, in the words of one staff member, "came and told us to issue a press release and retire." Goldwater was not a committee member. Others on the committee, particularly those actively involved in politics, wanted to do a quick job, keep the results brief, and adjourn. Staff members and Percy enlisted the support of Nixon to stop those efforts.

Through the philosophical and political maze, Percy steered a course of compromise in committee deliberations. For the most part the technique worked. Staff members remember him as a definite influence on the final document. "Chuck seemed to grasp that the committee could do great damage if it seemed to repudiate the President," one aide recalled. Percy's style of leadership was patterned after his management methods at Bell & Howell, and while that did not please all members of the committee, the technique was effective. Daniel C. Gainey of Owatonna, Minnesota, a committee member, wrote to Eisenhower staff members that "Chuck Percy has proved a young man of unusual competence and stature." Goldwater also wrote, not to compliment but to express concern that Percy did not look kindly on a preface outlining the principles of the party. A staff member suggested Goldwater meet with Percy to discuss the matter. The final report included a preface. Eisenhower took a hands-off approach to the report and wanted only to see the final product. Most of Percy's correspondence with the White House during this period was through Ann Whitman, Eisenhower's secretary and later the secretary to Nelson A. Rockefeller. Percy, in a letter to Eisenhower, called the committee "a dedicated group with virtually total attendance at all meetings." He specifically cited Hauge for praise: "Though my own admiration for him could never exceed yours, it does, I am sure, equal it." Hauge and Percy were to serve together on the 1960 platform committee for the Republican National Convention.

While the committee's deliberations did not receive excessive media coverage, the final document was widely reported and was circulated to Republicans in printed form. It ultimately received favorable critical comment. *Life* magazine editorialized about it, and publisher Henry Luce wrote Eisenhower to commend the effort. In discussing the report, Congressional Quarterly, a nonpartisan reporting service, said, "Despite its long look into the future, practical Republican politicians have found the report provides ready ammunition to use in Congressional, local, and presidential campaigns this year [1960]." Some measure of the moderate approach of the report can be taken in comments from the two extremes of political party philosophy. *Human Events*, a publication of the Republican right wing, said in its March 18, 1959, issue that the committee ought to adopt an earlier statement of party policy which proclaimed that "the major domestic issue today is liberty against socialism." At the other extreme, the March 7, 1960, issue of the *New Republic*, a liberal publication, said the report was "simply beyond criticism, as far above it as Hansel and Gretel, Cinderella, or any other first-rate fairy tale."

Percy acknowledged the report's political nature in a summary to

Eisenhower on February 8, 1960: "The report is, of course, a political document. That is what we intended it to be. We wanted an expression of the stand of the Republican party on fundamental issues. . . . It was the purpose of this committee to make known to every citizen the Republican approach to broad problem areas and to further make it a matter of record that the Republican party looks forward—indeed forward to 1976—rather than backwards."

The report, published under the title *Decisions for a Better America*, covered the four main topic areas: human rights and needs, impact of science and technology, economic opportunity and progress, and national security and peace. Eisenhower, in a letter to Percy on November 3, 1959, said he hoped that distribution of the report could be made to "each head of agency." The sections on national security and peace and on science and technology would be of special interest to the Department of State and Department of Defense, Eisenhower said.

Most statements in the report fit comfortably with Eisenhower's Republican philosophy and administration programs, with only minor exceptions. The recommendation on federal aid to elementary and secondary education did run contrary to administration policy. The report called for "matching federal grants for elementary and secondary class-room construction." The administration opposed federal grants to aid construction and called instead for support of school bond issues.

Many political observers said the final report would be used as the foundation for the Republican National Convention platform in 1960. To make the connection even stronger, Eisenhower and Nixon selected Percy to head the platform committee.

Percy had new stature in the party. He had passed the first critical test. Now he was being given a harder political test, one with far greater public exposure and visibility. The name that newspapers, magazines, and television had associated only with successes at Bell & Howell now was heard in association with political business. One opportunity to be heard publicly on a matter of general interest came while the platform committee debated the issues. Percy defended the way Eisenhower dealt with Nikita Khrushchev at the summit conference against the criticism of two-time Democratic presidential nominee Adlai E. Stevenson.

Stevenson's comments came after the summit conference of May, 1960, collapsed. Percy branded Stevenson's criticism as irresponsible. Percy said, "I would say that to denounce the President of the United States and to place blame on his shoulders for the breakdown of the summit conference are improper and not in the national interest." Percy said Khrushchev's "intention to wreck the conference before he came was clear. The methods he used at the summit were obvious to all. Unhappily, Mr. Stevenson has played into Khrushchev's hands by implying that, actually, the President is to be blamed for the wreckage rather than the man whom world opinion has already selected as the villain." Undoubtedly, Eisenhower did not need to be defended by Percy, but in his national convention policy role, the Illinoisan became a target of newspaper reporters. Percy seldom refused an opportunity to comment on national affairs. The defense of Eisenhower in the final months of the administration was a fitting expression of Percy's admiration for the president and epitomized how Percy had risen to the role of newsmaker without benefit of holding elective office.

The Eisenhower-Percy relationship did not end with the conclusion of Eisenhower's two-term presidency. The two kept in touch through the 1960s, the former president helping Percy whenever he could. In the Columbia University oral history project, Percy gave his perspective on the Eisenhower years: "I don't know that the Eisenhower years will go down in history as the most dramatic years, as for instance the Roosevelt years, because we had less dramatic problems. But what the country needed and wanted was a period of rest, of tranquility, of sitting down, catching its breath, and President Eisenhower enabled the country to do that, and they felt exceedingly comfortable with him."

Relations with persons of national prominence form an important part of Percy's development as a public person. By the time Percy began his own political career, the Republican cast of characters had changed. The names are familiar now: Nelson A. Rockefeller, William W. Scranton, Richard M. Nixon, George W. Romney, Barry M. Goldwater, Ronald Reagan. Percy had a special relationship with each of them.

When the Republican Committee on Program and Progress issued *Decisions for a Better America*, Vice-President Nixon said the report constituted "the most useful and constructive statement of goals and principles ever issued by a political party." Percy had made a point of soliciting the vice-president's comments so they could be included in the promotion of the contents of the report. Those close to the deliberations of the committee recall that Nixon, through his aides Robert Finch and Charles K. McWhorter, kept in touch with the work of the committee. One interest was in the subcommittee working on human rights. A staff member to the committee remembers Nixon expressing an interest in having a forward-looking document. Percy kept Nixon aware of the committee's work and at one stage arranged a dinner meeting of the full committee and Nixon. As one committee member recalls, "The vice-president's presence was felt much of the time." After the committee published its views, Eisenhower and Nixon saw that Percy got the prestigious assignment of platform committee chairman. For a Republican who had done some fund raising work and had made some ceremonial appearances on behalf of Eisenhower, the chairmanship constituted quite an achievement.

The stage was set for one of the more interesting episodes in Republican party history, involving four men, two of whom wanted to be president of the United States, one who held the presidency, and one who apparently wanted only to successfully complete his committee assignment. They were Nixon, Rockefeller, Eisenhower, and Percy. Each of the principals played a specific role in the unfolding of the party platform. Eisenhower was the protector of his eight-year administration against any hint of repudiation or revision. Rockefeller, the challenger, questioned much from the Eisenhower years, particularly military preparedness. Eisenhower also worried that Nixon would not fully support the administration and might be too willing to accept compromise language to appease Rockefeller. Percy guaranteed Eisenhower that there would be no repudiation, but he did not fault Nixon for wanting the platform to look beyond the Eisenhower years.

Percy found himself in a somewhat unique position. Most often chairmen of platform committees for the two national parties come from political ranks, which gives them a built-in point of view on many issues, some special interests of their own, and also a familiarity with the political process that brings about a platform. With Percy it was different. He had no constituency. Although there is no way to measure to what audience he might have been appealing, he wanted Nixon to be nominated and he wanted a platform that gave the nominee something to use in the election.

Percy also wanted an opportunity to place in the platform some of the more progressive parts of the document issued by the Republican Committee on Program and Progress. Percy had survived the treacherous business of trying to put a political party's ideals on paper with party leaders looking over his shoulder, and the platform committee assignment looked like more of the same.

It was different this time. First, the whole party was looking on. Sectional differences would surface more readily, and there were political careers at stake. Second, the committee's makeup differed. The members of the Committee on Program and Progress were handpicked, following the "blue ribbon" theory. The platform committee contained two persons from each state and some of the territories—more than 100 from the grass roots of the Republican party. Only in such a gathering does the party reveal itself, warts and all.

Before the platform committee met in formal session a week prior to the national convention in Chicago, Percy and aides of Nixon and Eisenhower had drafted most of the planks. It was to be Vice-President Nixon's platform, and it had to reflect his wishes. And so Percy became a go-between. He would determine the Nixon position and, without injuring the sensitivities of more independent members, see that Nixon's views were approved by the platform committee. Having no power base of his own, Percy could not challenge the Nixon position, but he could offer another opinion. So the role of middleman between Nixon and the platform committee, which suited Percy's abilities nicely, continued throughout the committee's deliberations.

Nelson A. Rockefeller, Nixon's major contender, was recognized as an important factor in the convention from the start. There were efforts to bring him and his aides into the preconvention process. Above all, President Eisenhower had to be considered. Rockefeller was principally interested in having the platform recognize the possibility of a missile gap and stress more defense spending. Eisenhower, recognizing this as contrary to the efforts of his administration, balked. Percy stood in the middle on this and other Eisenhower-Rockefeller or Nixon-Rockefeller issues. "My role was as mediator," he later recalled. "I had to get a document."

In the preliminary stages of work with the platform committee, Percy appeared to have everything under control and moving efficiently toward completion. The committee seemed willing to compromise in its week-long deliberations leading up to the convention. By the weekend before the convention convened on Tuesday, all that remained were some loose ends and minor compromises. The committee seemed agreeable to Nixon's wishes, or what they understood his wishes to be. The picture was deceptive. On another level involving Rockefeller and his aides and Nixon and his aides, the waters were less calm, and a collision seemed inevitable unless the two could get together. If Percy detected this tension, he ignored it, because it seemed to him that compromises could be reached without an open confrontation. Nixon had praised Percy's efforts as chairman, and Percy thought he had been able to satisfy Rockefeller interests. Percy had met during the week with Nixon and Rockefeller to go over some of the areas of difference, and all agreed they were closer together than anyone had imagined.

On the Friday night before the convention, Nixon and Rockefeller met secretly in New York City to work out what has since been called the Fourteen Point Compact of Fifth Avenue. Without consulting Percy or the platform committee and unbeknown to almost everyone except close associates, the two agreed to construct a mutually acceptable platform in 14 general areas. Percy and other platform officials learned of the meeting in a telephone conversation with Nixon and Rockefeller, but many of the committee members did not learn of the changes until Saturday morning. It was a rude awakening, and their anger was predictable. The whole episode had the effect of pulling the rug out from under Percy. Had he been experienced in handling sudden political shifts in events, he might have been able to pull the committee together, but from the moment the Nixon-Rockefeller compact was announced, Percy lost control of the committee. Nixon personally took over implementation of the Rockefeller agreements, but Percy stayed involved.

Percy remembers a critical moment when compromise over language for the military spending portion of the platform was reached. It came after the New York meeting and while Eisenhower was on the East Coast about ready to leave for the Chicago convention. Percy, hoping to have the platform worked out by the time Eisenhower landed in Chicago, wanted to use the flight time to best advantage. He placed a conference call to Eisenhower and Rockefeller. "I told Eisenhower that he could not leave until he made a decision on what we would say," Percy remembered. He also informed Eisenhower that Nixon was prepared to accept any compromise at that point. Finally, the need for accelerated defense spending was accepted by Eisenhower as long as the words "if necessary" were entered into the document. Rockefeller, having won a victory, accepted the qualifying words.

After the Friday night meeting and the Saturday explosion, it was a long three days until the convention opened on Tuesday. Most of the changes reflecting the Nixon-Rockefeller understanding were worked out by Monday night, but the civil rights plank remained. It proved to be the thorniest issue of the platform—and of almost the whole convention—and required some tricky parliamentary maneuvers before settlement to Nixon's satisfaction. In this case it was not a contest between Nixon and Rockefeller: it was a struggle that developed because the subcommittee was confused about Nixon's actual position on civil rights. The principals in this drama were Nixon, Percy, the subcommittee on civil rights, the chairman of the subcommittee, the full platform committee, and a variety of Nixon aides and associates.

The subcommittee had turned out a fairly conservative civil rights plank, but Nixon wanted an even more flexible civil rights document than the subcommittee had originally provided. The subcommittee report passed the full platform committee, thus providing Nixon with a dilemma. He personally took charge of having the matter reconsidered by the full platform committee, a parliamentary maneuver requiring some behind-the-scenes activity. With the help of Rockefeller and Percy sympathizers, Nixon persuaded members of the committee to reconsider the first plank and substitute language more to his liking.

Percy was an integral part of the strategy sessions for having the plank reconsidered and revised. He met with Nixon and vice-presidential aides and helped arrange meetings between Nixon and key committee members to persuade them to aid in getting the civil rights plank reconsidered. On the day of reconsideration, Percy relinquished the chair to Vice-Chairman Melvin R. Laird, who was more versed in parliamentary procedure. The committee used parliamentary rules from the U.S. House of Representatives, many of which were foreign to Percy. Laird succeeded in getting reconsideration and the final civil rights proposal was acceptable to Nixon. The party ended the 1960 presidential nominating process and election campaign with a flexible and moderate position on civil rights, thanks mainly to candidate Nixon.

To Percy's credit the revised civil rights plank and the entire platform document was presented to the full convention with no inkling of the battles that had raged for days and nights or of the intrigues necessary to work out parliamentary snarls. Many who observed committee proceedings believe that conservatives among the subcommittee membership became convinced of what they perceived as Percy's liberalism on the civil rights issue. The irony is that Percy earned such a reputation doing the bidding of Richard Nixon, who ultimately as president steered a cautious and conservative course on civil rights.

In later years Percy reflected, "I knew the issues, but I didn't understand how important tactics and maneuvers and parliamentary tricks can be. I learned a lot from that job and the main thing I learned was that knowledge is power." He may also have learned something about trusting those who have their eyes on the presidency. Reports have persisted through the years that Percy folded at the last moment and had to be replaced by Laird. The inference has been that Percy literally turned the committee over to Laird for the finishing touches. Eyewitness staff members temper that interpretation. Percy has always given credit to Laird's expertise: "I was not skilled in parliamentary procedures. I was more issue-oriented, but Mel Laird . . . proved invaluable and working together I think we did produce what both the nominee, Richard Nixon, and the contender, Nelson Rockefeller, wanted." A final satisfaction for Percy was that the media seemed to focus more attention and praise on the Republican platform than the one issued by the Democrats.

Percy felt he could make a contribution to the Republican cause during the campaign of 1960. He volunteered but seldom was asked to help in Illinois or elsewhere. Nixon reportedly asked Percy to be chairman of his national citizens committee, but Percy declined on the grounds that he was not the right man to get independent and Democratic votes. Years later, when Percy found himself in opposition to many of President Nixon's programs, he would find his greatest support among independents and Democrats. After Nixon lost to John F. Kennedy by a narrow margin, Percy said he felt guilty about the fact that Illinois had been lost by only 8,800 votes. He thought he could have made a difference in Illinois and that would have made Nixon president in 1960.

After those times of disappointment, Nixon and Percy went separate ways. Nixon went on to California and his abortive attempt to become governor in 1962. Percy returned to Illinois and, having achieved all available heights at Bell & Howell (he was named chairman in 1961), turned much of his attention to politics.

CHAPTER V

PERCY AND THE ILLINOIS TRADITIONALISTS

Gerald R. Ford may have put an end to the beautiful dream of Charles H. Percy and his followers that the White House would someday beckon, but the 38th president of the United States may also have spared the state of Illinois one of its more bruising political confrontations.

Until August 9, 1974, when resignation abruptly ended the administration of Richard M. Nixon, Percy was poised to put on a drive for the 1976 presidential nomination. The keystone of his push had been announced many months before—it was Illinois.

Percy repeatedly declared that he needed the support of his home state if he were to be nominated. His strategy had been to enter several presidential primaries, beginning with the one in Illinois. He said, "If I get at least 51 percent of the vote there, then I'll have a home-state mandate to continue on the presidential campaign."

The prospect of an Illinois-based presidential campaign even had a bit of romance to it. Not since the 1920 Republican National Convention played out in Chicago's steamy summer weather has Illinois had a serious challenger for the GOP presidential nomination. In the convention that made the "smoke-filled room" synonymous with convention shenanigans, Frank O. Lowden, governor of Illinois, occupied center stage as a prime contender for the nomination. Before it ended, with the nomination of Warren Gamaliel Harding, the convention had turned from Lowden, and he never gained such national heights again. For some Republicans now active in Illinois politics, Lowden is a kind of folk hero because of his reputed independence and reform attitude.

From the day Percy first showed an interest in the 1976 presidential nomination, speculators said his biggest obstacle would be to win his own home-state party blessing. That declaration rested on the belief that many Republicans, traditional and conservative to the core, would not give Percy the time of day. Even with Percy's presidential train derailed, the facts of Republican party life in Illinois indicate that Percy will always have difficulty establishing himself as a party leader of persuasion and respect in his own state. The story of Percy's continuing tussle with traditional Illinois Republicans is not just his tale: it is the story of grass-roots politics in one of the most influential states in the Union, no matter who is seeking the presidency.

For years political observers have tried to find a label that adequately describes the modern-day Illinois Republican party. Writers and politicians have used "conservative" as an all-encompassing descriptive term without attempting to define it. A characteristic of the party leadership in Illinois, and in many other states, has been a kinship with those politicians at the national level who take conservative positions on major issues and with those at the state level who associate themselves with organizations that profess a conservative leaning. These conservatives want control of the state Republican party because control means power, which lasts even in defeat, humiliation, and disgrace and so becomes even more important than winning to some party leaders. Power is achieved by having a grip on the party apparatus at the local government level, where longtime party supporters are rewarded with selection for elective positions or with appointments to key boards and agencies. At the local level, friendships are made in fighting the common enemy, the Democrat.

In addition to a conservative approach on issues, Republican party builders since the 1930s have stressed, and many have shared, certain basic—that is, traditional—characteristics. Roughly, these are close ties, with an emphasis on native-born Illinoisans; an independence of the national party; a rural background; party work at the grass-roots level; and a strong party loyalty. Thus, the term "traditional" may be more descriptive of the Illinois Republican party than the more frequently used "conservative."

Many state Republicans who have not had a rural base have felt closer to rural than to urban areas. This often made for a sense of joy in warring with city interests, a feeling that persists in much of Illinois. Another common bond among traditionalists has been the importance they attach to local power, allowing only those who have passed the test of time and loyalty into inner party circles, where control is exercised. Party leaders have been more willing to permit relative newcomers to become involved in the highly visible reaches of the Republican organization, but at the grass-roots level, party loyalty is necessary. No single "boss," such as Chicago's Mayor Richard J. Daley for the Democrats, has emerged, and this has made the Republican party often appear chaotic and disorganized. Though the party machinery does have some control over the rank and file, what is lacking is political dominance from the bottom all the way to the top. Nevertheless, there is party discipline among traditionalists.

The traditionalists' pride in their independence has often put them at odds with popular concepts of Republicanism, particularly as practiced at the national level. This was especially true during the administrations of Dwight D. Eisenhower and even to some extent in those of Nixon and Ford. Illinois traditionalists have been reluctant to admit to the inner party circles those Republicans who profess to be "moderate" or "progressive."

The fear is not so much that the outsiders might taint the party's philosophical base as it is simply a distrust of new faces and new ideas. Moreover, the traditionalists don't want to relinquish their power, some of which they lost in their confrontations with Charles Percy.

There is little question that Republican traditionalists have played a major role in Illinois politics and to some degree will continue to do so. Thus, a knowledge of the traditionalists' dollar power, their leadership, and their influence on public policy, both in the past and in the present, is important in assessing how Illinois might be viewed in any presidential sweepstakes, with or without Percy. Such information would provide the key to the degree of state party leadership Percy can expect to achieve.

Today the Democratic party in Illinois does well in some of the larger industrial Downstate cities and counties and in Chicago, while the Republican party has its strength in the Chicago suburbs and in Downstate rural-oriented areas. But it was not always this way. The current situation did not develop until well into the 1900s. Prior to 1900, party domination in the state—Democrats in the south and Republicans in the north—reflected settlement patterns. Persons in the southern part of the state came from the Deep South, while the northern part of the state was settled by persons from the Northeast. In the period from the Civil War to the Depression, Illinois was a fairly safe Republican state. Beginning in 1932 and continuing to the time Percy began his active political career, the two parties were fairly even in voter strength. On balance, the Democrats probably had the best of it. From 1932 through 1964 the Democrats won five gubernatorial contests, and the Republicans four. Over the same period Democrats won in seven presidential contests, and Republicans in two. During this time political allegiance in the geographic areas shifted too, and no longer was there a north-south division.

Some evidence of the durability of traditionalist influence can be seen in gubernatorial contests since the 1940s. During much of the 1940s, the handsome countenance of Dwight H. Green occupied the governor's chair. The popular Green gathered his support from traditional and conservative party elements. One of his strongest backers was the *Chicago Tribune* and its publisher Colonel Robert R. McCormick. Green served, with no particular distinction, from 1941 to 1949. In a third-term attempt in 1948, he lost to Adlai E. Stevenson.

In 1952 Illinois Republicans rode the Eisenhower tide and elected 38-year-old William G. Stratton as governor. He served until 1961 when Democrat Otto Kerner took over. Stratton's record in two terms reveals an administrative ability but little in the way of programs. He dealt with some programs he inherited from the Stevenson term—such as improvement of the state highway system—but did not confront any of the state's social problems of that time. Although giving the appearance of being a moderate politically, Stratton's philosophy actually was in line with traditional party supporters and leaders. His roots were conservative. While serving two terms in the U.S. House of Representatives as an at-large congressman, Stratton had shown isolationist tendencies before World War II by opposing aid to Allied nations, a stand that had endeared him to McCormick. The policies of the Eisenhower administrations had no effect on Stratton's political philosophy, and so when he sought a third term in 1960, traditionalists did not hesitate to renominate him instead of selecting Hayes Robertson, whose conservatism bordered on the extreme.

Beginning in 1940 and up to 1964, only those gubernatorial candidates closely aligned with traditional Republican forces had made it through the primaries and into the general elections, but in 1964 the pattern was changed. Conservatives and traditionalists first tried to rally behind Charles Carpentier, but he fell ill and died. Most of Carpentier's supporters jumped to Percy, and he became the front-runner for the party's nomination. A late entry, William J. Scott, attracted many traditionalists, but his campaign came too late. Percy's victory in the primary election broke the string of traditionalist domination, and the party began to seek candidates with a broader appeal to the electorate.

In the 1968 gubernatorial primary contest the conservative-liberal lines were drawn less clearly, but traditionalists were still able to find a candidate and support him. The traditionalists favored Richard B. Ogilvie. Other Republicans leaned toward John Henry Altorfer, an industrialist from Peoria and a friend of Percy. Of the two, Ogilvie appeared more conservative and had worked his way up through party ranks. Altorfer, considered a moderate, had not paid his dues in party work, and that is one of the most important principles to traditionalists. With strong grass-roots backing, Ogilvie became the Republican candidate, although his exposure Downstate was minimal.

Ogilvie, who bridged more gaps between party factions than other politicians in any wing of the Republican party at the state government level, served as governor from 1969 to 1973. His administration undertook a major reform of the structure of the executive branch and steered new courses in taxation and in the state's involvement in social questions. He ultimately angered many large Republican contributors and grass-roots workers, particularly by levying a state income tax. The contrast between Ogilvie's administration and those of the past is seen in the comment of the political scientist who said that until 1960 issues were never at the heart of Republican desires for control of the state. The goal was patronage. Ogilvie tried to adopt a broader view of goals, and this and the state income tax may have cost him reelection. However, a large part of the reason for Ogilvie's failure to win again in 1972 can be laid to an inability to expand his appeal and compete satisfactorily for independent votes. His problem underlined the difficulty any Illinois Republican has in trying to cultivate an independent constituency and still maintain healthy relationships with traditional Republicans.

Further traditionalist influences in Illinois politics can be seen in the

U.S. Senate races. Modern-day traditionalist lineage dates back to the early 1940s when the strong backing of Colonel Robert R. McCormick in the *Chicago Tribune* helped elect C. Wayland ("Curly") Brooks to the Senate. He had defeated James M. Slattery, the interim senator, in 1940. Brooks served from 1941 to 1949, during which time he spoke the McCormick rhetoric against the New Deal, foreign involvements, communism and those who sympathized, and Democrats. An indication of McCormick's devotion to conservatism was his support of Senator Robert A. Taft of Ohio for president in 1948 and 1952 against stronger party candidates. McCormick also deplored Republicans who adopted a nonpartisan stand on foreign affairs or did not fight communism with enough enthusiasm.

After liberal Democrat Paul Douglas defeated Brooks, the Democrats held both Senate seats for two years. Scott W. Lucas was the other senator from Illinois. In 1950 Everett Dirksen, a longtime member of the U.S. House of Representatives before an eye ailment forced his "retirement" in 1948, contested Lucas and won an upset victory. Dirksen charmed traditionalists throughout his career, though his credentials as a conservative were questionable since he frequently jumped ship on party issues. Most of his moves toward a moderate course were dictated by internal Senate considerations. His record never meant much to traditionalists. In payment for what they considered to be his undaunted loyalty, traditionalists maintained a special place in their hearts for Dirksen, despite his inconsistencies. Dirksen knew how important traditional appearances were to Illinois Republicans.

Since 1950 Dirksen and Percy have been the only Republicans elected to the U.S. Senate from Illinois. In 1954 Joseph Meek, a strong supporter of business interests and a traditionalist who was unable to excite the independent voters, challenged Senator Paul Douglas. This contest between Meek and Douglas was one of the party's most uncomfortable episodes. The incident speaks to the strength of traditional Republicans and their stubbornness. It is also evidence of the Illinois party's smugness toward the Eisenhower administration and its willingness to accept defeat before adopting a flexible ideology. From the start Meek's candidacy put a wedge between the Illinois party and the administration in Washington. Douglas had supported many Eisenhower programs, and the president and his aides knew it. Meek, on the other hand, took positions that clashed with Eisenhower's.

In the primary, Meek ran against eight other Republicans and led the field, which included Austin Wyman, who had the backing of the Eisenhower forces and the Marshall Field newspapers in Chicago. Meek won on the strength of support by Senator Everett Dirksen; the *Chicago Tribune*, which was loudly anti-Eisenhower; and other traditionalists.

After the primary, pressure was exerted on Eisenhower to break his pledge not to support any individual candidates in 1954 and to give Meek his blessing. Attempts were made by Meek's supporters to bring Secretary of State John Foster Dulles into the act, but Dulles declined to enter the controversy. To counterbalance these efforts, hundreds of Illinoisans, professing to be loyal Republicans, wrote letters to Eisenhower asking him not to endorse Meek.

Finally, a backhanded endorsement of Meek came late in July when the White House released an Eisenhower letter to Meek in which the president said he hoped to see Meek in Washington after the election. The media widely interpreted this statement as an "endorsement," but later behavior by Eisenhower indicated that his words were something less. In August at the Illinois State Fair, Eisenhower and Meek appeared on the same platform before a crowd of fairgoers. Eisenhower's address mentioned no Illinoisans by name, and Meek sat a comfortable distance from the president. Newspapers noted the "snub," and editorial pages opposed to Meek pointed out his unacceptability to Eisenhower Republicans.

Eisenhower and Meek disagreed over the latter's support of Senator Joseph McCarthy's Communist witch-hunts of the 1950s. Meek spoke strongly against communism, as most all candidates of the time felt obliged to do, but there were rumors that Meek supported the tactics used by the Republican senator from Wisconsin to fight communism in the United States. Meek's backers denied it, but the distance between the candidate and the White House widened because of the stories. While McCarthyism captured headlines across the nation and later became identified as one of the more pervasive influences in American political behavior, emotions in Illinois, particularly among Republicans, were not as intense as in other locations. Some reports have left the impression that Meek failed in his candidacy because of connections with McCarthy. Observers of the period are not inclined to blame his failure solely on that point.

The Meek affair ended up being an embarrassment to everyone. Eisenhower would have preferred a candidate who embraced progressive Republicanism and administration programs. Governor William Stratton and other Illinois Republicans who felt lukewarm about the national leadership still wanted smooth relationships with the administration. The Meek candidacy did not help the governor.

In retrospect, it is easy to see how reluctant Illinois traditionalists often have been to move with the national party if that meant movement away from what they thought was a straighter road. If control of the state and local party machinery were at stake, there was no choice but to protect interests closer to home. It is not out of the question that traditionalists concluded early in the campaign that no Republican could defeat Douglas, and so there was no reason to compromise with moderate Republicans. The Meek episode, combined with the Illinois Republican delegation's allegiance in 1952 to Eisenhower's opponent Robert A. Taft, clearly established the relationship between Illinois and Washington for the rest of the 1950s. Only rarely—when it suited all causes—did everyone truly unite. Charles Percy's rapidly warming relationship with Eisenhower and associates put the industrialist outside the mainstream of state party attitudes.

A moderate streak in the philosophy and practice of Republican candidates put traditionalist appeal on the skids in the early 1960s. Samuel W. Witwer, a well-liked progressive from a Chicago suburb, challenged incumbent Paul Douglas in 1960 and lost, even though he enjoyed steadfast traditionalist party support. Witwer later became president of the Illinois Constitutional Convention in 1970.

The trend away from conservatism coincided with the election of Democratic leaders John F. Kennedy and Lyndon B. Johnson at the national level and Otto Kerner at the state level. In 1968 Republicans Richard Nixon, who gained control of the presidency, and Richard Ogilvie, who won the statehouse, followed the middle ground and avoided open appeals to the fringes of the electorate. Traditionalists had little to cheer about in Illinois politics of the 1960s except for Everett Dirksen's reelection victories in 1962 and 1968. However, Dirksen's appeal to independents was limited because of his partisan image, thus preventing his carrying any other traditionalists to victory on his coattails.

While hard-core Republicans are not likely to admit that their strength has eroded, the trends indicate otherwise, particularly at general election time. Some of the deterioration of traditionalist influence is a result of the growth of independent voter patterns. Survey data from polls taken by Republicans in 1970 and 1973 add further evidence to the erosion theory. The 1970 data came from the campaign of Ralph T. Smith of Alton for the U.S. Senate. The 1973 data was compiled to help U.S. Representative John B. Anderson of Rockford decide whether he should run against Adlai Stevenson in 1974.

The Anderson survey, conducted by a Detroit firm in the fall of 1973 when Watergate revelations were frequent, revealed a significant decline in Republican party identification over the two previous years and attributed that drop to Watergate-related incidents. Between the 1970 and the 1973 surveys, Republican identification dropped 18 points, from 40 to 22. Democratic identification also dropped, from 46 to 38, while the independent total increased from 14 to 36. The Detroit firm said that, even considering the differences associated with the timing of the two surveys, the drop in Republican identification could hardly be considered an encouraging sign. The firm said the increased number of independents revealed an important drift away from the Republican administration in Washington and reflected an "anti-politics" sentiment. The 1973 survey also indicated that younger people were less likely to identify themselves as Republicans. Only those 65 years or older regularly chose Republican over Democratic or independent identification.

The same 1973 survey dealt with trends in Republican identification among high-income and highly educated voters, large numbers of whom traditionally label themselves Republicans. The survey indicated that Republican identification in this group dropped dramatically. The firm suggested that those defecting from Republican ranks now call themselves "independents." Survey information on the Cook County suburban areas supported this conclusion, which was strengthened by recollections that Democrat Adlai Stevenson, in his 1970 and 1974 victories, made strong showings in Republican suburbs.

Characteristically, the traditional wing of the Illinois Republican party ignores the trends. This happens because party machinery, county chairmen, and party officials remain closely allied and wary of opening the party to more moderate influences for fear of diminishing their power. In the wake of Richard Nixon's resignation from office in 1974, the state party convention convened. Many moderates saw the convention as an opportunity to broaden the attraction of the party to independents with a carefully worded resolution about the former president and Watergate. Instead, the 1,100 delegates approved a resolution condemning the activities of those who worked for Nixon but praising the ex-president's accomplishments in office. A resolution critical of Nixon failed to pass. The appeal of these actions could not have gone much beyond hard-core party supporters.

The Illinois Republican party had some of its worst moments in 1974, particularly during and after the fall elections. One series of incidents involved former state legislator George Burditt of LaGrange, the party candidate for the U.S. Senate. Except for a few conservative positions on major national issues, Burditt considered himself in tune with Percy's attitudes much of the time. When other stronger candidates failed to come forward to run against the easily recognized Senator Adlai E. Stevenson III, Burditt was drafted. Party officials all over the state pledged their assistance, which Burditt took to also mean financial help. As the campaign moved toward November, Burditt fell upon hard times financially. Money sources dried up. With little more than a month to go in the campaign, some Republicans, including Percy, requested the United Republican Fund of the state to loosen the strings on money for Burditt, but by that time nothing could help. Burditt suffered for the sins of the party: a lack of leadership, a disinterest, and an unwillingness to see the party through some of its tougher times with money.

Because of Percy's preoccupation with matters in Washington, resulting from the presidential crisis and concentration on his presidential campaign, the senator was unable to provide the needed party leadership to help Burditt. There is some question, however, as to just how much assistance Percy could have provided from a Washington base. After the election, a Republican disaster, Percy's attempt to provide some quick leadership was resented by some in the party who felt Percy was trying to take over in the vacuum. Percy called a meeting of party leaders and commissioned a special report on party affairs. Released on March 1, 1975, the report called for a variety of reforms within the Illinois Republican party, including abolishment of the United Republican Fund and efforts to open the party to a broader cross section of the population.

Republican voter strength is concentrated mainly in two geographic areas of Illinois. One is the suburbs of Chicago, which for purposes of this discussion will include some pockets of Republican strength in the city of Chicago. The other is Downstate—that is, all parts of the state excluding Chicago and suburbs. Despite its much greater area, Downstate is not dominant in voter strength because it has a more static population than the rapidly growing suburban areas.

Although the suburbs and Downstate are generally thought to vote alike, the party divisions are there, and they are growing. A moderate-conservative pull has developed among persons who might become future party leaders. While it is difficult to generalize, politicians in the suburbs seem to lean toward the conservative position. There are conservatives Downstate too, of course, but the growing trend toward moderate Republicanism among officials in the party is strongest outside the suburbs. Because they are able to function within the framework of traditionalism, moderates Downstate do not lose their standing with party loyalists. It is more difficult for moderates in the suburbs, for there the conservative constituencies and right-of-center officials have developed a more dogmatic approach to party affairs.

Getting an accurate count of conservative strength in the whole state is difficult. Political operatives in the party, and particularly those working for Percy, believe the base strength of conservatism is about 10 percent of a Republican primary vote, with influence over another 15 percent. The full 25 percent is possible when there is a strong candidate. In theory then, a strong conservative in a primary contest could count on 25 percent of the vote for openers.

A characteristic of conservative strength is strong voter identity at the congressional district level. Such conservative congressmen as Edward J. Derwinski of Chicago's Southwest Side, Philip M. Crane of Mount Prospect, and John N. Erlenborn of suburban Elmhurst, for example, have large sympathetic constituencies.

There is no single congressional district representative of all others in the suburban area, but a profile of one district, Crane's of Mount Prospect, provides a glimpse of a strong conservative constituency. The voters are young, mobile, and well-off, comparatively speaking. A profile based on the 1970 federal census reveals that the median age for this district is 24.8 years, the youngest in the state. Of those over 25 years of age, 22.3 percent had completed college, the second highest such figure in the state. Median income, a key figure to the analysis, was $15,173, second highest in the state. The median value of homes in the district was $32,696, also second highest, and the census showed that this district had more new housing units than any other district in Illinois during the decade of the 1960s.

The constituencies of Derwinski and Erlenborn are statistically similar to Crane's but generally reflect less affluence and a higher percentage of persons in blue-collar jobs. The voting records show that Percy does well in these conservative districts. Examination of the records of the 4th Congressional District, which has elected Derwinski to Congress since 1958, shows that in the 1964 Republican primary Percy received 25,805 votes and William Scott, 14,039, or 65 and 35 percent respectively. In the 1964 general election against incumbent Governor Otto Kerner, a Chicago area product, Percy drew 147,478 votes to 101,002 for Kerner. Derwinski's victory over his Democratic opponent was 59 to 41 percent, the same as Percy's. In the 1966 general election against Senator Paul Douglas, Percy received 102,762 votes and Douglas 50,211, giving Percy 68 percent of the total. Figures from the 1964 and 1966 elections are helpful, but because of the continuing shift of residents from Chicago's core area to the suburbs and the resulting reapportionment of congressional districts, they are of dubious definitive value today. Some people believe that these changes have made for a more conservative electorate in the ensuing time. However, the 1972 election results also show Percy winning a large percent of the votes in the 4th Congressional District: He defeated Roman Pucinski 137,643 to 67,413.

Even though Percy can attract a large percentage of votes in conservative districts, he is not looked upon with favor by the more powerful congressional segments of the party leadership. He does receive backing from moderate party leaders such as John B. Anderson of Rockford, who maintains a position in the U.S. House leadership; Thomas F. Railsback of Moline, who received attention as a member of the House Judiciary Committee during the impeachment process; and Paul Findley of Springfield, who first gained election to the U.S. House as a conservative but has become more of a moderate in his views on many issues, particularly on international questions. In Congress the voting records of Railsback, Findley, and Anderson are considered moderate. But the conservative and traditionalist leadership makes no secret of its dislike of Percy and any other moderate Republican. In the forefront of the opposition was Leslie C. Arends, who served in the U.S. House of Representatives from 1934 until his retirement as House leader in 1974. Today the party chiefs continue Arends's lead, but not as rigidly.

In the 1972 senatorial campaign, Arends once wore a campaign button proclaiming the candidacy of Percy's opponent, Representative Roman Pucinski. But even the most dedicated of opponents can break bread together when the occasion arises. Both Percy and Arends have September 27 birth dates. In 1973 Arends was 78 and Percy 54, and despite their differences they sang "Happy Birthday" greetings to each other.

Other congressmen have opposed Percy's views from time to time but with less boldness than Arends. In 1970 before the Senate vote on G. Harrold Carswell for Supreme Court justice, 11 Illinois Republican congressmen called on Percy and urged him to vote for confirmation. Derwinski, acknowledged spokesman of the delegation, said later, "We made it plain that this was the entire delegation [minus Findley] calling on him for the first and only time. He said, 'Thank you gentlemen,' and we left. And we haven't discussed legislation with Percy since." Percy voted against Carswell. Derwinski frequently has criticized Percy. In 1964 he served as Goldwater's Illinois campaign manager. During Percy's pursuit of the 1976 presidential nomination, the senator's supporters reached an understanding with Derwinski, who agreed to play down his critical comments publicly and privately. In return for Derwinski's cooperation, Percy supporters agreed not to seek a candidate to run against the congressman in the primary elections. Released from this understanding because Percy put an end to his presidential effort, Derwinski can be expected to resume his criticism of Percy.

The antipathy between Percy and the conservatives has lasted through the years despite occasional reconciliations. Late in 1973 Percy wrote each of the 12 Republican congressmen, urging them to vote for a bill that would have authorized the government's first subsidies to urban mass-transit systems. The House passed the bill, but Illinois Republicans voted 10 to 1 against it. Anderson, the most outspoken moderate in the delegation, voted for the bill, and Railsback did not vote. It may have been that the urban centers represented by the delegation would not have benefited from the proposal, but a slap at Percy is suspected.

The conservative nature of the Illinois Republican delegation is reflected in ratings made by Americans for Constitutional Action (ACA). The ACA ratings for 1973 showed two Illinois congressmen as having 100 percent conservative voting records. They were Derwinski of the 4th District, on Chicago's Southwest Side, and Crane of the 12th District, in the affluent northwest suburbs of Chicago. The ACA rated three congressmen as having conservative voting records of at least 80 percent. They were Robert P. Hanrahan of the 3rd District, on Chicago's South Side; Arends of the 15th District; and Robert H. Michel of the 18th District, which includes Peoria. Anderson received a 46 percent rating by the ACA. For comparative purposes, the ACA rated Percy as voting 17 percent with the conservative position. The liberal counter to the ACA is the Americans for Democratic Action (ADA). The ADA rated Percy's voting record as 60 percent favorable. All these ratings, based solely on philosophical determinations made by the organizations, are viewed with some skepticism by congressmen, who see them as oversimplified indicators.

With Percy not considered qualified by conservatives, the search for leaders to bring together the right wing as a nucleus of strong party support and influence continues. Some observers foresee possible future leaders among the loyalist congressmen in the Republican delegation, and probably the most articulate of these are Philip Crane and Robert Michel. At times Crane has openly led cheers in his district against Percy and the moderate to liberal point of view, but he has not attempted to seek statewide office or influence. Crane made no secret of his search for an alternative to Percy when it appeared the senator would be in the 1976 state presidential primary. His favorite for 1976 was Ronald Reagan, a native Illinoisan and former governor of California.

Publicly, Percy says nothing harsh about his congressional critics, but he is keenly aware of their barbs and their feelings. Peoria Republicans tell the story of a dinner in that city during a time when Percy had been particularly critical of Nixon. Michel, the speaker at the dinner, made references to the fact that Charles Dancey, editor of the *Peoria Journal-Star*, had stood by the president through hard times. Percy thought the comments were intended for the audience, but Republicans later told Percy that Michel's message had been directed at him: Stick by Nixon!

Edward Derwinski is considered by many members of the delegation as a possible successor to Arends in his conservative leadership role. But Derwinski's sphere of influence is limited to the Chicago area and his fellow congressmen.

There are some potential leaders among right-of-center legislators in the Illinois General Assembly, but none that have given indications of rising beyond the legislature. In Downstate areas Percy's severest public critic is John C. Hirschfeld, Republican state representative from Champaign, but his comments have failed to create any substantial following. Percy finds Hirschfeld more of an irritant than a threat because there is little indication that the representative could rally support from Percy's diehard foes in other parts of the state.

Among officials who have run successful statewide campaigns, State Comptroller George W. Lindberg is as close to being an issue-oriented conservative as any, an assessment based mainly on his previous legislative record. Although conservative in his approach to social-service questions, Lindberg earned a "progressive" label in the legislature mainly by sponsoring ethics and judicial reform bills. But the role of comptroller is administrative, and Lindberg would need a policy-making office from which to build broad statewide appeal.

The likelihood of some conservative rising from the ashes to revive the party on the short term is remote. For example, experience indicates that Lindberg, in a bid for higher state office, would abandon conservatism and seek a middle ground. The limited appeal of a conservative philosophy would severely restrict his chance for election. The dilemma for persons such as Lindberg, who has only basic financial resources, is that he must broaden his appeal but still must count heavily on traditionalist financial support. The middle of the political spectrum is increasingly attractive to Republicans, and it is most likely that the future party leaders will be persons with politically moderate views.

There are some Republican moderates in the congressional ranks who are possible contenders for high state office. The two most widely considered to be potential gubernatorial or senatorial candidates in the future are John Anderson and Thomas Railsback. Anderson nearly made the Senate race in 1974 against Adlai E. Stevenson III, but in the gloom of Watergate he backed off, preferring not to jeopardize his seniority in the House and his leadership position in the Republican House delegation. Anderson's 1973 survey of voter attitudes found that fewer persons than ever before wanted to be associated with the party and that Democratic fortunes, while sagging too, were far better on a percentage basis than the Republicans. The results of this survey helped Anderson decide not to run against Stevenson. Railsback received substantial television exposure in August, 1974, during impeachment hearings held by the House Judiciary Committee. He represents a district with major union strength but has managed to bridge the gaps in his constituency with a middle-of-the-road voting record. With only congressional constituencies from which to build party strength, Railsback and Anderson have to be considered dark horses unless a united party should turn to one of them for a specific contest, complete with pledges of financial support.

Without a strong personal leader at the gubernatorial level or in Congress, the Illinois Republican party is rudderless. The Democratic party, on the other hand, has been able to look to Chicago's Mayor Richard J. Daley for leadership whether the governor was a Democrat or not. Even if the mayoral situation were to change, the Democratic party's central controlling mechanism would still be far more successful at maintaining party discipline than any organization the Republicans have been able to build. Complicating the picture further for the Republican party is a greatly weakened Cook County organization and minimal party identification among residents of the city. Traditional money support had either dried up by 1975 or was pledged to more independent candidates, and the strong base from which Richard B. Ogilvie and William J. Scott began their political careers had eroded. After the 1974 congressional elections, many observers in the state felt that Illinois Republican fortunes had not looked so weak in decades.

That is the political situation that Percy must contend with as he looks to continued service in the Senate as a Republican from Illinois. Many traditionalists are not fond of him, but they recognize his drawing power on the ticket when he runs. Percy's trump is that these traditionalists will see him as a key to maintaining control of the state and local party apparatus and the means by which more Republicans can be elected at the courthouse level. Other traditionalists would like to defeat Percy regardless of the impact on the party, and though small in number, they are dedicated to his political demise. Even united, the two traditionalist groups have a waning influence in party affairs as long as strong candidates with appeals to independent voters, such as Percy and Scott, are around. Still, no one can rule out the possibility that traditionalists could put the muscle and money together to back a strong candidate against the senator in a primary election. The key, even more than money, is finding the personality. At the moment no one seems a likely prospect. If traditionalists can keep a minimal hold on party affairs until 1978 and find that elusive personality to back in an election, they will have one more chance at Percy if he seeks a third term in the Senate. Except for that possibility, traditionalists are more of a nuisance than a threat to Percy. The senator's best interests are served, however, by working with the traditionalists despite their animosity, just in case he should decide to face the voters again.

On many occasions Percy has needed a leveler in his dealings with traditional elements in the party, particularly in Illinois. The media has served this function by providing him with frequent opportunities to work outside the more confining framework of the established party to attract supporters and financing. Media treatment of his activities has always been a plus for Percy. Throughout his career Percy has made himself available to the media, and the media has responded, often to the anger of those who see this mutual availability as feeding the Percy ego and providing him with a disproportionate amount of exposure. From this has grown the opinion by many that Percy is little more than a media opportunist.

Even in nonreceptive sections of the country where he traveled when he was seeking the 1976 presidential nomination, Percy's overall press coverage must be ranked as favorable. In the metropolitan centers with large newspapers that have moderate to liberal editorial policies, Percy scores frequently. When conservative publications or journals have taken a swipe at him, the damage has been minor. There is no evidence that Percy has received favored treatment over the years from network radio and television personalities, although he is friendly with many of them and good friends with some. In the latter category is Walter Cronkite, the venerable dean of evening network news broadcasts.

Percy's stature as a renegade Republican, although overrated in fact, has earned him special recognition by the electronic media. Because the activities at the 1972 Republican National Convention were so carefully programmed, television newsmen on the convention floor often had little to do in the way of reporting breaking news, and they wandered about in frustration and boredom. If there were hints of a controversy or reports of a floor fight brewing, however remote, Percy, at the edge of the Illinois delegation, was often sought out and interviewed. Usually he knew nothing of the activity, and so the interviews often lapsed into discussions of Percy's political ambitions. These conversations usually ended with Percy declaring again that he was not a candidate for the 1976 presidential nomination.

Characteristically, candidates seeking statewide office in Illinois spend the early weeks of the fall campaign in Downstate areas and reserve the final month for Chicago and suburbs. While the concentration of voters in the metropolitan area is one reason for the strategy, another is access to Chicago media. Chicago newspapers will send a writer to follow a candidate in Effingham perhaps once during the campaign, but in Chicago the candidates can count on almost constant attention from the newspapers, radio, and television. It still is considered imperative for a candidate to have the endorsement of at least one Chicago newspaper if he hopes to have much of a chance at the polls. In 1966 Douglas's lack of a single Chicago newspaper endorsement seriously damaged his chances.

Historically, the dominant editorial voice in the Chicago area has been the Chicago Tribune, which was controlled by Colonel Robert R. McCormick. The grandson of Joseph Medill and the grandnephew of Cyrus Hall McCormick, the Tribune publisher had roots in conservatism and isolationism. In the McCormick heyday of the 1940s and until his death in 1955, the Tribune searched for attractive conservatives to back for high public office in Illinois and the nation. For putting the strength of his paper behind them, McCormick demanded loyalty. In looking back at the McCormick era in Illinois politics, it is commonly believed that the man and his newspaper had great influence over millions of persons. The counter to that theory, held by many who lived during the period, is that McCormick's importance was overplayed outside the state by an admiring and sometimes envious audience and that his impact inside the state was felt mainly among Republicans, who would have liked any Republican paper.

Since almost anyone can remember, Percy has been a whipping boy for the Tribune, which has given him the same invective reserved for Democrats, and particularly liberal Democrats. Only in recent years, with a relaxing of the strongly conservative editorial and news policies on the Tribune, has Percy attained an acceptable status with the newspaper. Still, the enthusiasm is restrained. For example, in 1974 when President Gerald Ford sought a vice-president, the Tribune said of Percy that he would not be a good candidate because "though an able man [he] has alienated the party's right wing."

McCormick had died almost a decade before Percy made his first run for elective office. Sitting in the editor's chair at the time was McCormick's successor W. Don Maxwell, who tried valiantly to continue the tenets of McCormick journalism. Downstate observers felt Maxwell to be less reasonable than McCormick on state political questions. To Maxwell and other editors at the *Tribune*, Percy never fit the image of a first-rate Republican candidate. He was too liberal, or rather, too liberal for the *Tribune*. On the occasions when some kind of alliance might have been possible, either Percy did not seek the paper's endorsement or the *Tribune* decided that Percy did not deserve it.

The 1964 campaign for governor had much to do with forming the background for the continuing relationship between Percy and the *Tribune*. Before Percy announced his candidacy for the nomination, he met with George Tagge, then political editor of the *Tribune* and literally one of the state's most influential persons. Tagge operated most effectively in Springfield by openly lobbying with senators and representatives for projects favored by the *Tribune*. The classic Tagge story concerned state financing for what eventually came to be McCormick Place in Chicago. Working with Maxwell, Tagge spent long hours smoothing the project's way through the legislature. Political wags called it "Tagge's Temple." Another of Tagge's roles was to find candidates the *Tribune* could support. He frequently had a personal hand in determining the endorsement fate of candidates.

After the meeting of Percy and Tagge, Percy made the error of going to Maxwell over Tagge's head. Tagge never forgave him for it. In a fit of childish pique and in an effort to demean Percy in the *Tribune's* news columns, Tagge referred to Percy as the "Chicago industrialist," knowing such a tag would alienate the grass-roots vote. That may also explain why the *Tribune* and Tagge were interested in getting William J. Scott into the 1964 primary against Percy. Tagge's feelings toward Percy could be laid to personal dislike rather than any deep philosophical differences. In 1964 Percy won the party's nomination for governor without the blessing of the *Tribune*, a rarity in Illinois Republican politics to that date. However, the *Tribune* did endorse Percy in the general election against Otto Kerner.

The importance of Percy's primary victory, regardless of his loss in the general election, cannot be underplayed. It broke the *Tribune's* stranglehold on the selection of Republican candidates and began a trend toward more moderate views in the party and among its candidates. It also meant less dependence on the *Tribune* and its political editor.

Because he was a Republican, more than for any other reason, Percy received editorial endorsements from the *Tribune* in 1966 and 1972. The *Tribune* had a way of making a recommendation of Percy sound more like a kiss of death than a pat on the back. The *Tribune's* endorsement of some Republicans is given reluctantly, but it seldom endorses a Democrat, except for Mayor Daley. So there was no thought of backing Percy's opponent.

The 1972 editorial endorsing Percy began with faint praise: "The contest for United States senator this year offers Illinois voters an interesting choice. Charles H. Percy, the incumbent, is a moderate-to-liberal Republican best known in the Senate for the breadth of his independent streak. . . . On balance, Mr. Percy would seem to have the wider grasp of statewide problems."

The *Tribune* finally got around to its reason for choosing Percy: "Our chief reason for endorsing Mr. Percy, however, is that his Senate seat is vital to President Nixon's post-election plans. If, as seems likely, Mr. Nixon should win reelection by a large margin, there is a good chance that the Republicans can win control of the Senate and break the stranglehold of the Democrats over administration bills. . . . While Mr. Percy has not voted with the party on many administration bills, he would vote for Republican organization of the Senate."

An editor in the *Tribune* organization wraps up the company attitude toward Percy and his Republicanism this way: "It's kind of like the colored fellow who doesn't know his place. Percy is too liberal for the Republican party. The *Tribune* would be more comfortable with someone like Philip Crane, the congressman."

The other two newspapers in Chicago are owned by the descendants of Marshall Field. The papers are the *Chicago Sun-Times*, in the morning, and the *Chicago Daily News*, in the afternoon. The Field newspapers speak with a common editorial voice, particularly on political endorsements and major policy questions.

The position taken by the Field newspapers toward Percy and his record is different from the *Tribune's* stand. While there is no indication that friendships among Percy and the Fields or other high-ranking officials of the Field organization have dictated the editorial approach to Percy, these associations haven't hurt him. During their Chicago days, the Percys' activities often involved them in social contacts with the Marshall Fields and with other top executives of the Field organization. To this day, editors of the *Daily News* and *Sun-Times* have a comfortable relationship with Percy and are visitors at the Percy home in Georgetown.

The liberal tradition of the *Sun-Times* began in 1941 when Marshall Field III founded the *Chicago Sun*—which was merged with the *Chicago Times* in 1948—to do battle with McCormick's newspaper. His successor, Marshall Field IV, was more conservative, favoring Republicans to Democrats, but still to the left of the *Tribune's* positions. Marshall Field III endorsed Harry S. Truman, but Marshall Field IV thought Eisenhower was the man. Percy has found sympathy at the *Sun-Times* and *Daily News* as noted by Paul Douglas in his memoirs. Talking about Percy's backing, the former senator said, "He would have the enthusiastic support of Marshall Field IV, who, in reaction against his liberal father and seeking the approval of his fellow millionaires, heartily disapproved of me. Field now owned the *Daily News* as well as the *Sun-Times*, with a combined circulation of about a million."

When Percy began his rise in Illinois politics, the Field papers were moderate on many issues and liberal on others. The papers might best be described as liberal Republican under the guidance of Marshall Field IV and Marshall Field V, the current master. Percy's approach to the issues, his style of campaigning, and his personality fit in nicely with the Field philosophy. In its endorsement of Percy in 1972, the *Sun-Times* began: "When we endorsed Charles H. Percy for the U.S. Senate in 1966, we described him as one of the new generation of Republicans who have the heart and courage to force squarely the problems of our age. His record in Washington in the last six years has more than justified our appraisal and we urge his re-election."

In glowing terms the *Sun-Times* pointed to Percy's independence of the party line and the administration, counted his labor support as a plus, and referred to him as a "champion of the consumer" for his efforts in attempting to create a consumer protection agency.

Percy's association with newspapers and their owners did not interfere with a vote he cast early in 1970. The issue was the Newspaper Preservation Act. The bill surfaced because newspaper ownership in 22 cities that had joint printing arrangements feared antitrust action by the government. The act would exempt joint operations from selected antitrust laws. Supporters argued that in some cities it was economically necessary to print two papers, either under separate or single ownership, in a single plant. Many newspapers across the nation supported the act and pushed for its adoption through editorials and professional lobbyists. The bill had been before Congress on several occasions, but early in 1970 it came to a vote. Everett Dirksen had been one of the bill's strongest supporters and, before his death in the fall of 1969, had helped to lay the groundwork for its passage in Congress. Percy and only 12 other senators voted against the measure. The act became law later in 1970. Some of the strongest lobbying on behalf of the act came from the Chicago newspapers, which do not have a joint printing arrangement. Officers of the Tribune Company, for example, telephoned editors and publishers across the state and nation to solicit support for the act.

Downstate Illinois media has given Percy a mixed reception. The Republican-leaning regulars—such as the *Waukegan News-Sun*, the Rockford newspapers before they became part of the Gannett organization, the *Peoria Journal-Star*, and papers owned in Kankakee and Moline by Len Small (whose father was a Republican governor in Illinois)—have editorial traditions only slightly less conservative than the *Tribune's*. Most have reluctantly endorsed Percy. The five central and southern Illinois newspapers owned by the Lindsay-Schaub organization, whose headquarters are in Decatur, have leaned more toward the middle editorially. The newspapers found Percy more desirable than Scott in 1964 but did not endorse either candidate in the Percy-Kerner conflict. Although they liked Percy in 1966, they did not back either candidate out of respect for the

Democrat incumbent. Finally in 1972, the papers endorsed Percy without qualification. Other Downstate newspapers with a moderate Republican tradition, such as the *Bloomington Pantagraph* (whose ownership includes members of the Stevenson family) and the *Alton Telegraph*, have supported Percy in most ventures.

Of importance to Percy are the attitudes of the St. Louis newspapers, which have substantial circulation in southern Illinois. The editorially liberal *St. Louis Post-Dispatch*, while usually more inclined toward Democratic candidates, speaks kindly of Percy and applauds his independence of the straight party line. Mainly because of its sometimes reactionary editorial policy, the *St. Louis Globe-Democrat*, a Newhouse paper, finds Percy less appealing.

Percy appears often on television and is heard on radio in Chicago and St. Louis and occasionally is seen on television in Champaign-Urbana, Springfield, Peoria, and Rockford. Percy used electronic media effectively in his 1966 and 1972 campaigns.

Charles Percy has shown the media and the party that he can work and win with the traditionalists—and without them. He recognizes, however, that traditionalism is as much a part of the state's Republican party as the familiar names of Dirksen and McCormick and that its roots are based on party loyalty and an appeal to the rural population. He is also aware that if the Republican party is to have a future in the state it must break with traditionalism at least enough to welcome those with less conservative views while still maintaining critical differences from the Democratic party.

When Percy came on the Illinois political scene, traditionalism had begun to show signs of impotence. He confronted the traditionalists almost every step of the way to his political successes. His enemies in the party never seem to give up trying to bring him down a notch. Yet Percy has shown no signs of abandoning his party, nor has he given up hope of reforming it.

When it counted, Percy received the backing he needed to win at the polls. Thus, as time passes, the extremes seem to be moving toward the middle ground, and in that movement is hope for the party's renewed strength.

CHAPTER VI

ON THE CAMPAIGN TRAIL

In less than 10 years Charles H. Percy went before the Illinois electorate on three occasions. The voters approved of Percy twice, and once, in the gubernatorial election of 1964, they preferred his opponent. Later he said that this defeat gave him the inner strength to try again for public office. Percy has made a conscious effort to view all defeats as pluses in his political career.

From election figures we know that, on the basis of his victories in 1966 and 1972, Percy established himself as one of the state's most successful modern-day campaigners. But in this same period, there have been defeats that did not involve his seeking office, such as the frustrations resulting from national political conventions.

In order to understand the actions of Percy today, it is important to have studied his political past in detail.

The tenacity of Percy's political opponents cannot be ignored, as Percy knows from his experiences in the 1964 Illinois gubernatorial election. While most Illinoisans have forgotten the bitterness and strain of that primary and general election year, the scars within the party remain. Despite the seeming friendliness of those who were directly involved, politicians cannot forget 1964 when they think about the future.

One of the principal players in the 1964 drama for the Republican gubernatorial nomination was Charles F. Carpentier, three-term secretary of state, former mayor of Moline, and party powerhouse. A thorough politician, Carpentier had assembled most of the regular party strength early in the contest, and he led the pack into 1964. Conservatives were in his camp, along with more moderate traditionalists and most of the remaining party mainstream.

Carpentier fancied himself the leading Republican influence in the state. He called himself "Mr. Republican," and the media picked up the label. His base strength was in Springfield, where he had served in the legislature and where as secretary of state he commanded one of the largest patronage armies in the state. Carpentier started flexing his gubernatorial muscles well in advance of 1964. In the 1962 off-year contests involving the offices of state treasurer and superintendent of public instruction, Carpentier handpicked two candidates for nominations. He backed Walter J. Reum against William J. Scott for treasurer and Louis F. Bottino against Ray Page for superintendent of public instruction. Any recommendations by the organization of state county chairmen, headed by H. G. ("Skinny") Taylor of Decatur, were pushed aside by Carpentier, who thought the chairmen were powerless and said so. The angered county chairmen supported Scott and Page in the primary, and both were victorious over Carpentier's pair.

A second principal in the 1964 race for the gubernatorial nomination was Percy, making his first bid for elective office. Long before 1964 Percy had it in his mind to run for high public office. No less a person than former president Dwight D. Eisenhower had urged him forward, and he found strength among party moderates who longed for relief from the usual run of candidates. From these eager persons Percy selected the volunteer organization that made it possible for him to compete with Carpentier.

Not all of Percy's friends and advisers thought he ought to run in 1964. William ("Pat") Patterson, chief executive officer of United Airlines and a member of the Bell & Howell board of directors, urged Percy not to seek the governorship because "it's a slum. It's a place where there's nowhere to go but down." Patterson did not see much hope for anyone who tried to govern Illinois. As journalist William Allen White stated at a much earlier time: "Under primary, under convention, under despotism, or under a pure democracy, Illinois would be corrupt and crooked. . . . It is in the blood of the people."

Nothing in the political climate at the time hinted that 1964 looked like a good election year for Republicans. Incumbent Democrats ran the nation and the state: John F. Kennedy in Washington and Otto Kerner in Springfield. Even if Percy got by the primary, he would surely be an underdog in the general election. Nevertheless, Percy began his quest for the nomination 18 months before election day.

The third principal in the race did not enter the picture until the filing deadline at the end of January. Thirty-seven-year-old William J. Scott, who only two years before had been elected state treasurer, got into the race when Carpentier could not campaign due to ill health. Scott and Richard B. Ogilvie, who had been elected sheriff of Cook County in 1962, were trying valiantly to reconstruct and broaden the Republican party in Cook County, and especially Chicago, and rid it of members who had ties with the underworld and who were more friendly with Democrats than Republicans. Scott and Ogilvie began a zealous crusade against the mob and "bad" Republicans, not to mention the Democrats. This enthusiasm for reform ultimately brought Scott into the primary against Percy.

On January 20, 1964, Carpentier suffered a heart attack, and it became immediately evident he would not recover to continue the battle for governor. He died on April 3 at the age of 67.

Percy made an immediate bid for Carpentier's support and campaign finances. Scott and Ogilvie had not supported Carpentier because of their belief that the secretary of state was backed by the very elements they they were fighting in the party—namely, the West Side bloc, which consisted of the legislators and their followers from the West Side of Chicago. Ogilvie and Scott believed this group to have associations with mobsters. Also those from the bloc who were in the state legislature seldom voted the Republican party line and usually joined forces with Mayor Richard J. Daley's Democrats. For Ogilvie and Scott to have joined the Carpentier team would have been to admit defeat in their attempt to reform the party in Cook County. Scott and Ogilvie had not joined the Percy team either. They wanted to be free to support a new candidate if they felt such a move was necessary.

When Percy picked up most of Carpentier's support, Ogilvie and Scott were concerned. They feared that Percy had aligned himself with the seamy side of the party. Scott now believes that Percy's desire to be the only candidate in the primary, coupled with his unawareness of party intrigues and his political naiveté and inexperience, caused him to make almost any deal to achieve his goal. Scott says he went to Percy to dissuade him from using any persons with questionable backgrounds in his organization. He also contends that some former Carpentier supporters were promised favors if Percy won. Percy denies making any deals. "I had nothing to offer," Percy said years later. "I had a rigid principle in the campaign: no promises." He also said that Carpentier's reason for personally urging his followers to work for Percy was that Carpentier had "responded positively to my campaign techniques." That meant Carpentier appreciated Percy's not indulging in personal references during the campaign. One of those who joined Percy as a result of Carpentier's appeal was Timothy P. Sheehan, a longtime Cook County Republican official, who later had a falling out with Ogilvie.

Finally, because of his reluctance to align himself with some of Percy's supporters, William J. Scott announced his own candidacy for governor. He did so, he now contends, even though he knew that his effort was futile and that Percy would win. Scott claims that his fight was not with Percy but with the influence of the West Side bloc, other unsavory elements in the party, and the crime element—all of which had originally been associated with Carpentier's campaign. Almost immediately Scott became the conservative, anti-Percy lightning rod. Scott says the contest did not involve political philosophies and that he had no particularly conservative views, but he became the conservative darling nonetheless.

All the reasons behind Scott's entrance into the gubernatorial contest have never been fully explained. Percy aides contend that Scott must have made a deal with the *Chicago Tribune* to receive support in future political ventures if he ran against Percy. Scott denies it, although he admits talking frequently with *Tribune* officials prior to his declaration of candidacy. He conferred with W. Don Maxwell, editor of the *Tribune*, and George Tagge, the *Tribune's* political editor and one of the smoothest political operatives in the state's recent history. Tagge did not like Percy and felt that supporting Scott was the only way to save the *Tribune* and the Republican party from Percy.

Members of the right-wing John Birch Society flocked to Scott. Some of Carpentier's supporters whom Scott considered legitimate abandoned Percy. As fringe elements became involved in the campaign, the charges against Percy grew. Birch followers published a broadside called "Mercy, Mr. Percy," which labeled Percy a "liberal" and cited as suspicious meetings of Percy and high-ranking officials of the Soviet Union. Such tactics were designed to question Percy's loyalty. Many of the state's newspapers responded with editorials against the smear effort, and Scott disclaimed any association with the right-wing element that was responsible for the broadside.

The meetings mentioned in the broadside occurred when Percy entertained Frol Kozlov, a member of the Central Committee of the Russian Communist party, and when he dined with Chairman Khrushchev on another occasion. In both cases the Russians were on official visits to the United States, and Percy's role in the events sponsored by the U.S. government was a ceremonial one.

As primary election day neared, it became obvious that neither Scott's campaign nor the efforts of Birchers to cast a shadow over Percy had caught on. One Downstate political writer explained some of the dynamics as he observed them: "Grass-roots workers felt that even though they preferred Scott over Percy, Percy had been out beating the bushes for many months before Scott backed into the primary. Somehow they figured he [Scott] was trying to take over Carpentier's rather awesome organization, and Carpentier was a very popular guy. Walking on Carpentier's grave, if you will." For that reason the reporter believes Scott never convinced the hard-core Republican voter of his sincerity.

Percy won an easy victory over Scott. Out of the 1,038,622 votes cast in the Republican primary, Percy received 626,111, or 60.2 percent. Scott received 388,903 votes, or 37.4 percent of the total. The remaining votes were spread among several minor candidates. Percy's control of the election was complete. He defeated Scott by 117,383 votes in Cook County, where Scott should have been strongest, and Percy won by 119,825 in the rest of the state, which was supposedly the stronghold of the conservatives.

Percy should have been cheered by these election results, but he knew there were more battles ahead within his own party. His victory had proved his drawing power against Scott, but not much else. Those loyal to Scott still needed a good reason to cross over to Percy's side. Many never would. Percy was the standard bearer for the party against an incumbent governor, but his primary-election victory had done little to improve his acceptance among party leaders. Almost immediately he had to look for an issue that would bring the party together again.

A major effort to build confidence with the electorate and within the party and to bolster Percy's image as a crime fighter came a few weeks after the primary election. Pressure mounted with the Ogilvie-Scott wing of the party to purge certain legislators who were associated with the West Side bloc. Percy had an unusual chance to do something about the persons singled out because the state legislature in the year before had failed to act on district reapportionment as required by the state constitution. Consequently, candidates for all 177 House seats that year had to run at large on a giant "bed-sheet ballot." The party getting the most votes in the general election would name 118 members to the legislature, or two-thirds of the total, and the defeated party would name 59. The nature of the ballot—long and with many unfamiliar names—favored straight-ticket voting, and it was conceivable that the nine West Side bloc members would be elected if they were nominated.

Besides the pressure of Scott and Ogilvie to unload the bloc candidates, a third party movement began in the state. Unless the Republican party could rid itself of the objectionable candidates, third-party supporters threatened to split the Republican vote and assure a Democratic victory.

Percy received some internal party pressures not to proceed with the purge but he was not deterred by them. He wanted to seize the crime-fight issue. Because of their image of often voting against anticrime legislation, the bloc members became prime targets. Also, the bloc was not considered loyal to the Republican cause in the legislature. In 1961 the bloc voted with Democrats for a Democratic speaker of the house although the Republicans had a majority of House votes and could have elected a Republican speaker. Such activity did not endear the bloc to regular Republicans.

At a party caucus early in May and again at the nominating convention in June, Percy sat by quietly while his forces and friendly delegates saw that the purge succeeded. Members of the bloc reacted angrily toward Percy. One said, "You may be dynamic, Mr. Percy, but you'd better learn how to aim the dynamite." Another said, "You who execute me today will never wash the blood off your hands." Percy got the brunt of the criticism but the bulk of the praise too. Political ramifications of the purge have lingered through the years. Many of the bloc members retired from politics, but some returned to the legislature later and continued to stir anti-Percy sentiment.

However, in spite of Percy's efforts in the purge of the West Side bloc, which gained him favorable reactions in newspapers across the state, he still could not win the confidence of Republican party leaders. Suspicious Republicans continued to deny Percy his place in the party leadership. This was the case when it came time to pick the chairman of the Illinois delegation to the 1964 Republican National Convention in San Francisco. Party regulars, who dominated the delegation, feared that Percy might be less than enthusiastic about Senator Barry M. Goldwater, the leading candidate for the nomination, in spite of Percy's 1963 pledge to support Goldwater's candidacy if he could win the nomination. Party loyalists considered this pledge a back-door endorsement. So the delegation denied the chairmanship, and even the cochairmanship, to Percy and instead elected as cochairmen Senator Everett Dirksen and Victor Smith of Robinson, who was the chairman of the state central committee. Under normal circumstances, granting Percy at least a share of the chairmanship would have been an act of courtesy, if for no other reason than that the exposure might have helped him in the gubernatorial election.

And so it was simply as a delegate that Percy attended the 1964 convention, his first as either a candidate or officeholder. The Illinois delegation had been correct about Percy's feelings for Goldwater. Percy really wanted to throw his support to a more moderate candidate than Senator Goldwater for president, but no one appeared likely to derail the Arizonan. Also, Republican support for Goldwater in Illinois and his 1963 pledge of support made it impossible for Percy to oppose the senator without losing important party strength.

When party moderates tried to involve Percy in preconvention efforts to stop Goldwater, Percy reminded them of the 1963 pledge. He told moderate William W. Scranton, governor of Pennsylvania, "If there were any way I could get out of this pledge, I'd do it. But I've made it, and I can't see that I can do anything else." Then at the convention the same moderate forces urged dissenters to consolidate behind the candidacy of Scranton to prevent Goldwater from being nominated.

Percy was at various times before and during the convention pressured to support Scranton. The Scrantons were good personal friends, and during the convention Mary Scranton went on television to denounce Percy for working against her husband's efforts to win the Illinois delegation. She later issued a statement admitting she had falsely accused Percy. Those were the emotions of the moment. Milton S. Eisenhower, a close friend of Percy, backed Scranton and placed the Pennsylvania governor's name in nomination. Dwight Eisenhower gave early support and strength to Scranton's candidacy but finally backed away and played a symbolic role in the convention activities. Percy was tempted by the pressure from his friends to support Scranton, but finally he refused, saying he would adhere to his pledge to support Goldwater if he were nominated by the convention. Percy had no choice if he wanted any kind of unified party behind his

Illinois candidacy. Later Percy said that the pledge was his "greatest mistake" and that this verbal alliance with Goldwater seriously injured his chances of winning the Illinois governorship.

Moderates, wounded by the Percy decision to support Goldwater, held Percy in low esteem. They could not be expected to fully understand the Illinois situation, but the picture could have been made clear to them had they bothered to inquire. The Illinois delegation supported Goldwater openly, although some delegates technically refused to back any of the candidates for the nomination until just before the convention. Hidden behind a facade of fairness to all candidates was a definite leaning by Dirksen toward Goldwater and an acknowledged friendship between the two senators of more than a decade. Dirksen withheld his public support of Goldwater until after Congress passed the Civil Rights Act of 1964, which Dirksen shaped and guided through the Senate and House in June. Dirksen wanted Goldwater to support the bill, but the Arizona senator finally voted against it. After that, and with no other candidates from which to choose, Dirksen finally made his support of Goldwater public on July 1, just a few weeks before the convention.

Civil rights played an important part in Republican party dramas in 1964. By the time the convention began, Goldwater definitely stood for a "soft," or nonprogressive, position on civil rights, which endeared him to Southern followers but caused great discomfort for Republicans in other parts of the nation. The Goldwater position was particularly upsetting to candidates for state office, such as Percy, who faced a Democratic surge and needed more than hard-core Republican votes.

According to some Illinois Republicans, such as William J. Scott, there had been a time when Goldwater did not appear overly conservative in his approach to civil rights. Scott recalls a meeting with Goldwater well before the 1964 campaign at which the Arizonan spoke moderately about civil rights, pointing out his part-Jewish heritage and how it had deprived him of entry to exclusive clubs. He also told Scott that his department store in Phoenix had been the first business in Arizona to hire large numbers of blacks. Scott in later years saw the final Goldwater position on civil rights as a betrayal. "I was shocked when it turned out differently, and Goldwater made a shambles of the party," he said. Regardless of Scott's surprise, Goldwater's conservatism had been well known years before 1964.

And so, even though Republicans, including Dirksen, had helped President Johnson pass the Civil Rights Act of 1964, it was clear to the public that a Republican administration headed by Goldwater would slow the process of equal opportunity that had been developing in the Kennedy-Johnson administrations. The thought of Goldwater as president sent chills through the black neighborhoods of the nation's cities, including Chicago. The implication for Percy was that the Goldwater position could cause him grief in the black areas of Illinois at a time when the Republican candidate wanted to project a moderate image to all citizens of the state.

Not only had Goldwater refused to support the Civil Rights Act in Congress, but he also insisted on a noncommittal civil rights plank in the party platform. As the leading candidate for the presidential nomination, he was able to get his way. Moderates at the national convention made a final try to alter the civil rights position from that proposed by the platform committee, but the attempt failed. Of the five civil rights amendments to reach the convention floor, only one—a proposal to liberalize the language of the civil rights plank—received a roll-call vote, and it was turned down 897 to 409. The platform that prevailed supported civil rights in general but omitted any specific proposals or positions beyond the status quo. It said the party supported the Civil Rights Act of 1964 and other existing statutes but made no promises about additional legislation. Goldwater said at a press conference, "I don't think it would be wise for either party to add to that [the civil rights law] until we see how this bill works."

Percy assumed a deliberately low profile toward the presidential candidate. During the campaign he often wore an all-gold lapel button on which the name "Goldwater" was visible at a distance of hardly more than a few inches. Publications of the day noted how Percy avoided campaigning with Goldwater in Illinois. On one occasion Percy showed up to introduce Goldwater but quickly took his leave.

As Time magazine pointed out, Percy and Goldwater "are miles apart on many issues." While Percy opposed an open-occupancy law for Illinois, one of several overtures to conservative voters, his general position on civil rights was far more liberal than Goldwater's. Just before the Senate vote on the Civil Rights Act of 1964, Percy said he would vote for the bill if he were in the Senate. However, Percy could not convince black leaders of his sincerity with Goldwater at the top of the ballot. Also, blacks did not like Percy's opposition to open housing.

Percy's positions on most national issues were the result of his work in 1959 on the Republican Committee on Program and Progress, an effort Goldwater did not favor. Percy endorsed low tariffs, cultural exchanges and trade with Communist countries, and improved opportunities for minorities. None of these were planks in the Goldwater program. Although Percy had not begun his drift toward dovishness on the Vietnam war, he did not share Goldwater's attitude that the government should use nuclear bombs or other aggressive strategies to win the war.

Percy worked hard to put together a winning campaign. To broaden his appeal, he had to maintain a tricky balance between party factions. He persuaded Eisenhower to campaign for him on the one hand and on the other hand held fast against an open-occupancy law for Illinois although it cost him dearly with Illinois blacks. Percy lost 89 percent of the black vote in the general election. One former aide from that period said the open-housing position illustrated that Percy did not have deep personal convictions on the issue and relied on the opinion of others in deciding his course of action. If circumstances changed, the aide said, Percy could and would change (in fact, before he sought public office again in 1966, he did alter his stand on open housing). In the general election Percy ran ahead of Goldwater by 240,000 votes but lost to Otto Kerner by 180,000 votes because of the Democratic governor's popularity and the strong showing of Lyndon B. Johnson.

After the 1964 election Percy spoke harshly of the party's stand on civil rights. He said at a meeting of Republican governors that the party would "never be known as the party of opportunity until we make it unmistakably clear where we stand as a party on civil rights." He called for a repudiation of those who led the party and who "waved our party banner in 1964 only as a means to promote hate and bigotry or only in the hope of discouraging the civil rights movement." Later Percy spoke at a meeting of the racially integrated Mississippi Council on Human Relations. The meeting was boycotted by Mississippi Republican leaders. During his remarks, Percy said, "What we succeeded in doing in 1964 was to drive practically the entire Negro vote in the United States into the Democratic camp." As a result, Percy concluded that "the Republican party won five Southern states by setting foot upon what has been called 'the shifting racist sands' and that was a triumph neither for Republicans nor conservatives."

In the aftermath of his defeat in the 1964 gubernatorial election, Percy had to decide what his next step would be politically. Before long he decided to challenge the aging but vigorous Paul Howard Douglas for the U.S. Senate in 1966. Many of Percy's followers urged him not to go up against the popular liberal Democrat but to wait instead until 1968 when he could run again for governor. They feared another defeat would bury Percy. Among those urging Percy to wait until 1968 were Thomas J. Houser, his 1964 campaign manager, and H. G. Taylor, a Downstate adviser.

One of the more persuasive voices urging Percy to run came from Richard B. Ogilvie, who was sheriff of Cook County at the time. By the mid-1960s Ogilvie had emerged as the new Republican strongman in Cook County. Percy recalled that in 1965 Ogilvie had said, "If you don't run, I won't run either." Ogilvie also said that "if the head of the ticket wasn't strong, the whole Republican campaign was likely to be a slaughter." (In 1966 Ogilvie ran for Cook County board chairman and won.)

Traditionalists such as Victor Smith of Robinson, chairman of the Illinois Republican central committee, pressed Percy to run. Percy's aides viewed traditionalist support as a conservative plot to get Percy out of Illinois or out of politics. Washington columnists Rowland Evans and Robert D. Novak observed that when traditionalists appeared eager for Percy to run, it was a "fiendishly clever trap prepared by his arch-enemies. . . . It will be a minor miracle if he wins."

Endorsements such as Ogilvie's and Smith's were helpful, but if Percy wanted to avoid divisions within the party, support had to come from the most powerful traditionalist of them all. That meant a blessing from Everett Dirksen. Republican officials, including Dirksen, eventually asked Percy to run. However, Percy wanted assurances that he would be allowed to be politically independent of Dirksen. So Dirksen wrote an unusual political letter in which the senator acknowledged that he and Percy had deep differences of opinion and that he respected Percy's right to a different point of view. That cleared the way for Percy and gave him the stamp of approval. He had no opposition in the primary, and through most of the senatorial campaign he kept warring party factions from quarreling publicly.

The 1966 senatorial campaign in Illinois began on a gentlemanly note. The incumbent, Paul Howard Douglas, then 74 years old, was trying for a fourth term in the U.S. Senate. His opponent was Charles Percy, who was 46 years old when the campaign started. These two had "faced" each other before: When Douglas was a professor of economics at the University of Chicago 28 years before, he had been one of Percy's teachers.

Early in the campaign Percy referred to Douglas as a "man of conviction and courage." Taking his turn, the white-haired Douglas called Percy "one of the finest men in public life, a splendid fellow . . . [whom] I would be honored to run against." Before the campaign concluded, the friendliness had faded, as it so often does in politics.

One of the more vivid descriptions of Percy during the 1966 campaign, although certainly biased, came from Douglas several years later. He remembered that "Percy was handsome, immaculately groomed, relatively young, and looked even younger. . . . Pleasant in his personal manners and very persistent, he had shown himself a master of the selling arts of public relations. He was, in fact, just the candidate for suburbia and middle-class youth: a kind of Horatio Alger hero in a Brooks Brothers suit."

The story goes that Douglas nearly retired at the end of his third term. In his autobiography, *In the Fullness of Time*, published five years after the campaign, Douglas said he decided against retirement because of the unfinished projects on his personal and congressional agenda. Despite his 74 years, Douglas was in excellent physical condition. He swam each day, weather permitting. Although he may have appeared bent and worn, he remained an indefatigable campaigner.

Among Douglas's unfinished business was his truth-in-lending bill, for which he had fought valiantly, although fruitlessly, in the Senate. Eventually the plan received congressional approval and became law in 1969. Another of the senator's pet projects was a plan to name the sand dunes along the boundary of Lake Michigan and the state of Indiana, near Gary, a national park. Douglas also feared that a Republican in his Senate seat would mean another vote cast against his favorite liberal projects, which included ending poverty, supporting federal aid to public schools, and promoting aid for the nation's cities. So the warhorse liberal, former professor, and ally of the Chicago Democratic organization (which he fought unsuccessfully in 1942) decided once again to take his case to the streets and the small towns, to the people who somehow felt Douglas could help them. They were his strength.

As one of the first acts of the campaign, Douglas made a full disclosure of his personal finances. Over the years of his public service, such disclosure had become a fetish with the senator, and he remained one of the few persons in Congress to voluntarily bare all his finances. His 1965 income—compiled from Douglas's ledger books, tax forms, and other lists—totaled $35,537.32. His net worth hit $130,000. Douglas liked to talk about the difficulties of a man of modest means raising large sums for campaigning—and particularly the difficulties of raising money to run against someone like Percy, who has seemingly endless resources. Percy did not disclose any personal financial figures that year but said after the election that his personal fortune exceeded $5 million.

Percy had worked toward this campaign since the early 1960s. His organization had learned some lessons in the 1964 gubernatorial campaign, and so had the candidate. To many, his image during the race for the governorship had been of a stiff, formal, and uncomfortable businessman working at a game he did not fully understand. While self-confidence has always been one of Percy's characteristics, it did not always come across sympathetically in those crush-the-body-up-against-the-candidate situations. Campaign observers noted before and after the 1966 contest that Percy's smile came across more naturally and with more appeal than in 1964. Although he still had mannerisms that irritated some people, his general approach seemed friendlier. He earned the reputation for being a tireless campaigner and a willing worker.

Percy needed all he could get going for him, because from the outset the campaign would be an uphill battle. The senatorial contest came at a critical time for the Republican party in Illinois. In 1964 Democrats had swept offices from the courthouses to the statehouse in Springfield. The Republican party needed a major victory, and it looked to Percy for it, although perhaps with some trepidation.

Before long the campaign thrust became clear. Douglas pointed with pride to his 18 years of service in the Senate. "In the case of a Senator," Douglas said, "what is chiefly needed are judgment and experience. Here I certainly have the edge." He stoutly supported the Vietnam escalation policies of the Johnson administration in a time of increasing national challenge to such escalation. In an editorial endorsement, the *New York Times* said, "In every generation there are a few men who by force of mind and character become moral exemplars to their contemporaries. . . . Senator Douglas is such a man."

Douglas pointed out what he called the "unparalleled prosperity" of the nation. Percy's counter: "I think most Americans take little joy in prosperity that is based on war." Douglas praised the Great Society for its social programs, many of which he had supported, and most of all he reminded the public of his good intentions, his responsiveness to the people, and his fights against the power-hungry interests. Douglas did not make up his record, although he was prone to overplay it.

Percy did not need to mention the age difference between the candidates because his youthful appearance made it obvious. He told audiences that the state and the nation needed leadership with a fresh viewpoint and characterized the Douglas approach to issues as coming from the past without vision for the future. He referred to Douglas and the Democrats as "my opponent and his old-fashioned party of the thirties."

Douglas let out all the stops to win. He brought various Democratic national luminaries to Illinois to campaign for him, including members of the Kennedy family. Percy on the other hand campaigned without the help of outsiders. It gave him an opportunity to comment on Douglas's helpers. He jokingly welcomed the visiting politicians to Illinois, saying that Illinois could benefit from some of the Kennedy money.

During the Douglas campaign Percy began dabbling in a national issue on which he would comment during his entire first term in the Senate: Vietnam, a made-to-order issue for someone bursting on the national scene as Percy did. Percy criticized the Johnson Vietnam policy. He opposed escalation of the war but did not suggest that the United States should withdraw unilaterally until a satisfactory settlement could be reached. He challenged Douglas to say how far escalation should go.

In one of his first major proposals on the war, Percy suggested an all-Asian conference to settle the conflict. He believed that an Asian war could be settled best by Asians. The idea did not originate with Percy, but he was the first national figure to promote it. In some GOP quarters, mostly among those seeking an alternative to Johnson administration policies, the proposal rang a bell. Republicans who supported the policies of Johnson—and chief among them was Illinois Senator Dirksen—did not think much of Percy's idea. Nixon was hawkish by then and had been warning that demands for negotiations by doves in the United States only encouraged the enemy to fight harder in Vietnam and thus prolonged the war. But Nixon always understood the importance of helping fellow Republicans whenever it did not run contrary to his own ambitions, and he could see that the Percy-Douglas contest would be a close one. Nixon also could see an advantage in the Republican party having an alternative to the Democratic program. In a press conference Nixon made an argument for the all-Asian conference. Later Percy said,"The only thing that bothered me was that he probably didn't believe a word of it." It may have been one of the few times, such as when Nixon later proclaimed his intention to end the war, that Percy and Nixon were in public agreement on Vietnam war policy.

Douglas called the all-Asian conference idea "half-baked" and told audiences that it was not the first time it had been suggested. Percy replied that "anything half-baked is also fresh and not just a warmed-over idea." So went the campaign rhetoric.

In the preliminaries for the 1966 contest with Douglas, Percy had commented on racial unrest in the state. On national television in January, 1965, Percy said that the Republican party had to rebuild in the wake of the Goldwater loss. He declared the party had a moral commitment to the civil rights movement and deplored the fact that Goldwater won the five states of the South for what Percy called the wrong reasons. Also in 1965 Percy changed his position and declared in favor of a federal open-housing law. In his 1964 contest for governor, Percy had opposed a state open-housing law. In explaining his switch Percy said that real estate brokers who had promised to liberalize housing sales to minorities did not honor their pledge, and so he now supported action on the federal level. Percy's opponents took some glee in recalling that Percy had opposed an open-occupancy law for Illinois when it seemed the thing to do in the more conservative atmosphere of the 1964 gubernatorial campaign. Although Douglas worked hard to belittle his opponent's turnaround, Percy's new stand helped his image and broadened his appeal. But he failed to convince blacks that he supported favorable civil rights legislation. This failure was reflected in the 1966 voting figures: In the black neighborhoods of Chicago, Percy was badly defeated by Douglas.

After the election Douglas reflected that Percy began to hedge on the open-housing question when he saw it might hurt him with many Republicans. Douglas also said that in the black wards of Chicago Percy supporters circulated pamphlets supporting open occupancy and civil rights, but Republicans elsewhere carried on a campaign against open occupancy. Douglas, the veteran of many battles in Congress for improving opportunities for the underprivileged and the disadvantaged, smarted at the idea that Percy, a relative newcomer, could get votes for being a supporter of civil rights.

During the summer of 1966 Percy wooed the black wards of Chicago. Then in midsummer, riots erupted on the city's West Side, doing millions of dollars of damage and bringing tempers elsewhere to the surface. Shortly thereafter Dr. Martin Luther King, Jr., held a series of marches in the Chicago area and made plans to lead a march in Cicero, a bastion of ethnic-white sentiment. Only at the last minute, under threats and the possibility of bloodshed, did King cancel the march.

The reaction in white suburban areas to the racial agitation worked to the advantage of Republican candidates because of the party's conservative stance on civil rights during the Goldwater campaign and because the voters tended to associate Democrats with sympathizers of the civil rights cause. For that reason Thomas Houser, Percy's campaign director, said the racial conflict of 1966 worked to Percy's advantage by putting the white backlash vote in his column.

By early fall, polls taken by both parties showed Percy slightly ahead of Douglas. From within the party Percy had encountered only mild resistance to his candidacy, and those who were not interested in him simply stayed out of the road. Dirksen, still the rallying point for Republicans who disliked Percy, blew hot and cold during the campaign. It is difficult to say whether he helped or hindered Percy. Dirksen admitted privately that he had grown fond of Douglas and would miss him in the Senate if he were defeated. He told friends that the Democrats would lose an able debater, one Dirksen considered a worthy rival on the stump. There is no indication that Dirksen's remarks about Douglas had public exposure, and while there may have been a "distant cousin" relationship between Douglas and Dirksen, there were sharp differences between them on issues and priorities for the nation.

So it was "a strong new voice for Illinois," as the Percy posters said, against what might have been called "the same sure voice for Illinois" in the battle of their political lives until the morning of September 18, 1966. Shortly after 5 A.M. the world learned that Valerie Jeanne Percy had been murdered in her bed in the Percy home. Persons unknown had entered the fashionable Kenilworth mansion north of Chicago and bludgeoned her to death.

The crime brought the 1966 campaign to a halt. Douglas, years afterward, felt that the cessation of campaigning broke the positive momentum he had built. Douglas supporters knew from the first moment that the event would have a serious impact on the senatorial campaign, but hardly anyone imagined that it would be the deciding factor. Democratic officials in Cook County investigated the death, and Douglas, recognizing the potential for rumors and innuendo in a political situation, made a special trip to Chicago where he asked the party's leadership not to take advantage of the situation. The Valerie Percy death dominated the news media throughout the rest of the campaign. Columnist Stewart Alsop, writing later, said the death changed the public image of Percy from a rich and ambitious young man to a suffering person. The feeling of sympathy for the Percys, the valuable time lost to Douglas, and the preoccupation of the public with questions other than the issues led to a Percy victory of large proportions.

The 1966 battle with Douglas had been difficult, but in the final tally Percy had 55.6 percent of the vote, and Douglas 44.4. The plurality for

Bell & Howell board of directors gather on October 27, 1948, less than three months before Percy succeeded Joseph McNabb, his benefactor, as president of the company. McNabb is seated at the far right.

During a visit to the White House in February, 1960, Percy presents President Dwight D. Eisenhower with a copy of *Decisions for a Better America*, the report on which Percy and the Republican Committee on Program and Progress worked for a year. Thruston B. Morton (left) was chairman of the Republican National Committee.

Dwight D. Eisenhower encouraged Percy to seek elective office. Here the former president joins the Illinois gubernatorial candidate in a 1964 campaign appearance.

Percy and Senator Barry M. Goldwater pose together during a 1964 campaign appearance at the Illinois State Fair. The handholding was a gesture, the two not seeing eye to eye politically.

Decatur Herald and Review

During the 1966 Senate race, Percy campaigned by train throughout Downstate Illinois. At a stop in Effingham, he is surrounded by two of his children, Mark and Sharon, and by School Superintendent Ray Page (right) and Harris Rowe (left), the Republican candidate for state treasurer.

Decatur Herald and Review

Percy and William J. Scott, both of them Republican candidates for governor, meet on the campaign trail in February, 1964. They waged a bitter campaign for the nomination, but after Percy won in the primary, he and Scott became political allies.

Wide World   Kenneth V. Schmid

LEFT: During the inquest into the murder of Percy's daughter Valerie, he and his wife Loraine testified about what had occurred in their Kenilworth home on the night of the tragedy.

RIGHT: On a trip to Vietnam in 1967, Percy (in light shirt) is forced to take cover when the Communists opened fire on the abandoned village he and his party were visiting. The man with the rifle is Dennis Smith, a member of the Percy party. When the shelling began, Smith gave his pistol to Percy. Percy suffered only minor scratches.

Wide World

Percy introduces Governor and Mrs. Nelson A. Rockefeller at a Chicago political gathering on July 29, 1968. Percy had previously announced that Rockefeller was his choice for the Republican party's presidential nomination. At this time, it was rumored that if the New York governor were nominated, he would choose the senator from Illinois as his running mate.

Wide World

Everett M. Dirksen, senior senator from Illinois, shares the spotlight with Percy, his junior colleague, at a 1967 press conference in Chicago.

Arthur E. Scott

The top contenders for the 1968 Republican presidential nomination—Ronald Reagan, Richard M. Nixon, George W. Romney, and Percy—meet the press at a "victory gala" dinner in Washington on March 1, 1967.

Longtime Illinois Republican associates—and sometimes opponents—Governor Richard B. Ogilvie (left), Attorney General William J. Scott, and Senator Percy meet with reporters during the strategy-planning days of the 1972 Republican National Convention. These men held three of the state's top elective positions, but Ogilvie lost his reelection bid that fall.

Sharon Rockefeller was the only family member not present at the 1972 election-night activities in Chicago. Seated (left to right) are Loraine, Gail, Percy, Roger, and Mrs. Elisabeth Percy, the senator's mother. Standing are Mark and Roger's wife Penny.

Aboard the presidential plane in June, 1973, Richard M. Nixon listens as Percy tries to explain his May "sense of the Senate" resolution, which called for a special Watergate prosecutor to be appointed by the chief executive and approved by the Senate.

Percy talks with Henry Kissinger before the Senate Foreign Relations Committee begins its hearings in September, 1973, on Kissinger's qualifications to become secretary of state. The two men have maintained close contact ever since they first worked together in the 1950s on a Rockefeller Brothers Fund project.

Charles Meissner

On a trip to the Middle East in 1975, Percy talks with King Faisal of Saudi Arabia. The king was assassinated less than three months after the senator's visit. James Akins (left) is the interpreter. As a result of this trip to the Middle East, Percy changed his attitude toward continuing unlimited U.S. aid to Israel.

Vivian Jacobson   United Press International

LEFT: Percy and Thomas J. Houser, his longtime friend and political adviser, participate in the 1974 annual staff "olympics." The winner receives a token award.

RIGHT: In January, 1975, Percy appears with Edward H. Levi at the Senate Judiciary Committee hearings that were held prior to Levi's confirmation as U.S. attorney general. Percy had sponsored the former University of Chicago president's candidacy for the nation's top legal office.

the new senator was 422,302. Percy won 93 Illinois counties, and Douglas 8. The significance of that margin was caught by Douglas in his auto-biography: "I would be one of the worst-defeated candidates in the state's history." That was true only until 1972 when Percy received 62.2 percent of the votes and swamped Roman Pucinski by a margin of 1,146,047 votes.

In the 1966 campaign Percy and his supporters earned the reputation of having a well-organized, hard-charging campaign complemented by an ambitious candidate. Although there is a tinge of sour grapes in his recollections, Douglas's description of the Percy effort should be a warning to any prospective Democratic candidate in the future: "Percy . . . carried on a skillful and costly public-relations campaign from three floors of offices in Chicago's Loop. He was well packaged and sold to the public as the advertisers would sell toothpaste or a new breakfast food. Handsome pictures of him appeared discreetly everywhere."

After the election the two men resumed a gentlemanly posture toward each other, with the exception of some edgy remarks in the Douglas autobiography, *In the Fullness of Time*. In 1972 Percy found it difficult to refute what Douglas had to say because "he [Douglas] is an honorable man, because political actions are susceptible to various interpretations, and because it is pointless to dredge up six-year-old controversies." However, in his book Douglas also remembers that "no one could have been more considerate to a defeated rival than Percy has been since that election."

During much of 1967 the new senator's name was suggested as a potential presidential or vice-presidential candidate for 1968. As prepara-tions drew nearer for the selection of Illinois delegates, it became apparent that both Dirksen and Percy wanted to be chairman of the Illinois delegation. Percy was not a candidate for any state position in 1968, so he could not claim the chairmanship for the reason of exposure. Dirksen was on the ballot for reelection. Also in the picture and in need of some publicity was Richard B. Ogilvie, the Illinois gubernatorial candidate. Only two of them could share the chairmanship.

Percy supporters hoped that, in addition to being appointed chairman of the delegation, the senator would be named the favorite-son presidential candidate from Illinois. Percy's vice-presidential ambitions needed the boost. Combined with the chairmanship, the favorite-son designation would have meant considerable exposure and a demonstration of influence. But Dirksen stood in the way. One Illinois Republican said, "Chuck has about as much chance of being the favorite son as I have of being the queen of the Ziegfield Follies." Dirksen wanted to be chairman of the Illinois delegation and the Illinois representative on the platform com-mittee. As a final service to his ego, he wanted to be chairman of the platform committee, a position Percy held in 1960. In sum, Dirksen did not want anyone taking any limelight from him.

Those Republicans opposed to Percy reacted quickly to stifle any thought by Percy or his followers prior to the primary election of starting a battle to elect those delegates who wanted Percy as the favorite son. In September, 1967, the *DeKalb Daily Chronicle*, which circulated in an area that could be considered more Dirksen country than Percy land, praised Dirksen's service to the nation and then said of Percy:

"There can be no place in our Republican party for those who have only their own political aspirations in mind and in heart.... A decision by Mr. Percy to involve himself and his colleagues in the upcoming delegate contests might well cause further damages to our party, which we can ill afford.... Senator Dirksen, by right of experience and known integrity, deserves this public acknowledgement as another tribute to his great leadership in the government of these United States."

Growing differences between the two senators on national issues added impetus to the movement to choose Dirksen as the chairman of the Illinois delegation. By early 1968 Percy strongly opposed escalation of the Vietnam war and proposed a halt to the bombing in North Vietnam. He crossed Dirksen on the war issue while Dirksen remained arrow-straight in his support of the Democratic administration. Since the delegates' attitudes on the war issue generally leaned toward Dirksen's, they would naturally prefer Dirksen as chairman of the delegation.

Some of the more outspoken Percy opponents pointed to Percy's attitude toward Goldwater in 1964 as a reason for challenging his selection as favorite son. Mrs. Phyllis Schlafly, a conservative spokeswoman from Alton, said, "There is still bitterness toward Senator Percy for his failure to support Senator Goldwater more strongly in 1964." On the other hand some party officials supported Percy for favorite son. Timothy P. Sheehan, Cook County Republican chairman, said, "If neither Nixon nor Reagan could win, Senator Percy would be an ideal candidate and would have special appeal to a broad cross section of both conservatives and liberals." But gubernatorial candidate Richard B. Ogilvie spoke for many Republicans when he said, "I would be favorable to Senator Percy as a favorite son. I think he could be a favorite son—with the cooperation of Senator Dirksen."

On Tuesday, June 11, in a letter to Victor Smith, chairman of the state central committee, Percy refused to seek the favorite-son designation. Percy told Smith that all along he would have accepted the favorite-son role "only if Senator Everett Dirksen did not want it, it represents the genuine will of the Illinois delegation, and it served a truly useful purpose." That capitulation put Dirksen in the saddle. He became cochairman of the delegation with Ogilvie and reigned as chairman of the convention platform committee. Of Dirksen's delegation chairmanship and his failure to achieve it, Percy said, "We're undergoing a period of unification in the party, and this is a step in that direction."

Talk of Percy as a presidential candidate had started and grown in speculative stories in the media during 1967. Reality dictated that George W. Romney, Nelson A. Rockefeller, and Richard M. Nixon were all more prime candidates than Percy; but the new senator's fast pace in Congress, his frequent public comment on issues, his attraction to the media, and his public affairs posture seemed to be the actions of a man seeking the White House. According to Percy and those who worked for him at the time, he took himself out of the presidential contest fairly early, although speculation continued well into 1968. Percy claims to have eliminated himself from the presidential contest in a face-to-face meeting with Nixon before Nixon was an announced candidate. The meeting took place in Baltimore on November 2, 1967, at the home of Milton S. Eisenhower, then president of Johns Hopkins University. Eisenhower, a personal friend of Percy, invited the two men in hopes that Nixon would find Percy an attractive possibility for vice-president. The three men discussed party politics and foreign and domestic issues for four and a half hours. Percy later recalled a Nixon question about Percy's intentions: "Nixon said, 'You know you are one of the four candidates that are potentials for '68. The national committee has your picture in the national head-quarters with three others, me included.'" Nixon then supposedly asked about Percy's plans regarding the presidency. "I said no," Percy recalled. Nixon seemed surprised, and Percy added that the reason was his lack of qualifications for the job: "If I was qualified after serving less than two full years in the Senate, the only time I'd held public office, to run for President of the United States, there is something wrong with the political processes in this country." Percy said he knew that Sears, Roebuck and Company would never appoint an officer with only two years' experience as chairman of the board of directors, and he felt that the nation should not do the same with the presidency. Percy's recollection of the subject matter discussed over dinner is at odds with that of Eisenhower, who declares that no mention was made of presidential or vice-presidential plans.

At that meeting Percy himself closed the door on the presidential nomination in 1968, but he did not make himself unavailable for the No. 2 position on the ticket. In January, 1967, Senator Stephen M. Young of Ohio, a Democrat, had predicted that Nixon would run for president and that Percy would be his running mate. It is doubtful if at this time Percy had his eye set on the vice-presidency when he was very possibly still considering his chances at the presidential nomination. But Nixon's aides fueled the vice-presidential fire. One aide said, "If Dick wins, I think he's got to have Percy with him."

Percy recalls that Nixon wanted to discuss the vice-presidency specifically on two occasions, once at the Baltimore meeting and once later at a meeting in Chicago. He declined to discuss the question, Percy said, because he knew the press would be asking if they had talked about the vice-presidency, and he wanted to be able to say no.

In the spring of 1968 the vice-presidency was enough of a possibility for Percy to ask his friend and political adviser Thomas J. Houser of Chicago to take a six-week leave of absence from his law practice and open an apartment in Washington, D.C. The objective of Houser's stay in Washington was to determine Percy's chances for the vice-presidential nomination. Houser was not authorized to seek the nomination or to commit Percy if it were offered. Houser's job was to monitor the Nixon political community. During this time Houser became personally acquainted with John Mitchell, then Nixon's close political adviser and later attorney general. He also had contact with Nixon and Richard Kleindienst, a Nixon operative and later a successor to Mitchell as attorney general. It was clear to Houser that Nixon wanted Percy on the ticket and that Nixon could have convinced potential objectors, such as the Southerners, that a moderate like Percy would give Nixon added muscle in the midwestern and eastern states.

The substance of Percy's chances as a vice-presidential nominee have been in dispute. One of Nixon's speech writers, Richard Whalen, has said that Percy's candidacy was a media buildup and that in reality Percy was a "straw man." Confirmation of Percy's consideration as a vice-presidential candidate comes from the Mitchell camp. Mrs. Rita Hauser, then an associate of Mitchell and a campaigner for Nixon, recalls Mitchell asking for a balance sheet of pluses and minuses on Percy. This type of evaluation was also done for several other potential nominees. In the report Mrs. Hauser wrote of Percy as a centrist in the party. She does not remember his name being at the top of any list, but she recalls that Percy "made good sense to a lot of people." Mrs. Hauser says a number of others, including Senator Mark O. Hatfield of Oregon and Mayor John V. Lindsay of New York City, were under consideration for the vice-presidential nomination. Mrs. Hauser is now a lawyer and banker in New York.

During this time, when Houser became convinced that Percy could be the vice-presidential nominee, Percy and staff members held a number of meetings to discuss both Nixon and his challenger Nelson A. Rockefeller in order to decide which man Percy should endorse. Percy said later, "They each had public records. I had seen something of Richard Nixon and campaigned with him [and] ... with Rockefeller." Percy viewed Rockefeller as an abler and more-desirable presidential candidate than Nixon, but the New York governor had lost some of his appeal because of his indecisiveness. As early as 1966 Rockefeller declared himself not available for the nomination, but on April 30, 1968, he announced his candidacy. He did not campaign in any primaries. Percy felt that

Nixon was better equipped to bring peace in Vietnam, though Nixon openly supported much of the Johnson war program. Houser, by this time, had become personally involved in the vice-presidential question. He cheerfully supported the Nixon presidency and wanted Percy to be allied with Nixon.

By the early summer of 1968 Nixon had won most of the Illinois delegation's votes. Most state party leaders were publicly committed to him, but by mid-July Percy still had not announced his support of any candidate. Talk of Percy as vice-president persisted. The *New York Times*, in a June 26 story, said that many people regarded Percy as most likely to be on the ticket with Nixon. The *Times* said Nixon held no views that would preclude Percy from taking the vice-presidential spot. It reported that Nixon aides saw Percy as a bridge between the urban blacks and Republican liberals.

Not long before the convention began, Percy called together aides and family members to consider an endorsement. There was a full discussion of the question, according to Houser, and he told Percy why he should not endorse Rockefeller. Houser considered it a political mistake because Nixon had the nomination virtually won. Houser said later, "To my everlasting dismay, I found out everybody in the room except for a couple of us were for Rocky. I went down in flames." Percy's staff, most of whom were opposed to Nixon, had been at work. Additionally, Percy had heard from Senate colleagues who urged endorsement of Rockefeller. Principal among those were Hatfield of Oregon and Jacob K. Javits of New York, who was obviously a strong supporter of Rockefeller.

On July 25 Percy, with Houser in the office, informed those concerned that he would endorse Rockefeller's candidacy. Until that time Percy had not conferred with Rockefeller or any of Nixon's people. He then called Rockefeller, Nixon, Richard Ogilvie in Illinois, and Hatfield and walked over to tell Dirksen. Later in the day, before Percy announced his endorsement of Rockefeller to the news media, Houser talked with Mitchell. Houser said he felt ashamed to confirm the Percy decision. Later Percy commented, "Obviously, according to John Mitchell, we took the opportunity, looked it in the face, and threw it away which he considered pretty stupid politically." So did Houser, but he felt that Percy considered the endorsement a question of principle rather than politics. Houser, injured and mad, supported Nixon at the national convention and during the 1968 campaign.

The Percy decision to endorse Rockefeller made no sense politically. Hardly anyone believed Rockefeller had any chance at the nomination. Even today many of Percy's supporters remain puzzled about the endorsement and identify it as the beginning of difficult times for Percy with many members of the Republican party, and particularly with Nixon and his staff. Shock waves hit the Illinois delegation, and Percy's standing among party loyalists sagged. To the Illinois delegation, which over-whelmingly supported Nixon, Percy's choice of Rockefeller seemed a desperate attempt to deny Nixon the nomination. Percy knew that his endorsement of Rockefeller ruined any chance he had of being on the Nixon ticket. He said of Rockefeller: "We urgently need a leader who can establish an orderly society at home and who can regain respect for America through the world." While Percy endorsed Rockefeller, he did not criticize Nixon. He said the party was lucky to have two well-qualified persons seeking the nomination.

Richard Ogilvie, the Republican candidate for governor of Illinois and subsequently the victor, had supported Nixon, but he remained loyal to Percy too. After Percy's endorsement of Rockefeller, Ogilvie said, "If I were to make a recommendation for vice-president, I would recommend Chuck Percy."

At convention time, even after his endorsement of Rockefeller and his differences of opinion with Nixon on the Vietnam war, many people thought Percy still had a chance at the vice-presidential nomination. Those on the inside, however, no longer gave Percy's candidacy any serious consideration. In comments to Nixon personally, the party pros turned thumbs down on him. Southern delegates, who held sway with Nixon at this stage of the convention, refused to support the Illinoisan. The Southern strategy was formed, and a moderate like Percy had no place in it.

Even before the convention Southerners had been opposed to Percy. Upon hearing Melvin Laird's prediction about the vice-presidential con-test—"It should be either Reagan or Rockefeller, but it's going to be Chucky-boy"—J. Strom Thurmond, the South Carolina senator who often appeared to be whispering in Nixon's ear, said, "I'll get up on the floor of the convention and denounce him [Percy] and that will cost him [Nixon] the election." Percy received little support in subsequent meetings.

Some other party moderates made the list of vice-presidential possi-bilities, but Southerners blocked any efforts to name them too. Percy was one of four persons guarded by the Secret Service prior to Nixon's choice of a running mate, but it meant nothing. Late in the discussions the names of Governor John A. Volpe of Massachusetts and Governor Spiro T. Agnew of Maryland were added to the list of potential nominees. Nixon appeared to have had Agnew's name in mind all along because he wanted a vice-president who could take orders.

Soon after Percy's endorsement of Rockefeller, his relationship with Nixon and his aides deteriorated. Herbert Klein, later to be Nixon's director of communications, accused Percy of making a deal with Rocke-feller for the opportunity of being Rockefeller's vice-presidential nominee. Percy called Klein's remark "ludicrous on the face of it, obviously untrue, politically and totally unfeasible." He later said the accusation was a "blatant lie. We felt that was a pretty dirty deal and a cheap shot."

Percy said his decision on Rockefeller reflected a belief that the New York governor would broaden the base of the party: "The only benefit we could see was for the country and ultimately for the party. We had what I considered to be a man extraordinarily well qualified to be President, who could win big and would do what I've tried to do for all my life in the Republican party—broaden the base of this party to make it a truly national party and representative of the entire country and not just a select segment of a part of the country."

Only five of the 58 delegate votes from Illinois were cast for Rockefeller, and one was Percy's; 50 were for Nixon, and the rest were scattered among also-rans. Percy made polite but noncommittal comments about the selection of Agnew for vice-president—"a distinguished governor"—and left Miami Beach along with the rest of the Republicans. As in the aftermath of the 1964 convention squabbles, Percy's standing with fellow Republicans hit a low point from which many predicted he could not this time rebound.

The years from the 1968 convention until 1972 were difficult ones for Percy with Illinois Republicans. Percy's endorsement of Rockefeller in 1968 was only one count against the senator in the minds of many Republicans. They saw Percy's Senate activity—his lack of complete support for Nixon—as an extension of his previous disloyalty. They voiced their displeasure with many of Percy's votes in the Senate, and when it came time to think about Percy's reelection in 1972, the old arguments were raised, the old battles remembered, and traditionalists across the state looked for a way to renew the fight. By 1971 it looked as if Percy might be vulnerable. Early in that year his popularity sank, reflecting his public disagreements with the Nixon administration and voter response to them. Besides, Percy never had fully recovered from internal party setbacks that developed in the 1968 Republican National Convention.

By spring of 1971 Percy's popularity had rebounded somewhat. It is hard to isolate specific reasons, except that his national profile had moderated. Polls taken in Illinois by both parties showed Percy to be clearly the biggest potential vote getter for 1972, and the Democrats had no clear challenger for Percy's Senate seat. In a well-executed stroke Percy invited two planeloads of state party leaders, totaling nearly 200 persons, to a two-day unity celebration in Washington. All factions of the Republican party—including old adversaries and new friends—were represented in the group. Percy gave places of honor to Governor Richard Ogilvie and Attorney General William Scott. Before the meeting Scott had been rumored as a potential primary opponent for Percy. But Scott, a veteran campaigner by then, could see the danger of trying to unseat an incumbent senator. The major result of the trip was to cement Percy's position within the Illinois party as the person other candidates in 1972 wanted at the top of the ticket.

As 1971 wore on, it became increasingly clear that other Republican candidates would need Percy, whether they wanted him or not. The national picture remained cloudy, with Democratic presidential challengers showing well in polls against President Nixon. In mid-October, Ogilvie extinguished the last flicker of a challenge to Percy. Mayor Robert V. Sabonjian of Waukegan, a frequent candidate for public office in the state, thought he would run against Percy in the primary and become the sweetheart of traditionalists. The goal was simply to embarrass Percy because everyone knew Sabonjian could not defeat him. Sabonjian came within an eyelash of announcing his candidacy. At the last minute Ogilvie convinced the mayor that for the good of the party he ought to forget about becoming a candidate.

By spring, both Democrats and Republicans knew that Percy, the senior senator from Illinois, would be the one to lead the Republican ticket and that he might take Governor Richard Ogilvie with him. Since at this stage Nixon still expected to have difficulty in Illinois, all state Republicans united behind Percy.

Percy's popularity in the state actually worked against him in one instance—when the chairman of the Illinois delegation to the 1972 Republican National Convention was named. Governor Ogilvie needed public exposure more than Percy, and so instead of pushing for the chairmanship, Percy let it pass again.

Percy had no illusions about his role in the 1972 convention. It was orchestrated by aides and followers of President Nixon, and the love feast had no place at the table for critics such as Percy. Those who wrote the script ordained that Percy would be ignored. The snub even extended to Percy's activity in the social area. In contrast to the hotel suites of other mainstream Republican senators, the Percy suites at the Playboy Plaza were uncommonly quiet, and the Percys were not invited to the gala events surrounding the nomination of President Nixon.

Percy buried himself in the affairs of the rules committee before and during the convention. Congressional moderates and liberals proposed a plan to equalize the delegate-selection system among the states by using the one-man, one-vote premise. This reform favored Illinois and the other more heavily populated states. Percy put in long hours on the committee and battled at the hearings for the reform, which was not passed because the moderates could not gather the needed convention votes. When the time came for debate and voting, moderates did not make a serious floor fight. Percy refused to take the rostrum. He said, "I've done my fighting in the rules committee, and now it has involved personalities." The reference was to comments by some Republicans that Percy favored the reforms because of his presidential ambitions.

After the Democratic National Convention nominated George S. McGovern, everyone realized that Nixon was a virtual shoo-in for another term. Percy saw that the potential Republican victory gave him a chance to promote a theme of independence. He could avoid commenting on major issues, except for those on which he had an established viewpoint. Percy's only shift of position during the campaign was the hardening of his dovish line on the Vietnam war. He became particularly critical of the continued bombing of North Vietnam.

Percy's Democratic opponent in the 1972 senatorial race was Roman Pucinski, a U.S. representative from the 11th Congressional District on Chicago's North Side. Residents of Pucinski's district, and even residents of other parts of Chicago, knew the affable, smiling congressman, who had been sent to Congress in 1958 after working for 20 years as a news reporter in Chicago. In his years in Congress, Pucinski's claim to fame came from his work on the House Education Committee. He wrote or sponsored many of the key education programs passed during the Johnson administration. Since the late 1950s Pucinski had changed some of his attitudes toward social legislation. Early in his tenure he had struck a moderate-to-liberal position on many issues, but as more ethnic spirit surfaced in his district, he turned conservative on such questions as busing schoolchildren for desegregation purposes. Pucinski had a reputation, acknowledged even by Republicans in Congress, as one of the most tireless workers in Washington. In fact, Pucinski worked so hard in the House that during the campaign he seldom got to Illinois to seek votes.

Pucinski's campaign never got beyond the popgun stage. His theme "a workhorse, not a showhorse" was devised in an attempt to picture Percy as a headline grabber and showboat. But it did not work.

Downstate Democrats knew immediately that Pucinski would have difficulty with name recognition and image in their areas, and so they spent much of their time telling reporters and editors about the hardworking congressman. Most Downstaters never saw Pucinski, who made few personal appearances in the area, and they were unimpressed with his record as told by his friends and as outlined in the congressman's weak and uninspired media campaign. And when Pucinski did appear publicly, his style ran to long-winded diatribes.

During the campaign Pucinski made a variety of charges against Percy. He called Percy a "faker" on revenue sharing and claimed the senator voted against an amendment that would have benefited Illinois. He accused Percy of delaying action on a minimum-wage law, and he used the term "waffling" to describe how Percy supposedly took both sides of an issue.

Joseph A. Farrell, Percy's campaign manager, published several statements refuting Pucinski's charges, saying they were "not substantiated by the record." Percy called most of Pucinski's charges either untrue or based on misinterpretations of his voting record. In some Downstate areas

Pucinski accused Percy of a "woeful lack of knowledge—or concern—about the problems of the family farmer," but Pucinski did not convince the farmers that he knew or cared any more about them than Percy did.

Because the polls showed him winning easily, Percy usually ignored Pucinski. A couple of "debates" were held early in the campaign, but Percy ended his participation before they became a habit. Pucinski angered Percy, and especially Mrs. Percy. At one point Mrs. Percy refused to appear in public with Pucinski. Finally, Percy resisted all attempts by organizations to bring the two candidates together.

Percy got through the campaign without unnecessarily angering Republicans. He followed the lead of other campaigners, including Nixon, by planning separate Citizens for Percy organizations that would be independent of the county Republican organizations. Founded primarily in most large areas of the state, these groups could do their own fund raising and campaigning. Some party regulars saw in these new groups an opportunity not to get involved in the Percy effort. As he campaigned, Percy avoided entangling himself in internal Republican party issues, and although he came down hard on ending the war, he praised Nixon's action in withdrawing troops from Vietnam. When a labor union endorsed him, Percy heralded it as the dawning of a day when the Republican party could earn labor support. He emphasized his independence, saying there was nothing un-Republican about it. Percy said, "The President, above all, understands that I am trying to build the party. He is doing the same thing himself."

The inevitable came to pass on election day. Percy received 2,867,078 votes, or 62.2 percent of the total cast, and Pucinski, 1,721,031 votes. Of the three major political areas of the state—Chicago, suburbs, and Downstate—Pucinski won only in Chicago, and the margin was much too slim to offset the Percy landslide elsewhere. Percy took Pucinski 67 to 33 percent in every county outside Cook, and he took the suburbs of Cook County 69 to 31 percent. There are no accurate registration figures available to show how far Percy went beyond the potential Republican vote.

Throughout his career Percy's campaign funds have been scrutinized by foes in the other party and antagonists in Republican ranks, although no claims of illegal activities have been raised. Persons whom Percy met during his years at Bell & Howell have been faithful contributors. These connections and the cultivation of organizations ranging from labor unions to large law firms give Percy a financial base that makes him largely self-sufficient and independent of traditional Republican sources of funds. More than one candidate in Illinois has wooed the traditionalists for money, thus giving the donors an influence greater than their numbers. Percy dutifully calls on these sources of funds, or friends call for him, but his campaigns do not depend on their money, and he has never had to beg for contributions. Percy's financial support from business and industrial leaders has been supplemented by large sums of "small money" from individuals. This financial combination leaves critics suspicious but unable to focus on any particular inappropriate activity. Still they try. In 1973 the conservative publication *Human Events* reprinted a column by Robert S. Allen, a Washington writer. In addition to referring frequently to Percy's supposed liberalism, the column contained statements such as the following: "Contributors included bankers, businessmen, labor organizations—and notably Cyrus Eaton of Cleveland, multi-millionaire board chairman of the Chesapeake & Ohio Railroad and a longtime friend of top Kremlin leaders with whom he has exchanged expensive gifts."

Conservatives have not been the only persons to call attention to the financial support Percy receives. During the 1966 contest with Douglas, Percy's wealth was a frequent topic of conversation. Douglas wrote petulantly in his autobiography, *In the Fullness of Time*, that "Percy, would, of course be backed financially by the large corporations, by the wealthy Eastern Establishment, and by the oil and gas interests." He linked Percy's friendship with Marshall Field IV, the Chicago publisher, to large donations from Chicago banking interests.

There are no detailed campaign figures available for Percy's first two election contests in 1964 and 1966. Because of a federal law calling for complete disclosure of donations and expenditures after April 7, 1972, details are available on Percy's finances for the 1972 reelection contest against Roman Pucinski. If patterns of financing are similar from one campaign to another, some insight into previous campaign funding can be gained from the 1972 figures.

Percy's prowess in eliciting contributions for a campaign was never more apparent than in 1972. According to documents filed under the federal law, contributors to Percy's campaign gave $1,399,374. This financial statement was made after April 7, and so the total amount contributed to the campaign was undoubtedly larger. In this same period contributions to Pucinski totaled $339,402. Percy's total expenditures were $1,408,822. Pucinski's total expenditures of $335,482 earned him the dubious distinction of being the most outspent candidate for the Senate in 1972. Percy's campaign spending placed him among the top four incumbent senators. He was outspent by John G. Tower, the Republican from Texas, whose campaign cost him $2.3 million. Robert P. Griffin, the Republican from Michigan, equaled Percy's expenditures at $1.4 million. Howard H. Baker, Jr., the Tennessee Republican and son-in-law of Everett Dirksen, spent $831,000.

Percy received large sums of money from banking interests and from businessmen, including some with sizable fortunes and influence in the East. In 1972 there were small contributions from the Political Awareness

Fund of the Union Oil Company, the Action Committee for Rural Electrification of the Association of National Rural Electric Cooperatives, the Kerr-McGee Corporation, American banking interests, Natural Gas Retailers, and the Savings and Loan League.

The largest individual donations, aside from Percy's own $10,000, came from Mr. and Mrs. Sam Wyly of Dallas, who gave $8,910, according to figures researched by Common Cause, the national citizens' lobby led by John Gardner, a former member of President Johnson's cabinet. Wyly was an executive for Bonanza International at the time and has been a friend of Percy since his early political battles in Illinois. Others who made contributions of more than $6,000 included Seymour C. Graham, an executive with Marpak, Inc., in Chicago ($7,500). Mr. and Mrs. Irwin Miller of Columbus, Indiana, and Roger L. Stevens, executive director of the Kennedy Center for the Performing Arts in Washington, each contributed $6,000. Also high on the list were Mr. and Mrs. Charles Wyly, who gave $5,947.

Common Cause said Percy's major source of funds was from individuals in Illinois. "During the period April 7 [1972] through January 26, 1973, Percy received $705,000 in individual contributions of over $100 each. Nearly $560,000 of that amount came from Illinois citizens."

Several longtime Percy financial supporters and friends were contributors to his 1972 campaign. One was Richard Duchossois of Flossmoor, Illinois, president and treasurer of Thrall Car Manufacturing Company. In 1972 Duchossois gave $5,650, according to Common Cause. He also contributed $5,000 in 1973 to set up the committee to explore Percy's chances of winning the 1976 presidential nomination. He was one of the committee's organizing members. Duchossois was also linked with a 1967 effort to raise $100,000 to help offset expenses Percy incurred in operating his Senate office. Another longtime Percy associate is William B. Graham, chairman of the board of Baxter Laboratories. He gave $4,996, Common Cause reported. Graham purchased Percy's Kenilworth home. James A. Linen III, chairman of the executive committee of Time, Inc., and a friend of Percy, gave $1,000. Several Rockefeller names were on the list, reflecting friendships and the family connection through his daughter Sharon's marriage to Jay Rockefeller. Jay gave $3,000 in 1972; his father, John D. III, gave $2,500. David, chairman of the Chase Manhattan Bank, and Laurence, of New York, each gave $1,000.

One familiar Republican, who has been the patron saint of many party candidates in Illinois and on the national scene, contributed to Percy's campaign. He was W. Clement Stone of Chicago, the multimillionaire who made his fortune in the insurance business. His gifts to favored Republican candidates in 1968 and 1972 totaled more than $7 million. Stone's 1972 contribution to Percy of $2,500 was much less than he spent on a gala poolside party for the Illinois delegation and their friends at the 1972 Republican National Convention.

Percy did well with labor unions. Republicans as a rule do not fare well with union political committees, but Percy worked that side of the fence hard during the 1972 campaign. Two organizations of the United Auto Workers gave amounts totaling almost $10,000. The UAW Volunteer Community Action Program donated $6,300, and the UAW Committee for Good Government, of Detroit, offered $3,400. Unions giving less than $1,000 each represented operating engineers, retail clerks, and workers in graphic arts, transportation, and service occupations.

The bulk of Percy's fund-raising program—manpower as well as dollars—came from the business world. Several large corporations had executives on various Percy fund-raising committees, and some firms had large numbers of employees who made individual contributions. The firm with the most individual contributors was Commonwealth Edison, the large utility company serving Chicago and the northeastern part of Illinois. High on the list were the First National Bank of Chicago and Marcor, Inc., the holding company for Montgomery Ward.

Percy has said that his business-related contributors are long-standing "personal friends." Of the union contributors he said, "These have only known me politically."

An important bridge between Percy and the business and professional communities is Thomas J. Houser, an attorney in Chicago. Houser ran Percy's 1964 and 1966 campaigns and maintains an important role in charting Percy's future. The relationship of the two dates back to 1962, when Houser was an attorney for the Burlington Railroad. Although Houser's position in the strategy councils has diminished with the growing influence of Washington-based advisers, Houser's recommendations often carry more political reality than those from the Washington inner circle. He leaves matters of principle to Percy. From his base in Illinois he can survey the political situation in the state for Percy.

In 1972 Houser did not have an official role in the Percy campaign. Joseph A. Farrell, who was Percy's administrative assistant in Washington and a major political strategist, was appointed campaign manager. Houser became the Illinois chairman of the Committee to Reelect the President. He took this post because of his long-held respect for Nixon and John Mitchell. Houser explained the 1972 arrangement: "Percy is a close friend, and I discussed working for Nixon with him and he approved. I believed Nixon had done more for the cause of world peace in his first term than any other President."

Houser was not implicated in the affairs of Watergate. He said, "There was no knowledge of Watergate or other activities out here [in Illinois]." Houser had some associations with Jeb Stuart Magruder of the reelection committee staff, and he also knew Magruder from the days when Magruder had worked for Illinois Republicans—Donald Rumsfeld, for his election to the U.S. House of Representatives, and for Richard Ogilvie. Houser's work for the Nixon committee consisted of fund raising in Illinois. His job was to get in touch with persons who would donate to the campaign. "Illinois was No. 1 in the number of people contacted in the nation," Houser said with pride.

Because of his insight into the complexities of the Republican party in Illinois, Houser today plays the same watchdog role for Percy in the state as he has in the past. In 1974 when Richard Ogilvie, the former governor of Illinois, flew to Washington and made it known to Percy that he would like to be the senator's Illinois campaign director for the 1976 presidential campaign, Houser was alarmed. He knew that Ogilvie had left a considerable trail of disillusionment in the party after his defeat in 1972. Houser asked those people in the state who were close to Percy to call Washington and complain. Meanwhile, he appealed to Percy to limit Ogilvie's role to organizing lawyers and raising money. The statewide pressure Percy received ended Ogilvie's chance to become campaign director. Percy then had to announce that Ogilvie's participation was something less than that which the Ogilvie aides had indicated to the Chicago newspapers in well-timed leaks. Through the years, such episodes as this one with Ogilvie have established Houser as Percy's political eyes and ears in Illinois.

It is unlikely that Percy's pledges of independence, his Senate voting record, and his defiance of some presidential positions are all happenstance. Without questioning the sincerity of Percy's approach, it is possible to identify the cause and effect relationships in his public positions.

The pressures from Illinois are fairly easy to identify. The degree to which they influence Percy's votes or style is more difficult to pin down. Percy is proud of his strong 1972 showing in the black areas of Chicago's South Side. This traditionally Democratic territory cast a majority of its votes for Percy. He became the first Republican to carry that part of the city since the 1930s. One reason for the voter shift may have been the retirement of U.S. Representative William Dawson, the dominant force in the black areas of that district for nearly 30 years. Increasingly, the influences on black voters in Chicago are Reverend Jesse Jackson, a former lieutenant for Dr. Martin Luther King, Jr., and now leader of People United To Save Humanity (PUSH), an organization for upgrading blacks of the city, and U.S. Representative Ralph H. Metcalfe, an outspoken Democrat. They are attempting to keep the black vote flexible, so that blacks are not entirely dependent on the Democratic machine for opportunities. Percy's appeal in this area constituted quite a turnaround. In the 1964 campaign he lost 89 percent of the vote in the black areas of Chicago. Estimates from the 1966 election indicate he might have done a couple of percentage points better. In both cases the incumbents against whom Percy ran were strong vote getters among blacks.

Percy's stance as an advocate of human rights undoubtedly has helped him with the black vote. His fairly consistent voting record on behalf of civil rights is available to show to black political leaders. He has favored busing to desegregate schools without declaring it the only, or even the most desirable, form of achieving desegregation. The careful cultivation of this constituency has erased memories of his opposition to open housing more than a decade ago. While the Percy record looks good to blacks, it is not so blatant as to alienate more conservative persons. Percy has not proposed much in the way of civil rights legislation as it would apply to blacks. His votes on civil rights matters have been without detailed explanation or public declarations.

Another segment of the Illinois constituency that Percy has cultivated is organized labor. During the 1972 campaign officers of the Illinois AFL-CIO helped Percy campaign at the gates of large industrial plants. They told workers passing through the gates that they supported Percy. Not only did some of the more socially conscious unions, such as the United Auto Workers (UAW), endorse Percy and contribute to his campaign, but Percy had enough subtle support in other unions to be embarrassing to Pucinski, whose voting record was pro-labor. Percy won the UAW's favor by stressing his independent voting record. In Ottawa, Illinois, during the campaign, he spoke to a UAW gathering: "You know how many times the Republican county chairmen said to me, 'We sent you to Washington to vote for us.' And when I didn't, they said, 'We're going to get you in the primary.' Well, the primary came and went, and here I am." During the campaign Robert Johnston, the UAW's regional director, explained why the union, with large membership in Peoria and Decatur, endorsed the incumbent: "Chuck Percy stands head and shoulders [above others] in the U.S. Senate on the basis of voting his convictions rather than voting his party's position."

While Percy cannot expect formal endorsement from many unions because of labor politics, he has received back-door support from many of them. His independence theme sounds good to labor leaders, and his occasional running battles with business interests help persuade labor of his good intentions. Financial contributions to the Percy campaign in 1972, while far from the kind that might turn his head on key votes, are symbolic of the inroads he has made into traditionally Democratic voting areas. The word has spread among unions over a period of years, and in another election Percy could find stronger and more vocal support of his candidacy from labor.

The Percy constituency includes great numbers of Democrats and independents, who are not inclined to be persuaded by traditional Republican positions on major social issues. This group of voters, which provided substantial funds in small contributions for Percy in 1972, was undoubtedly pleased with Percy's votes against Nixon programs. Their financial support may have been in response to his votes against two Nixon Supreme Court nominees, the escalation of war in Indochina, and other well-publicized departures from administration positions. Percy's generally pro-Republican voting record in the Senate has been overshadowed by his singular efforts to undermine proposals attributed to the Nixon administration. It is important to keep this segment of the electorate firmly in his corner. He undoubtedly will find it necessary to choose some issues on which he can differ with the Ford administration so he can continue to appeal to Democrats and independents.

Another significant element of Percy's support has been the business community. As a rule these persons, representing large corporations all over the nation, are friends from Percy's business days at Bell & Howell. But a younger generation of businessmen is also influenced by Percy's friends. The list of contributors and workers on behalf of Percy in 1972 reveals the impact of business. Perhaps this influences such Percy positions as opposition to a tax cut and encouragement of less federal spending as a means of fighting inflation. Percy is generally considered a conservative in fiscal matters, and his effort to have the government steer clear of any form of wage and price controls adds strength to the contention. At the same time supporters fear Percy has alienated too many businessmen with his strong support of the consumer protection agency. The agency would represent consumers before federal organizations. With business interests well aware of his developing friendship with labor, Percy is increasingly under pressure to prove his worthiness to business and industry, which makes for a delicate balancing act.

Percy has also received support from party officials at the state level who want Percy to act in their behalf to strengthen their hold on state affairs. Percy has been pulled in the direction of programs that Republican officials needed on several occasions. Most important of these were revenue sharing in 1972 and efforts to federalize welfare payments. Both issues were pushed by a Republican governor, Richard Ogilvie, who hoped to stay in office more than one term if the proposals passed. The success of both measures did not help Ogilvie win reelection. At least until 1976, Republicans do not hold key policy offices at the state level, and the pressures on Percy to support certain national proposals because they might benefit the Illinois party should not be too great. Attorney General William J. Scott has carried on a continuing battle against corporate polluters, and he could bring pressure on Percy to support stronger antipollution laws. That issue could cause Percy some uneasiness with his business constituency. Revenue sharing will also come up for renewal in advance of the 1976 elections, and Republicans are expected to use it as a major issue at the state level. Many municipalities in Illinois, and across the nation for that matter, have come to appreciate federal funds being returned from Washington with few strings attached. Percy should be able to handle that pressure as he has maintained a position in favor of revenue sharing from its inception.

If Percy has served all those masters fairly well in his Senate years, how well has he done for the rank and file Republican party voter? The fact is that unless the Republican voter falls in one of the categories mentioned, he may have been overlooked, and that is one of Percy's continuing dilemmas. Percy's advisers have urged him to devote his attention to some subjects with consumer appeal, even if they are not hot issues. Percy's interest in economic issues may be an indication of this strategy. Percy fought hard for congressional budget reform, and he has been active in suggesting ways for the federal budget to be trimmed. He battled for removal of economic controls and has been more vocal in addressing questions of energy conservation. These are nonpartisan activities for the most part and may be designed to comfort Republicans who feel they have been ignored too often by their senator.

The likelihood of Percy being able to win the hearts of Republican voters is remote, but he recognizes the importance of playing the issues in that direction occasionally. When Republicans are faced with deciding the Percy future again, they will need more than state pride as an incentive. The accurate feeling toward Percy by many in his party is embodied in the statement of one reluctant Percy voter: "He's a son of a bitch, but he's our son of a bitch."

CHAPTER VII

PERCY'S REPUBLICAN PHILOSOPHY

Charles H. Percy's Republican party credo is embodied in a quotation from Colonel Robert G. Ingersoll, one of the most famous orators in the last half of the 19th century: "I am a Republican, I tell you. There is room in the Republican air for every wing; there is room on the Republican sea for every sail. Republicanism says to every man: 'Let your soul be like an eagle; fly out into the great dome of thought, and question the stars for yourself.'"

Throughout his political career Percy has spoken of his Republicanism, more so than many Republican politicians of equal stature. One reason is that his loyalty to the Republican party has been challenged frequently from within. Another reason is that Percy has strong feelings about his Republican philosophy and likes to express it whenever an appropriate occasion presents itself. And such a time often arises in the wake of criticism.

Despite the more than 15 years he spent trying to convince Republicans of his loyalty to the party and to a set of principles he believes is compatible with Republicanism, Percy is viewed with suspicion by many. These suspicions were generated early in his political career. Since then isolated actions by the senator have been used by influential traditional elements in the party in a determined effort to discredit him and to deny him state and national party status. Their efforts have created some doubts even among more moderate party officials and workers. Few stop to analyze Percy's loyalty. Any effort to evaluate the depth of Percy's Republicanism must include a review of the apparent reasons for conservative distaste for Percy's principles and actions as well as an analysis of the senator's statements on his philosophy.

When Percy's political activity began to get public notice late in the 1950s, party stalwarts in Illinois and across the nation were basically conservative on such issues as civil rights and other social concerns, particularly if compared to current approaches to these problems. This posture was a reflection of post-World War II attitudes of the party, a loyalty among party leaders to many of the tenets of Republicanism as espoused by Senator Robert A. Taft, and the trials and woes of the Joseph Mc-

Carthy era. These factors outweighed any influence of President Dwight Eisenhower. The general was a phenomenon but hardly a permanent fixture in the party or a philosophical influence on the likes of Barry Goldwater, Everett Dirksen, William Knowland, Charles Halleck, or Richard Nixon. The day of moderate-liberal Republican senators and congressmen with voices in party affairs was yet to come. About the only notable major officeholder in the party with a national voice who held some moderate social views was Nelson Rockefeller of New York.

Percy began his political career as a protégé of Eisenhower. While that endeared him to many progressive Republicans, it did not make him an instant member of the GOP insiders' club. A suspicion of Percy was combined with a resentment of Percy's ability to begin his political career at the top of the heap while others supposedly had to work their way up through party ranks.

Republicans who guarded the party work ethic in those times saw the young industrialist from Bell & Howell using his business position as a jumping-off point for political office. It was not supposed to work that way. The traditional beginning from which to achieve success within the party was grass-roots political work, preferably at the county level or lower. Prior to his first run for office in 1964, Percy's grass-roots activity, perfunctory at best, mainly consisted of some precinct work and fund-raising efforts. Party loyalists manifested their fears about Percy in practical questions: Could he be counted on to parcel out jobs to the right people? Would he keep the system going? With no experience on which to base an opinion, party workers and officials leaned to the suspicious side.

At least one incident back in his days at Bell & Howell placed Percy at odds with economic conservatives. While he guided the fortunes of the company, Percy became an advocate of free trade. In his own industry, most executives and the industry association clamored for high tariffs and quotas to protect domestic-made camera equipment from competition by German and Japanese products. Percy consulted his own investment bankers about the effects of free trade on Bell & Howell, and they advised against it, saying that free trade would put the firm out of business in a decade. But Percy insisted on expanding into foreign markets. The financial success of Bell & Howell over the last quarter of a century was based in part on the energetic foreign business that Percy initiated. He recalls that "many in my own industry thought I was a traitor."

Percy contends that his position on free trade is the true conservative position and that those who would have high tariffs for protection are the liberals. Percy belittles the protectionist position: "I've always looked upon the position of conservative businessmen as hypocrisy.... [he's] saying he's for the free enterprise system but wants protection at home. In fact he doesn't want protection in any industry other than his own. He wants freedom in all others. He wants to be able to buy everything else without restrictions, but he does want protection for his own industry." Further, Percy believes the consumer should not be denied the right to buy products that are available on other markets in the world.

While some attitudes toward free trade have changed in recent years, making it a more acceptable practice in some quarters, Percy believes the strong opposition of businessmen when he started the free-trade battle has lingered to the present day.

Another specific episode from the past that Percy feels may have injured his reputation with businessmen and politicians in Illinois involved his testimony in favor of the creation of a Fair Employment Practices Commission for Illinois in the early 1960s. Percy supported an FEPC in the face of strong opposition from business interests, particularly from the Illinois Chamber of Commerce. After his testimony before the Illinois Senate, a Chamber of Commerce official told Percy, "You've just broken our backs." The first leader of the commission was Charles Gray, a Bell & Howell personnel executive, who turned out to be controversial. One of the first cases before the FEPC involved the Motorola Company. Gray accused the firm of discriminating in the use of ability tests for hiring. Robert Galvin, the president of Motorola, was and remains a personal friend of Percy's. Although he thought the accusation to be false, Percy did not interfere. Ultimately Motorola successfully defended its position in court. Galvin, now chairman of Motorola, has been a major financial supporter of Percy. Gray left Bell & Howell smarting because Percy did not support his position more strongly.

Percy believes another past event that hurt his political reputation was his support of federal open-housing legislation in 1966. He felt Republicans at that time saw support of open housing as contrary to party policy.

During those early years of political activity, Percy flailed at those Republicans who he felt twisted the meaning of Republicanism. "I've never really felt they had a right to say who is a real Republican and who isn't," Percy said later. "After all, I'd been chairman of the platform committee, chairman of the committee that had chartered the Republican course for the next 25 years. What right did they have to suddenly set up their own definition of what a real Republican is?"

In a speech after the 1964 presidential defeat of Barry Goldwater, Percy tried to straighten out persons who felt there was something to cheer about in the crushing Republican loss. He said, "In retrospect, the Republican party made a critical error in 1964, not so much because we lost ... but because we gave the leadership of our party to men who do not accurately reflect its attitude and aspirations, its traditions and philosophy. The philosophy of some of these men does not even reflect conservatism as it has been practiced in the GOP by such men as Senator Robert A. Taft, Senator Arthur Vandenberg, and President Herbert Hoover." His speech went on to castigate the racist appeal of the 1964 national election campaign and the resulting success of the party in the Southern states, concluding, "Let us not boast of these inroads, for they are nothing to be proud of."

Percy has not been able to make some Republicans forget their early suspicions of him. As he gained a greater national image in the 1960s, influential traditionalists from Illinois made contact with persons of similar persuasion on the national level, and the suspicions spread. The challenge to Percy's party loyalty camouflaged a fundamental fear: Untried politicians cannot be trusted. Many felt that defeat by the Democrats was better than victory for a renegade Republican.

Some party loyalists and right-wing elements tried to deny Percy success the first time he sought public office, but they failed more through a quirk of fate than by a show of strength. In 1964 Percy sought the party nomination for governor. His chief opponent and front-runner, Charles Carpentier, was a true-blue Republican with a long and visible record of party reliability. He was the politician's candidate because he demonstrated an understanding of patronage and party traditions. Most persons concede that Carpentier would have defeated Percy in the primary, but Carpentier became ill and later died. Percy became heir to the party blessing, angering ultraconservatives who supported a last-minute challenge to Percy. The effort failed. Carpentier's death gave Percy victory, something he could not have earned on his own at that stage in his career. It was the beginning of a continuing love-hate relationship between party professionals and Percy, the degree of which usually depends on who needs whom at what time.

Many Illinois Republicans resented the circumstances that gave Percy the gubernatorial nomination in 1964, and this attitude increased their doubts about his worthiness. Chief among these Republicans was U.S. Senator Everett Dirksen, a party regular and a major influence in state and national circles. With Democrats in control of state government and holding the other U.S. senate position, Dirksen ranked as party leader, despite his being out of the state much of the time. And it was inevitable that Percy would be compared with Dirksen. Dirksen could express his Republican ideals eloquently—although he did not always vote them in the Senate—while Percy's style was clipped and businesslike. Dirksen was comfortable; Percy seemed formal. Dirksen had been through the Republican wars; the battle was new to Percy. Dirksen knew Republicans everywhere; Percy didn't. Dirksen liked politics at the courthouse level; Percy did not understand it.

There were other powerful Republicans in Illinois who held Percy at arms length and contributed to suspicions about loyalty. One was U.S. Representative Leslie Arends. Although Arends, a traditionalist, represented a rural district in Downstate Illinois, his position as party whip in the House from 1943 until his retirement in 1974 gave him great influence in Washington. Arends's influence on the Republican congressional delegation was testimony to his strength in the Illinois party. He never warmed to Percy, and his influence among party officials made it clear that befriending Percy was frowned upon. Arends at one time pledged not to vote for Percy if the senator should become a candidate for the 1976 presidential nomination.

After Percy's election to the Senate in 1966, his critics in the party took some time finding new ammunition with which to continue the crusade against his style of Republicanism. By 1970, Percy had given his ideological opponents the fuel to mount a renewed offensive. The senator's votes against President Nixon's programs in 1969 and 1970—particularly the antiballistic missile, the confirmation of two Supreme Court justices (Clement F. Haynsworth, Jr., and G. Harrold Carswell), and the Cambodia invasion—had raised the ire of Republican loyalists.

Illinois newspapers long associated with Republican causes and under the ownership and guidance of unabashed Republicans began to point out how Percy had veered from the path charted by President Nixon. By spring, 1970, the newspapers—including the *Waukegan News-Sun*, published by longtime party loyalist Ward Just; the Rockford papers; the *Peoria Journal-Star*, in the Republican heartland of the state; and the *Chicago Tribune*, the biggest anti-Percy cheerleader of them all—were shrill with accusations.

Editorials in the Waukegan, Rockford, and Peoria papers castigated Percy's voting record and called for the senator to switch parties. A *Rockford Register-Star* editorial in May, 1970, was representative:

"Somewhere along the line Percy apparently not only has forgotten the party banner under which he was elected, but also the views of the majority of the constituency that put him in office.

"We have a suggestion for Sen. Percy, and there is ample precedent.

"Sen. Wayne Morse of Oregon originally was elected to the U.S. Senate as a Republican. But after he got to Washington, he found he was uncomfortable as a Republican. Republican Oregonians were uncomfortable, too.

"So after one successful run as an independent, Morse changed labels and became a Democrat. . . .

"Then, there is Sen. Strom Thurmond of South Carolina, a longtime Democrat who resigned from the Democratic party in 1964 to join the Republican ranks.

"We recommend the same route to Sen. Percy inasmuch as he chooses regularly to oppose the Nixon administration's foreign and domestic policies and shows little responsiveness to his party and the folks back home.

"Percy has cast his lot with the Eastern liberal political establishment, whose members include senators from both parties.

"He has abandoned the position of a traditional Midwestern Republican. . . .

"Since Sen. Percy continues to talk and act like a member of the opposition party, he may as well become a Democrat and take his chances at being slated by Chicago Mayor Daley's Democratic machine. . . ."

As impractical as the suggestion may have been, it represented the attitudes of many Illinoisans, and word of these feelings reached national audiences through conservative publications. Republican loyalists in other parts of the nation got a version of Percy's activities that was hard to change.

Although by the 1970s his image could not be altered in the minds of many Republicans, Percy continued to try. In reply to criticism about his effort on behalf of Republican candidates, Percy said, "I am very much a Republican and deeply believe in the two-party system. I have been working to help elect Republican candidates for every office from county clerk to president since at least 1947. . . . I am again campaigning for Republicans whenever I am asked and whenever I believe the candidates are honorable men even though I may not subscribe to their particular interpretation of Republican principles." He proved this point by campaigning in Illinois for Ralph T. Smith of Alton, the interim senator, against Adlai E. Stevenson in 1970, although Percy and Smith did not enjoy a close personal or philosophical relationship.

While the debates concerning his loyalty to the party continued, Percy occasionally wrote of his Republican philosophy. Traditional Republicans are not likely to find much comfort in the overall thrust of his attitudes. In his writings the depth and consistency of Percy's Republicanism is revealed, and it is clear in which direction he believes the party should be headed.

One of the earliest expressions of Percy's philosophies came from his experience in 1959 as chairman of the Republican Committee on Program and Progress. He took the assignment with the blessing of Eisenhower. The committee's goal was to draft a document that could stand as a primer for modern Republicanism for 25 years—1976. Percy helped shape much of the content of the document, working with a paid staff and reserving the right to make final editing as he saw fit. The result of nearly a year's work received a warm party and media reception. Percy has credited the experience with having a major impact on the development of his public attitudes.

The report, published under the title *Decisions for a Better America*, reflected the mixed philosophical character of the committee members and their attempt not to step on President Eisenhower's toes. Some of the statements in the report were vague; others surprised traditional Republicans of the day. At the outset the report said the party "must pursue definite goals, safeguard enduring values, yet be flexible and imaginative in welcoming change as the key to all progress." The preface said: "The Republican program for a stronger America ... is the application to the specific problems and challenges of the future of the great human principle: faith in the individual. ... This principle underlies our determination to guard against the heedless growth of the central government in Washington." Numerous references to the presence of centralized federal government dotted the report. The preface continued: "Republicans believe in a central government vigilantly alert to the needs of the people and strong enough to defend the people, to help keep the economy in balance and to make certain that a life of dignity is within the reach of every American."

National defense was a major question in 1959, and the section of the report dealing with national security and peace raised no serious questions contrary to the Eisenhower point of view. It said: "Republicans stand for the strongest military defense against the threat of tyranny—and proceeding simultaneously on all fronts with the positive job of helping to bring peace with justice—to ensure dignity and self-respect for all the people of the world." Republicans of traditional standing would not have been jolted by those words—or these: "We must assure these people [in former colonies] that we affirm their right of self-determination in choosing the type of government under which they wish to live, and that once they have made their decision in free elections we will respect and work with the government of their choosing."

The principle of reciprocal trade, an area of some disagreement within the party, was spelled out in the section of the report on national security and peace. It supported the gradual, selective, and reciprocal reduction of the "barriers to a freer exchange of goods and services among free nations." The only hesitancy voiced was for avoiding adverse effects on business and labor. The report endorsed trade with Communist nations so long as it "does not increase their relative military strength." That was about as close as the document could get to endorsing free trade.

The report reflected current thoughts on foreign nations, and particularly those in the Communist world, although the days of Joseph McCarthy were not long past. It opposed diplomatic recognition of Communist China and its admission to the United Nations, both of which occurred during the administration of Richard Nixon and were roundly applauded by all elements of the Republican party except the extreme right. However, the report did seek agreements with the Soviet Union and other countries for cultural exchange, disarmament, and control of nuclear weapons. Cessation of nuclear testing was another point on which the report said cooperation with Russia should occur.

One of the report's more important segments dealt with human rights and needs and offered some opportunity to veer slightly from traditional party positions. In one part the document dealt with the obligation of the government to individuals:

"There are gigantic jobs that only government can do and must do, and others where the government must exert positive leadership and wise co-operation. In identifying those tasks that are properly government's, Lincoln established guidelines:

" 'The legitimate object of government is to do for a community of people whatever they need to have done, but can not do, at all, or can not so well do, for themselves—in their separate and individual capacities.

" 'In all that the people can individually do as well for themselves, government ought not to interfere.' "

The civil rights portion of the report called for removal of "unconstitutional barriers" to voting and development of "vigorous programs" to assure equality of opportunity in employment, education, health services, and housing. It gave "high priority" to eliminating segregation in public places. While endorsing these fairly "safe" areas, the report only mentioned more controversial subjects such as school desegregation.

This section of the report contained an outline of basic rights for individuals. Some of the wording obviously had impact on the politically young Charles Percy:

"We Believe:

"That government has a positive responsibility to its people to maintain the conditions for a sound, productive economy. Without this there can be no opportunity, no assurance of a meaningful life for anyone.

"That every American must have access to the best education his individual endowments enable him to use. To achieve this requires the strongest combined efforts of government at all levels to stimulate the pursuit of excellence in our schools.

"That every American should enjoy every reasonable protection against those conditions or accidents that threaten him with economic disaster through no fault of his own.

"That every American of whatever race or creed must have the chance to make his best contribution to society, to himself and his family and to earn a status of respect."

No part of the report declared the traditional Republican line any better than the economic-progress section. The four basic principles for economic progress, as laid down in the report, were:

"1. The best means ever devised to plan and organize the production people want is through private initiative exercised in competitive markets.... We reject the idea that government price fixing, wage control, production planning, or materials control make sense in peacetime....

"2.... No such forced distribution of economic gains, and no amount of compulsion or state planning, will make for economic progress in America unless we preserve and enhance the stake for individual effort....

"3. A dependable dollar is essential to the strong and steady economic growth we seek. . . .

"4. Government has a responsibility to move effectively against either depression or inflation. . . . This approach calls for maximum reliance on monetary and fiscal policies, and a minimum emphasis on direct federal spending or direct controls over wages, prices or production in the private economy." The report missed the contradiction in terms.

Most of these tenets for economic progress were bent considerably by Republicans in the 15 years after the report appeared.

The report discussed economic growth. It predicted a $900 billion gross national product by 1976 and said that this growth "will give us the means to remove the last blights of poverty from the land . . . to wipe out slums, rebuild our cities . . . to reduce substantially further the insecurity now caused by sickness, indigent old age, or unemployment." The report often made such pledges but ended up warning about government growth and intervention. Some economists believed that the goals enumerated in the report signaled a desire to alter time-tested Republican economic theories.

Establishing the value of the committee's work beyond its initial impact and use in the 1960 election campaign is a task several political scientists have addressed in the years since. Cornelius P. Cotter, now a professor of political science at the Milwaukee campus of the University of Wisconsin, had a unique vantage point from which to make some judgments. He served as executive director of the committee. He doubts if there was any long-term impact of the report on the party. In fact, Cotter remembers being more concerned at the time about its potential damage to the party rather than its long-term benefits. He and others were concerned that the committee might report findings that clashed with those of President Eisenhower or those of the candidate in 1960, Richard Nixon. He feels now that "incumbent administrations probably ought not to do anything like that again."

Cotter believes that for a brief time the Republican party was one up on the Democrats. "In a partisan sense there was a temporary benefit," Cotter said. "The Republican party for a brief time had gained ascendancy in organizing for grass-roots political activity." In the history of party affairs Cotter believes Percy had the same kind of impact on Republicans as the McGovern Commission had 10 years later on Democratic National Convention affairs.

Percy's political and philosophical roots were planted in this 1959 effort of the Republican Committee on Program and Progress and in his association with President Eisenhower, Nelson Rockefeller, and other party moderates. This philosophy served him through his election defeat of 1964 and into the 1966 campaign for the Senate against Paul Douglas. In the October 29, 1966, issue of Saturday Review, Percy expressed his views of Republicanism and his comments about the direction of the party with more personal perspective and clarity. Written and published before election day, the article sounded a theme that would be familiar to those who followed the Percy political career: "If we will forget our liberal-conservative obsessions and devise solutions that are responsible and realistic—if we do these things, we can regain the confidence of the American people."

Those words, and others from the article, were directed at a party that in 1966 still had not fully recovered from the overwhelming Goldwater defeat in 1964. Many officials, Percy included, sought a renewed and vigorous party.

The article included a review of the party's traditional position on issues confronting the nation, and Percy observed that the party's stance had often been negative: "We have not even been soundly conservative. All too often, we have been merely negative both in word and deed." Having stripped away the facade, he decried the party's caution: "Unfortunately in recent years Republicans have not always been in the vanguard of social and economic development in this country." He offered an alternative to the negativism by saying the party should be suggesting "constructive—and superior—alternatives" to Democratic programs.

He attempted to identify the common denominators of a Republican philosophy but withheld any agreement with them. "I suspect that the tie that binds all Republicans is a sincere and stubborn belief in the individual," Percy stated. He carefully listed another bond between Republicans as "their alarm at the diminishing role of state and local government. But holding to those tenets isn't enough," he said. Percy observed, for example, that in 1966 Republican governors in many states had progressive programs under way. He inferred that the federal government could try some such programs too: "These states are moving ahead in education, civil rights, medical care, mental health, conservation, and highways. In some cases, they are taking the lead away from the federal government." Percy's solution was that the federal government, under Republican leadership, should fill the void. That concept put Percy outside the traditional Republican framework of a decentralized government.

If some traditional Republicans stood uneasy about Percy before the article, its substance surely gave them the jitters. Percy's idea for a Republican domestic program included a thrust in civil rights and housing for the poor. On civil rights, he wrote that "the Republican party cannot approach this issue timidly.... We must do what is necessary to guarantee the legitimate rights of every citizen, whatever his color, his creed, his cause."

Percy came to the civil rights movement later than many, but observers of his early years in politics believe he was sincere in his views.

As one said, "Before that he was a guy who was ambitious and had little time for activity in any kind of movement. He had very little concept of the civil rights struggle until he was in his late 30s and early 40s, which is late for most persons." Percy lived in one of the most restricted of residential neighborhoods in suburban Chicago. No Jews or blacks lived in this area. When Percy began to seek public office, he argued with real estate brokers and residents of Kenilworth about the closed aspect of life there. Percy did not succeed in opening up his former residential area.

In the early 1960s it was hardly chic to embrace civil rights or even talk openly about the subject, particularly if one wanted to win Republican plaudits. Percy knew the limits of involvement, although he went further toward support of civil rights than many others in the party who had long-term political ambitions. Percy did not march; he did not link arms with Dr. Martin Luther King, Jr., and parade through the suburbs of Chicago or appear before Mayor Richard J. Daley demanding concessions for blacks. But Percy did not avoid the issue either.

Percy began commenting on the civil rights issue early in the 1960s as he prepared to run for governor of Illinois. His involvement from 1964 to 1966 was more a case of his relationship to the issue rather than his leadership in it. In the Republican context of the time, this constituted a kind of "liberalism."

It may be that Percy's attitude on civil rights early in his political career contributed to the liberal tag he acquired. However, Percy suggests that his civil rights position actually is conservative: "My position has been to support the institution of the Constitution on human rights and that kind of position normally is viewed as a conservative approach. Actually those who would alter the Constitution to serve some selfish viewpoint are the liberals on civil rights."

Since his election to the Senate in 1966, Percy has developed a reputation as an advocate of civil rights causes. Whether he deserves that reputation in the total view of his comments, proposals, and actions requires some assessment. In the Senate, he does not have a reputation as an outspoken advocate of new approaches in the fight for civil rights, although his colleagues recognize him as sympathetic.

In the 1966 senatorial campaign, Percy's standing on an open-housing law received publicity. When he reached Congress, the freshman senator found an opponent of some consequence in his senate colleague from Illinois, Everett Dirksen. Civil rights was but one of many issues on which they differed. In 1967 Percy voted to kill a Dirksen amendment prohibiting the use of federal funds for busing students and teachers to correct racial imbalance in school systems. Dirksen's amendment failed. In those early Senate years Percy occasionally made public comments on civil rights activities. In May, 1968, while Washington experienced

Tent City and the Poor People's Campaign, Percy endorsed the effort as long as it remained "nonviolent and reasonable." He said, "We must be receptive, we must listen, and we must learn." A month earlier Percy had traveled to Atlanta, Georgia, for the funeral of the slain Dr. Martin Luther King, Jr.

As he stated during his 1972 campaign for reelection, Percy is on record in favor of most of the major civil rights legislation during his years in office. He opposed frequent efforts to prohibit the use of busing for desegregation of schools, although he often said busing is not the ideal method. He did vote for a measure to give local school authorities the option of requesting federal aid for busing rather than requiring federal aid to be used. As an example of his congressional activity, in 1968 he advocated creation of new financial institutions to funnel private capital into large city ghettos. He supported establishment of community development banks as proposed in the Community Self-Determination Act of 1968. The record shows a degree of involvement in civil rights affairs, if not outward leadership. Few major civil rights efforts have taken place in the Senate since the early 1970s, which is one perspective on his efforts.

In reviewing his Senate activity on civil rights, Percy prefers to look at the total picture, which includes efforts on behalf of the elderly, women's rights, the physically handicapped, and young people. In the area of women's rights, which he believes is an important civil rights advocacy, Percy supported the Equal Rights amendment. Percy has said, "I wouldn't say it's a prime preoccupation [civil rights for blacks] of mine as senator. I have greater expertise in these other rights fields."

In his 1966 *Saturday Review* article, Percy offered some generalities for pursuing world peace and easing tensions among nations. The article reveals him to be an expansionist and foreign affairs activist. He saw the party bringing "more imagination and more flexibility in our foreign policy." Percy encouraged greater cooperation with the United Nations, efforts for cooperation with Russia in exploration of space (something achieved by President Nixon in 1972), and negotiation of a nuclear non-proliferation treaty (achieved through the SALT agreement in 1972). The Republican party strategy according to Percy must be "to seize these opportunities."

By the spring of 1971 Percy's political fortunes and standing in his home state were rebounding from a low point reached during 1970. He took the opportunity to establish himself as the chief party spokesman in Illinois. In March, 1971, Percy wrote an article for a group of Illinois newspapers that contained a plea for party unity and expressed the Percy feeling that the Republican party should be open-minded enough to accept almost anyone: "Not only will all points of view fit comfortably under the rubric of Republicanism, but the party, if it is to endure as a national force, must actively seek to be as inclusive as possible. All responsible groups and ideas must be assiduously courted; none should be rejected out of hand."

Again fighting the negative image of the party, Percy said that the party should be a confederation of individuals and groups and should avoid being a "monolithic mass marching in lockstep." Rather than having specific attitudes that bind the members, Percy called for common dedication to general principles, with the goal of broad representation. He addressed Republican preoccupation with loyalty. "Administering ideological litmus tests to each other" distracted the party from solving problems, Percy said, and made the atmosphere poisonous for dissident Democrats and independents who might seek refuge in the GOP. It seemed natural for Percy to draw Democrats and independents to Republicanism because much of his vote strength comes from the other party and independents. In 1972 Nixon used the same strategy, attempting to attract unhappy Democrats to his "new majority."

Percy spent much of the article defending his Senate actions in the context of separation of powers. He noted that his party loyalty had been challenged but suggested that such talk was irrelevant. "If all we were designed to do [in the Senate] was to parrot the views of the executive branch, we would not function in the check and balance role the Constitution clearly intends us to fulfill. . . . As an active Republican for more than a quarter of a century, I believe I understand the need for party loyalty wherever possible. I make every effort to support the President and Republican programs wherever I can conscientiously do so."

Percy wrote about his loyalty to other party members, regardless of their points of view. He said that during the 1970 off-year elections he had campaigned in 14 states for a variety of Republican candidates whose views he did not always share, including Charles E. Goodell, the liberal incumbent in New York, and George L. Murphy, the conservative incumbent in California. Both Murphy and Goodell were defeated. Percy said it was not inconsistent for him to work on behalf of individuals with whom he was not always in agreement.

Percy sounded his theme of independence in the article: "Not only is blind partisanship in the exercise of public duties an impediment to progress, but it also is a fact that Republicans do not have a monopoly on sound legislative ideas." He admitted an obligation to the party and to the president "as the leader of my party," but he pronounced the independence premise by pointing to a higher obligation: the people of Illinois and the nation. He admitted that in 1972 he and the president would be linked in their fortunes, but he again suggested that his votes and actions in Congress would be determined by a higher calling—namely, "good government and good politics." He said, "I believe that if we Republicans think of the next generation, we will have begun the job of winning the next election. If we serve our country well, we will serve our party well. If we further the public interest we will further our political interests." It read like a preamble to the independence theme that he sounded with frequency throughout his campaign for reelection in 1972.

Charles Percy spent an unpleasant and restless time during the 1972 Republican National Convention. President Nixon's aides did not give Percy any role in the nationally televised festivities, and even in his own Illinois delegation some of those who had been critics of his party loyalty for a decade attempted to thwart the senator's attempts to catch a headline or two. His only battle took place in the convention committee that considered rules for the 1976 convention. Senator Percy had more than a passing interest in the rules, because they would influence the relative strength of industrial states in the next convention. After the convention, Percy explained his actions and his fears for the party.

The way to build and maintain a majority party is to encourage membership and participation in party affairs, he said. One way to achieve this is to make every delegate's vote count the same. He argued that rules supported by conservatives and Southerners in the party built in an imbalance for 1976 and gave added weight to delegations from less-populated states. Percy's alternative would have evened things in the tradition of one-man, one-vote.

Percy pinpointed sectionalism and idealism as the foes working against equalization of delegate votes: "Representatives from smaller states fought hard to protect their advantage in the party's nominating process. At the same time, conservatives from all the states organized to combat what they perceived as the 'liberal' threat from the more populous urban states." Those forces won. As Percy said in the article: "Those of us who tried to open further the door of the Republican party, in a way that more fairly and justly balanced population and Republican strength, had the door slammed in our faces." This decision reflected the atmosphere of the convention and the ideological leanings of the delegates.

Although the congressional moderates and liberals in the party lost the rules fight—because they were unprepared as well as outnumbered—Percy saw clearly that the rules question must become the challenge for the period between conventions: "If we are to win in the future, we must be better organized, better coordinated, and more committed to an agreed upon strategy." He said that challenges to the rules must be made in the courts. The continued fight, Percy said, would impress upon the party "that how and from where delegates are selected for a national convention is one of the most important factors influencing the long-term strength of our party."

While Percy could exhort the party, he also found ways of defending it. During the revelations of Watergate and related incidents, Percy spoke in defense of the party and noted the lack of involvement in campaign abuses by those running the official party mechanism. Whenever possible, he called attention to the advances brought about by a "Republican administration." One of these occasions occurred in Chicago at the Lincoln Day dinner of the United Republican Fund of Illinois on February 8, 1974. Percy was the speaker. During remarks on the subject of Watergate, he identified some of the party's principal themes and applied them to current events.

"The Republican party has long stood for fiscal responsibility in government," he said. He applied this to the battle for congressional budget reform, which became law later in the year. Percy was a sponsor of the legislation. He stated that "the business end of government needs to be run with more fundamentally sound business principles."

"The Republican party traditionally has been skeptical of an ever-more centralized government," he said. He applied that principle to federal revenue sharing and decentralization of government: "We must continue to fight to shift more revenue and responsibility from Washington to our states and communities."

On the subject of government decentralization, Percy has shown some minor inconsistencies in his public statements over the years. Percy has spoken of the need for decentralizing government while at the same time acknowledging the need for some federal government intervention. The two views need not clash, assuming that Percy sees some issues clearly in one camp and some in the other. The trouble is that in practice differentiation is not easy. His public statements have not dwelled on the fine points of difference, but his voting record in the Senate has demonstrated that Percy sees some important issues as clearly in the federal domain. As far as is known, he does not feel that his support in Congress of many social issues, such as civil rights and medical care, for example, is contradictory with his support of revenue sharing and other programs designed to give states and local governments more responsibility.

In the Lincoln Day speech Percy also said, "And through the years, the Republican party has been a persistent guardian of individual liberties." He made a direct application to the "excesses of Watergate" and called for a rededication "to the preservation of those liberties."

Developments within the Republican party in 1975 permitted Percy to express his long-held feeling about the need for broadening the party's membership base. Early in 1975 conservatives in the party held meetings in Washington to discuss a possible third party. The apparent reasons were a moderating drift of the national party and a lack of faith in President Ford's philosophical strength. The meetings followed the moderates' call for changes in the party after its overwhelming setback in the 1974 congressional elections. Not long after the meetings, a movement began among congressmen to gather support for a statement of

Republicanism. Illinoisans had a major role in drafting the statement and rounding up support for it. They included Percy in the Senate and Representative John Anderson in the House. With the exception of Philip M. Crane and Edward J. Derwinski, Illinois conservatives in the House delegation—including Minority Whip Robert H. Michel of Peoria, leader of Illinois conservatives in the House—supported the statement. Crane and Derwinski considered it unnecessary to reaffirm their dedication to Republican principles.

The statement reaffirmed efforts to rebuild "the party in the wake of our recent setbacks and to broaden our political base." It spoke of an "open door" and an "open mind" and added, "We welcome all segments of our party as well as those disaffected with any political party to join us in this challenge of shaping a modern-day Republican Party which can effectively serve the legitimate political interests of a large segment of the American people within a strong, two-party framework."

Almost in reply to the conservative complaints, the statement said, "We believe the Republican Party must build anew, not split apart. . . . We acknowledge that within our own party there is a wide range of views on particular issues, yet feel that this competition of views and ideas can be healthy in terms of broadening our base of support and strengthening our party in the long run." The statement also supported President Ford, saying, "We recognize that no party leader can please all of the party all of the time, particularly if he also serves as President of all the people."

Through many of his writings and in his public appearances, Percy has talked hopefully of a large party umbrella big enough for anyone who wanted under. In one television appearance early in 1971, when asked by a reporter why the senator had voted to admit conservative party member James L. Buckley of New York to the Republican caucus in the Senate, Percy replied, "I did so because he is a registered Republican. He proclaimed himself to be a Republican, and though I do not necessarily believe in hyphenated Republicans, we have so-called progressive, liberal, moderate Republicans. If he wants to call himself a conservative Republican, all right. . . . I think the umbrella of the Republican party has to be a large one. It has to embrace and take into its ranks people of differing views."

CHAPTER VIII

UNITED STATES SENATOR

Congress holds a distinctive place among American institutions as the single most continuous source of material for the nation's comedians. Mark Twain dished up one of his memorable one-liners about Congress: "It could probably be shown by facts and figures that there is no distinctly native American criminal class except Congress." Will Rogers kept them laughing on his lecture circuit by depicting Congress as a gathering place for lazy and uninspired hacks. Hardly a Bob Hope monologue passes without a congressional quip.

Its humor value notwithstanding, Congress is the source of great power and influence. For those who come to play the game, the rules are strict and the action intense. This is particularly true among the 100 members of the U.S. Senate. Those who come to watch or observe the action can about do as they please, and few will bother them. But they had better not ask for a share of the power. Philip M. Crane, congressman from Illinois, caught the flavor of it all: "Control of Congress is more important to a political party in long-term politics than control of the presidency."

It is accurate to describe each of the 100 members of the Senate as lord of a fiefdom. There are few unifying causes among the senators, and for many of them party affiliation means little beyond internal power plays for leadership positions. Often senators are preoccupied with traveling, serving a state constituency, or promoting a pet project. Last on their priority list is worrying about concerted Senate action on any subject. Senior senators are primarily interested in preserving their prerogatives, mainly large committee staffs and more square footage of office space. It is, as one senator said, 100 individuals heading in different directions.

More often than not a new senator is ignored by his colleagues until he gains seniority or demonstrates he has a following that others cannot ignore. If he comes on too boldly, he'll get the freeze treatment until he simmers down. If he minds his own business, he might get cordial treatment, but he'll have to wait his turn for recognition and responsibility. Most new senators quickly sense that it takes time to achieve acceptance. They turn their attentions to matters of personal and parochial interest because they recognize that a senator does not need to dabble in the big picture to keep busy. For many senators that pattern of activity lasts for their full tenure. For others it is only a temporary direction.

Charles Percy came to the tradition-laden atmosphere of the Senate in 1967 fresh from victory over Paul Douglas and high on the shoulders of an admiring press. Political columnists such as James Reston and Tom Wicker mentioned his name. The gossip columnists buzzed, and within weeks his name was whispered and then spoken aloud as a possible candidate for president. In November, 1966, an Associated Press dispatch after the election referred to Percy as a member of the party's "big four for 1968." Reston of the *New York Times* wrote in April, 1967: "The hottest political article in the Republican party here [Washington] these days is the junior senator from Illinois, Charles Percy." Many other people were taken with the former industrialist. But the record does not show any open enthusiasm by his fellow senators. If Charles Percy did not know his place, his colleagues did. He was at the bottom of the seniority list. That summed it up.

Percy maintained a brisk pace in the Senate through most of his first year, making it one of his most active and public years in Congress. By midyear he was booked heavily with speaking engagements, and his name frequently made headlines, particularly in Illinois. But if he intended to take the Senate by storm, he found it unmoving and begrudging. By year's end Percy had little more than clippings to show for his efforts.

In those early months Percy learned that the road to some measure of success and acceptability in the Senate must include making friends and playing the game. He also found out that now, unlike his days as a business executive, he could not give orders that would be carried out instantly. The Senate, he later observed, takes patience and persuasion and a high tolerance for frustration. As George Reedy, one of President Lyndon B. Johnson's press secretaries, said, "A successful congressman will get maybe 25 percent of his proposals through, and most of them will be drastically altered. It isn't a business where success is measured in anything but inches."

In Percy's freshman year, Vietnam rhetoric picked up, and each time Percy commented, he made headlines. He supported a statement by Senate Republicans that questioned many aspects of U.S. policy in Vietnam. Later in the year he favored limiting the bombing and warned against escalation of the war. In October, Percy introduced a sense of the Senate resolution—not binding in law—that called on President Johnson to make a more determined effort to obtain increased Asian military support for the Vietnam war. This suggestion was to recur. Percy said the United States should make it clear to its Asian allies "that we have no intention of indefinitely protecting their interests without their full cooperation and participation."

Late in 1967, Percy, his wife, and a small group of aides and friends took a 14-day around-the-world trip, which included a stop in Vietnam for a firsthand view of the devastation. After arriving in Vietnam, the Percys and seven of their traveling companions hired a private helicopter and took an unescorted trip to an abandoned and demolished village named Dakson. After landing, Percy and four members of the group had just left the helicopter when Communist gunners, who only days before had driven the village residents from their homes, opened up with mortars and small arms. One of the mortar shells hit within 15 feet of the senator and his fellow travelers. Percy received small scratches on his arms as he crawled behind some wood huts for cover. Mrs. Percy and the others still in the helicopter left for a nearby village. A rescue party returned to Dakson, and Percy and his companions were removed from the village without further incident. Mrs. Percy said of the episode: "I've learned after living with him for 15 years that life is never dull around him." Percy had asked for no military escort in Vietnam. After the scare he said the thought of an attack "never really occurred to me." Newspaper editorials were critical of the senator's apparent carelessness.

Although Percy started in the Senate at the bottom of the seniority lists, he quickly gained headlines for a major legislative proposal. In 1967 he submitted a home-ownership bill that would have created a private, nonprofit corporation for housing. This corporation would have had the authority to float bonds and use the proceeds to make loans to private sponsors for rehabilitating, buying, or constructing homes for eventual resale as low-income housing. After Percy explained the bill to his fellow senators and members of the Johnson administration, 36 Republican senators endorsed the plan. A long and difficult fight ensued in the Senate Banking and Currency Committee over the senator's housing plan, and alternatives were offered by the Democrats. The Democratic administration, through the Department of Housing and Urban Development, balked at the home-ownership idea. Bitterly argued, the proposal was carried over in the Senate to 1968, when a compromise bill from the Senate combined the Percy proposal with that of Joseph S. Clark of Pennsylvania, Abraham A. Ribicoff of Connecticut, and Walter F. Mondale of Minnesota—all Democrats. The administration formally endorsed the proposal in 1968 after further revisions were made in the total package. Both the Senate and House of Representatives concurred on the Housing and Urban Development Act of 1968, which proposed spending $5.3 billion over three years to provide housing for low-income families. In the final bill, signed by President Johnson, the revised home-ownership provision enabled low-income families to purchase their own homes by providing a federal subsidy that could bring down the interest costs of home mortgages. Percy voted for the 1968 law.

Through the next several years Percy established himself as an articulate spokesman, who was always available to the media. His comments on the nomination to the Supreme Court of G. Harrold Carswell and Clement F. Haynsworth, Jr., were sought and gained wide distribution. He spoke frequently on the antiballistic missile program and the supersonic transport. His remarks on these subjects as well as his running commentary on Vietnam established Percy as a source of comment on a broad range of topics. While this may have earned him recognition with the public, it irked some of his aides and associates, who felt he spread himself too thin, was associated with too many anti-Nixon issues, and did not select a key issue with some consumer appeal for comment.

When pressed for Percy's possible shortcomings in public life, Peter G. Peterson, a longtime associate of his, said that in the past Percy may have tried to cover too many issues at the same time rather than focusing on a few. Consequently, Peterson felt, some people do not have a clear image of what Percy stands for. However, Peterson thought that Percy may have begun to overcome this shortcoming when he started to focus on a few issues such as congressional budget reform and consumer protection, both of which became critical subjects later in his Senate service.

If Percy has enjoyed any measure of success in the Senate, it is due to his standing in regard to the three ruling forces of the Senate: seniority, secrecy, and committees. In a term and a half Percy has moved to the edge of power. He has not entered the charmed circle of committee chairmen and party leadership, but he is only a short distance away. Another term, for example, could make him one of the Senate's most powerful members.

Working one's way to the edge of power takes skill, but it cannot happen without paying heed to one of the Senate's ruling forces: seniority. Percy started at the bottom of the seniority ladder in 1967. At the end of six years he was 18th in seniority on the Republican side, out of 43 members, and there were 39 Democrats ahead of him in total Senate seniority. After eight years Percy had moved even closer to the top. The Republican setbacks in the elections of 1974 and the resignations among senior Senate members helped him. When Percy started the 94th Congress in 1975, he was tied for 14th in seniority with two other Republicans, Howard H. Baker, Jr., of Tennessee and Edward W. Brooke of Massachusetts. Among moderates and liberals on the Republican side, only Clifford P. Case of New Jersey, Jacob K. Javits of New York, and James B. Pearson of Kansas had more seniority. Attrition in the Democratic ranks permitted Percy to stand tied for 50th in total Senate seniority. Further progress on the seniority ladder will be slow because those now ensconced are long-term senators who are least likely to think of retirement or to be defeated since they come from relatively safe constituencies. Nevertheless, Percy could find upon completion of his second term in 1978 that further retirements, deaths, and defeats have made him one of the Senate's senior members. Regardless of this fact, one of Percy's strongest-held views about the Senate is that the seniority system should be revised and reformed.

Some new faces in the Senate were behind a flurry of proposals in the early 1970s to reform the committee seniority system. In 1973 Robert A. Taft, Jr., of Ohio and Robert W. Packwood of Oregon, both Republican senators, proposed a new nomination and election procedure for choosing top-ranking committee members. After some modifications were made, the Republican Conference adopted the plan, which gave Republicans on each committee the right to choose the ranking member without concern for seniority. These choices are subject to approval by the Republican Conference, which means there is still an opportunity for such a vote to be blocked or overturned. Common Cause, the citizens' lobby, hailed the policy change as an "important reform."

Percy has shown a willingness to deal harshly with another ruling force in the Senate: secrecy. He dates his interest in doing business in the open to his days at Bell & Howell, which operated contrary to businesses in which privacy is insisted upon by company executives. Percy said, "I felt too much was done behind closed doors without shareholders, employees, and the public knowing what a corporation is doing—and after all, most of these companies are public companies."

One senator believes Percy prefers to work in the open and cloakroom operating just is not his style. "Successful business executives don't operate in a cloakroom," this senator said, "and you can't expect Chuck to do it. It's just not his nature. But really, I'm not so sure it would make him any more effective if he suddenly became an operator. That would be too out of character for him." Percy's unwillingness to adopt the cloakroom style of other senators should not mislead anyone into concluding that he avoids using the system to get what he wants. An analysis of Percy's complete style indicates he has effectively worked within the committee system to achieve his goals, or part of them.

Committees are the third ruling force in the Senate. By a circuitous route, but with skill, Percy has threaded his way through several committee assignments. He went from Banking and Currency (now called Banking, Housing, and Urban Affairs) and Aeronautical and Space Sciences in his first year as a senator to the prestige of Foreign Relations and the Joint Economic committees. Almost unnoticed, he became the ranking member of the Government Operations Committee and thus took a share of the internal Senate prestige that comes with such a position. Being ranking member means that he would likely become committee chairman if Republicans were to gain control of the Senate. It also means he has access to committee staff and can consult directly with the administration on bills the president wants to get through the committee. Percy also is a member of the Special Committee on Aging and is ranking Republican member on the Select Committee on Nutrition and Human Needs. By design or by chance Percy has had many committee assignments that fit neatly with his interests and background. He likes foreign travel and knows his way around overseas (Foreign Relations), his experience and background in business give him a working knowledge of economics (Joint Economic Committee), and his executive experience with Bell & Howell makes him conversant with the structure of government and organization patterns (Government Operations).

Percy started in the Senate with the Banking and Currency Committee, thanks to help from Senator Everett Dirksen. Percy wanted the assignment because it would help him bring to the Senate an idea for a home-ownership program. His assignment to that committee lasted until the congressional session beginning in 1971. Percy gave up seniority on Banking and Currency for a seat at the bottom of the Appropriations Committee, one of the most powerful in the Congress. In a television interview at the time, Percy listed several reasons for his decision: "First of all, the committee is the most powerful ... in the Senate. Generally it takes many years to get on it, and I was fortunate this year to be given this opportunity. Secondly, I think the most important thing we face ahead are the priorities of spending for America, and this will be decided, of course, by the Appropriations Committee. And third, I was pleased to know that the Democrats—if I went off the banking committee—would put Adlai Stevenson on so that Illinois will be represented on that committee still."

Early in his first term Percy took a seat on the Joint Economic Committee, which has members from both the House and Senate. Membership on this committee has enabled Percy to comment on economic subjects, a field in which Percy feels he has special expertise. There is little on the public record to indicate that Percy had much interest in work of the Aeronautics and Space Sciences Committee, his second major committee assignment when he came to Congress. He moved from it to the Government Operations Committee midway in his first term.

The greatest controversy over any of Percy's assignments occurred when he moved from Appropriations to Foreign Relations. The Senate Appropriations Committee is widely considered to be one of the four most powerful and prestigious committees in Congress. The other three are the House Ways and Means Committee, the House Appropriations Committee, and the Senate Finance Committee. Not surprisingly, all four deal directly with money matters. If there is a ranking as to the relative strength of the House and Senate appropriations committees, the nod goes to the House, where the money bills originate. It is not unusual to find all four committees headed by Southerners. It takes many years of service in the Senate to become a committee chairman, and that is particularly true on these key committees. Because Southern Democrats generally have the longest tenure of all Congressmen, they eventually have become leaders of the most influential committees. Senator John L. McClellan of Arkansas, who came to the Senate in 1943, is chairman of the Senate Appropriations Committee. He took that job after the death of Allen J. Ellender of Louisiana. When Percy came to the committee in 1971, Ellender served as chairman.

By the fall of 1971 Percy complained about the obscurity of working on the Appropriations Committee, the fact that the committee did not originate legislation, the tedious work of reviewing appropriations bills, and particularly the disadvantage he felt on questioning military expenditures. Percy told a group of editors in 1971 that the senators were not given adequate information with which to rebut evidence and figures presented by the Department of Defense.

When an opening occurred on the Senate Foreign Relations Committee in 1972, Percy took it. The move stirred a furor in Illinois among those who felt his value to the state would be greater on Appropriations, before which must come most local, regional, and state pork barrel requests. His critics—including Representative Roman Pucinski, who ran against Percy in 1972—pictured the change as an example of Percy's desire for publicity rather than the gut work of the Senate. Percy responded that Foreign Relations gave him a regular forum for comment on the Vietnam war, an issue that concerned him greatly. He also reminded voters of his life-long interest in foreign travel, and he played down the importance of membership on the Appropriations Committee to the welfare of Illinois. He found the work on Appropriations stifling. Turnover occurred infrequently on the committee, meaning that movement up the ladder toward leadership would be slow. The chairman of the committee was in his 80s, and dealing with him was at best unpredictable. On Foreign Relations, Percy had an eager audience for his opinions on ending the war, although by being low man in seniority he had to wait patiently for his turn to question witnesses or comment on affairs. And if that assignment helped boost Percy's visibility at a time when presidential thoughts were not far from his mind, then membership on the Foreign Relations Committee was even more advantageous.

After he had moved from the Appropriations Committee, Percy criticized the amount of power that rests with the chairmen of Senate committees and the inability of committee members to deal with it. "It is so grossly unfair because the ranking member and the chairman run the committee, particularly on Appropriations—they move millions of dollars around, and nothing can be changed in committee—maybe 50 percent. The power is unbelievable." Percy has supported a mandatory retirement age of 70 for senators and limits on the number of committee and subcommittee assignments a senator can have. In an interview after he had moved to the Foreign Relations Committee, Percy again challenged the power of the chairmen: "The code is to leave everything in the hands of the chairman, but the code is wrong, because it places too much power in his hands. And precedent is so heavy here that it is difficult to operate."

Percy also complained of delays in committee work: "So much time is wasted here. A meeting is called for 10 and we sit around until 10:20 waiting for the chairman to show up. . . . I think at the scheduled time the majority member with the most seniority should bang down the gavel and start."

Percy did praise the care with which the Appropriations Committee reviewed budgets, calling this thoroughness important to congressional responsibility in national fiscal planning. But he complained of the large number of hearings that are necessary for a single appropriation to be approved in Congress and urged more joint committee hearings with the House.

Despite the problems of the committee system brought out by Percy and other senators, the committee is the place where the main work of Congress is done. And this work has usually been done in closed sessions, a fact that Congress seemed reluctant to change. Debate and voting on the floor of the Senate chamber have been open to the public, but little is really accomplished at this final stage to change a vote; floor debate was never more than a forum—a place for occasional high drama and a showcase for visiting schoolchildren and tourists. It was this reluctance to open committee deliberations to the public that has contributed to the reputation of Congress as one continuous series of cloakroom deals and big-money stakes.

The real work is done in committees that function differently from what most people would imagine after watching committee hearings on television. Committees may meet for what is called a "markup session." At these nuts-and-bolts meetings, details of the proposed legislation are explained, and resource persons pour over the fine points. It is at these "working sessions" that legislation is shaped. Those senators who wanted more openness in the committee system thought that these working sessions should be made public.

Supporters of the principle of openness also wished to see the conference committees open their doors. These committees are formed when different versions of a single bill are passed by both the House and the Senate. Then members of each body are chosen to meet in conference and work out a bill that is agreeable to both houses. One senator said that in a conference session "a few men can sit down and undo in one hour the most painstaking work of months of effort by several standing committees and the full membership of both houses." George W. Norris, longtime (1913–44) senator from Nebraska and a fighter against conference committees, had called them the third house of Congress.

Slowly reforms have been made which Percy and other senators have supported. Also working for reforms were Ralph Nader and his organization; Common Cause; and individuals such as Louis Harris, the public-opinion pollster. In supporting the fight for openness, Percy said, "As I look at it, the public is barred simply because senators don't want their conversations ... and the positions that they take open and available. I wonder what the reaction is from the tens of thousands of visitors that pour through the Capitol, thousands of schoolchildren every day, when they walk by a committee room where a sign says, 'Committee in Executive Session. No Public Permitted.'"

Pressure for more openness in government increased as newspapers began making public the secret activities of the Nixon administration. At this time Percy spoke more often of the problems with secrecy: "I maintain that money and secrecy are the two things that have caused the downfall of confidence in government. First, large amounts of money to buy influence, and particularly cash, and second, the fact you can do business behind closed doors." Percy's activity against secrecy would appear to be partially a result of his frustration with a system that does not pay much attention to those outside the inner circles of power.

As a result of increased public concern for what was happening behind closed doors—even the Senate's—several breakthroughs were made by Congress in the early 1970s to unlock committee sessions. The 1970 Legislative Reorganization Act came first. It declared that all committee roll-call votes were to be made public. In 1972 the Federal Advisory Committee Act was passed. It originated in the Government Operations Committee, of which Percy was a member, and it required all government advisory committees and commissions to conduct their business before the public. Percy said he became interested in the proposal when he learned that "something like 1,600" advisory committees in the executive branch were meeting in secret.

In 1973 the Senate rejected a proposal to open all committee meetings to the public. However, later in the year, the Senate did change its rules to permit committees, by a vote of their members, to open all sessions to the public. One of the few committees agreeing to do this was Government Operations, on which Percy served as ranking Republican. Congressional Quarterly said that in 1974 the Government Operations Committee held the fewest secret meetings of all Senate committees. Four percent of its meetings were closed to the public. Two other committees with low percentages of secret meetings were the Interior and Insular Affairs Committee, which closed 5 percent of its meetings to the public, and the Banking, Housing, and Urban Affairs Committee, which held 10 percent of its meetings in secret. Ranking Republican on the Interior committee was Paul J. Fannin of Arizona. Ranking Republican on the

Banking committee was John G. Tower of Texas. Both committees had sizable membership from the liberal-moderate ranks on the Republican side of the aisle.

After a trial period in which his committee's meetings were open to the public, Percy said, "There has been no disruption, no delay, no demonstrations, and the effect has been remarkable." He contended that the committee's decision to conduct open sessions helped get senators to meetings on time and to be more attentive to business. "Most of all," Percy said, "the openness rule has removed the suspicion that so many people have about what goes on behind those closed doors when we really do the work of the Senate by writing bills."

In 1974 some conference committees held public sessions to test whether secrecy was really necessary for the efficient functioning of the conferees. Until then all but a few of the conference sessions were conducted in secret. The committee members found that conferences could be opened to the public without injury to the conference process. In 1975 the House agreed to conduct public conference-committee sessions unless a majority of conferees voted for secrecy. This decision constituted a major breakthrough in congressional reform.

The most sweeping secrecy reform to surface in years was a proposal by Senator Lawton Chiles, a Florida Democrat. Percy, among others, co-sponsored the bill, which was first considered by the Senate in 1974. Intended by its sponsors to dispel growing cynicism by the public about the work of Congress, the bill would have made all congressional activities, including those of federal regulatory agencies and government commissions, open to the public except in cases of "national security" or a few other special situations. Percy preferred a system by which sessions could only be closed by a roll-call vote of the members, and with the reasons fully stated for public consumption. The Chiles proposal met strong opposition from those senators who felt that such comprehensive changes would totally destroy the system by which they had reached positions of power and influence.

The constant pressure for more openness in Senate committees, and on the House side too, has reduced secrecy substantially in recent years. Congressional Quarterly reported that only 15 percent of all congressional committee meetings in 1974 were held in secret. The percentage was 16 in 1973 and 40 in 1972. In the Senate alone, 25 percent of the committee sessions were closed to the public in 1973, and there was no improvement in 1974.

There are many senators who, for a variety of reasons, still oppose any attempts to open the committee system to the public. If Everett McKinley Dirksen were still a senator from Illinois, he undoubtedly would be a leading spokesman for continuing business as usual. He looked dimly upon internal Senate reform of any kind, as expressed in his comment on a plan in 1968 to require financial statements from senators. Dirksen said such rules would be "impertinent" and would make senators "second-class citizens." His sweeping justification for secrecy: "After all, all life is a conflict of interest."

Since Percy's first year in the Senate, his work generally has drawn plaudits, particularly from those outside the halls. The Nader Congress Project of 1972, which analyzed the records of senators seeking reelection, stated that an eagerness and willingness to compromise "has made Charles Percy one of the most diligent, well-prepared, and effective men in the Senate." His colleagues are more cautious in their assessment. George D. Aiken, the former Vermont senator who ranked No. 1 in Republican seniority until his retirement in 1974, found the words that best describe the feelings of the senators. He said Percy is "ambitious and hard-working."

Few senators doubt that Percy takes his work seriously. He has become an articulate spokesman for the prerogatives of Congress and the specific roles that are important to the concept of separation of powers. Percy knows the roles of a senator, and he explained them in a 1971 article entitled "Separation of Powers" in *Today's Education* magazine. The article discussed the responsibility of a senator and the relationship of the Senate and the executive branch. Percy used the appointment of judges and the appropriation function of Congress to make his points about the separation-of-powers principle.

"All too often pro forma acquiescence to the President's wishes is expected," Percy wrote. "The Senator who, in the course of discharging his constitutional obligation, finds it necessary to express reservations about a nominee is construed as attacking the President, or the courts, or both." Part of that responsibility, Percy wrote, is recognizing the difference between judicial nominations and routine presidential appointments. "The Senate's role in assessing the fitness of potential federal judges differs markedly, I think, from its position in the confirmation process for executive appointments, such as those in the Cabinet," Percy said. "The President is held accountable politically for the performance of his appointee. . . . Moreover, an executive appointee ordinarily serves only as long as the President who appointed him; judicial appointments are for life."

Public reaction to Congress exercising its responsibilities in appropriating money is similar to the judicial situation, Percy wrote. "When the legislative branch uses its power over the purse as a check on the executive, its action is frequently regarded by the public as obstructing the smooth functioning of government." Percy argued that the reverse is true. Congress determines the nation's priorities by exercising its rights in appropriating money. Abdicating the control over funding to the executive "would upset the delicate balance that must be maintained if the separation of powers principle is to really work in actual practice."

In the same article Percy used the separation-of-powers argument in defense of his votes on the supersonic transport (SST). He wrote in regard to the SST: "Many of us in the Congress believed that the SST was a bad economic and environmental risk for the nation and that pressing domestic needs—such as urban mass transit systems—had a much better claim on the limited federal funds available to us. The Administration disagreed, assigning a relatively high priority to the SST. It was not necessary to support our position to agree that we were well within our rights in using the principal weapon in our arsenal—the power to approve or withhold appropriations—in the SST fight. The alternative would have been a program created by executive fiat."

At another point in the magazine article, Percy offered the separation-of-powers argument when discussing the right of Vietnam doves in the Senate to criticize the administration's policy in Indochina: "The minority of Senators and Congressmen who courageously advocated an end to the escalation of the war in Indochina long before these views became popular did not deserve the censure they received from many quarters, particularly from self-proclaimed super-patriots. Even if one disagreed with them—or disagrees today—it is incontrovertibly true that they were constitutionally entitled to speak out. And I submit that it was this exercise of their constitutional prerogative that was responsible in large measure for the reversal of the overall American policy in Indochina—from escalation to withdrawal."

How does Percy rate with fellow senators? As Percy himself says, "I feel that most senators feel that I do my homework on the positions I take and then work very hard at them." He sees himself as persuasive with a "large group" of senators, particularly on economic issues. He likes to think he and a few others put together enough votes to defeat any chance for extension of economic controls in 1974. Percy says, "I exposed the SST for the fraud that it was. I did my homework, not on ecology, but as a return on the investment. It was a true 'flying Edsel' as I called it, but I had to analyze and appraise it." Percy has good acceptance for his views from the Democratic side, occasionally including some Southerners on his committees and some committee chairmen. "We disagree on social issues," he says, "but there are many issues on which we are in agreement." While Percy and Sam J. Ervin, Jr., former Democratic senator from North Carolina, hardly agreed on social questions, they worked together on passage of the budget reform bill in 1974 and cosponsored much of the legislation originating from the Government Operations Committee. Still, Ervin fought tenaciously against a proposal, cosponsored by Percy, to create a consumer protection agency.

Percy's self-appraisal cannot stand as the final word on his performance in the Senate. Most any member of Congress could select one or two instances in which he has been successful with his colleagues or persuasive on issues, particularly in the span of six or eight years. It is difficult to analyze the performance of a senator because no one has established a universal list of tests or comparisons. The nature of parliamentary activity—switching votes at a crucial time, voting one way on amendments and another on the final tally—adds up to a highly subjective business. It is far easier to ask "What kind of senator has Charles Percy been?" than it is to come up with the answer.

Any senator or representative can fill the *Congressional Record* with statements, speeches, editorials, reprints from friendly newspapers, and even poetry. Any senator can have a near-perfect voting record and not do much else. Out of 100 persons in the Senate, there is always at least one who will say something nice about a fellow senator and one who will make him out to be a villain. It all depends on what is expected of him. Analysis of a senator's record does depend to some extent upon his colleagues' appraisals, but more important is the public record of his statements and votes and his reactions to statements and votes. Some additional information can be obtained by listening to colleagues compare a senator with others.

Senators understand the unreliability of off-the-cuff comments about colleagues that often get mileage in newspaper and magazine articles. One senator, when asked to assess other senators' attitudes toward Percy, said, "It is hard to evaluate the comments of other senators. Much of it has to do with how deeply, how penetrating, the analysis goes, and much of it is flippant and not worth considering." Even if some of a senator's public remarks should be lightly considered, the astute political observer can generally put the remark in its proper perspective. One Democratic senator, who shares a committee assignment with Percy, watched him closely during the 18-month push for the 1976 presidential nomination. During this period there was little doubt that the demands on Percy's time influenced his performance in the Senate. This Democrat observed, "There is a lot of public relations mixed in with his work. Anybody who wants the presidency develops a tendency to make an increasing number of stump speeches. He projects very well on the media and has a built-in advantage there. He's established a national prominence in a relatively short time, and he has considerable charisma." The same Democrat observed how the demands on Percy's time affected his committee performance: "He wasn't always informed. He had to rely on his staff person or the committee staff to brief him, and sometimes that wasn't done sufficiently." As a result Percy would ask the same questions others had asked. "It's darned irritating sometimes, but he's a victim of circumstances. He has to rely on staff work. First of all he has the problem that any senator from a big state has, and that is time. Put that together with his ambitions for president, and he's spread pretty thin." Percy has worried about the demands on his time. "I'm on eighteen committees [including subcommittees], and we are spread too thin," he said in 1972. "As a result we are overly dependent on the committee staff, and when it is not too good, the price is pretty high." Percy's Washington staff ranks fairly high in the eyes of other congressional staff members, so Percy's situation may not be as critical as that of senators with smaller and less experienced staffs. Subcommittee assignments vary from session to session but take a large share of the senator's time. In 1975, for example, he was serving on four subcommittees of the Government Operations Committee.

The pressures of ambition and Senate work make for long days and nights. "When I was at Bell & Howell, the job had weekends and vacations and nights," Percy says. "But many is the day that I come home with a full briefcase and work until bedtime, and there is no such thing as vacation time, and most of the weekends are filled with trips back to Chicago or campaigning."

Percy's Senate colleagues may understand him and sympathize with some of his views, but that does not mean they automatically will come rushing to his side on Senate business or in support of his candidacy for higher office at some future time. This is particularly true of moderate Republicans in the Senate. Jacob Javits of New York, with whom Percy worked in the long battle over a consumer protection agency, has voted against reforms aimed at opening committee sessions to the public. Percy and Edward Brooke from Massachusetts voted together on many questions during the Indochina war, but they parted company on the subject of a presidential resignation in 1974. Brooke called for a Nixon resignation while Percy steadfastly opposed that course even to the last minute. There is a group of Senate moderates who often vote together on major questions, and Percy can count on their help with some questions. They include Mark O. Hatfield of Oregon, Richard S. Schweiker of Pennsylvania, and Charles McC. Mathias, Jr., of Maryland. Robert A. Taft, Jr., of Ohio, while not a liberal on most questions, is a good friend of Percy's and the two often agree on substantive issues. Although the small group of moderate Republicans differed with Nixon during much of his administration on such issues as Vietnam and attitudes toward social questions such as busing of schoolchildren, overall Republican support seldom failed the president. The affairs of Watergate and the resulting discussion of impeachment had a strange effect on alliances in the Republican party as individuals wrestled with how far they could go along with the president when he obviously was losing ground with the public. Moderates, liberals, and conservatives ultimately found themselves in step. When the president's resignation finally came, it was not at the insistence of moderates and liberals. Conservative leaders such as Barry Goldwater and James L. Buckley were the ones who finally got the president's ear and persuaded him that resignation was the best course. While Nixon stood as a source of many Republican party divisions in the Senate, at the last they were united on the question of the president's involvement in Watergate and the need for him to be removed from office.

The division between conservative and liberal Republicans remains, regardless of occasional agreement. Only a few months after virtual unity on the question of removing Nixon from office, the factions split openly over who should be chairman of the Senate Republican Conference. Liberals and moderates supported Jacob Javits, and conservatives voted for Carl T. Curtis of Nebraska. Curtis won handily, 23 to 14, with Percy not voting because he was in the Middle East on a trip. His vote would likely have been with the liberal-moderates. Ironically, Curtis was one of Nixon's staunchest supporters and, after the former president's resignation, stood as one of only a handful who remained loyal and said they would not have voted to convict Nixon if it had come to a trial in the Senate. After returning from the Middle East, Percy noted that while the House of Representatives seemed to be reforming its structure, the Senate remained a basically conservative body.

Substantial opposition to any Percy proposal can be expected from the bulk of Senate Republicans, particularly ones with roots in party wars dating back 15 years or more. Most of these senators vote a conservative line on issues in the Senate, preferring to stand by themselves or with Southern Democrats on social questions and money matters. This wing of the party, perhaps best identified as traditional, has strength in party affairs far beyond Senate halls. It runs the machinery that produces delegates for the national convention, and it turned the party toward Robert A. Taft and Richard Nixon and Barry Goldwater at presidential nomination time. For the most part the conservative senators represent the less-populated states with rural constituencies in the southern, western, and plains states. Since the days of Dwight Eisenhower they have dictated the party's direction, the cries of more moderate, liberal, and less easily led Republican senators notwithstanding. Charles Percy could hardly be considered in step with the sum of these conservative senators. Their views differ not only on party appeal and thrust, but also on many of the issues before the nation. Although their opposition has not hurt Percy at the polls through the years, on the inside of party affairs they have denied him certain political fringe benefits, the frosting that feeds an ego. This has happened particularly at national convention time, when Percy has been denied the prestige of leadership positions. If there is a frustration in Percy's dealings with conservatives, it must be from the quadrennial experiences of selecting a president.

Senate conservative Republicans are not likely to be joining Percy on many issues of singular importance to the Illinoisan. Leaders among these conservatives are Goldwater and Buckley. One colleague put it practically: "I wouldn't expect the old guard to be strong for Percy. They could be practical, I suppose, but usually when the Republicans divide up, they stay divided." Percy claims his relationship with Goldwater, probably the most outspoken conservative in the Senate, is "friendly." Evidence of this, according to Percy, is the fact that Goldwater campaigned for Percy in 1972 and wrote several hundred personal letters urging reelection of the Illinoisan.

Before Gerald Ford became president and Percy was a committed presidential candidate, Goldwater told an interviewer, "Right now I wouldn't give Chuck Percy a 10 percent chance. I don't think he can get the delegation from his own state. It's not that he's too liberal—but he's too inconsistent. He wanders all over hell's half acre." Later Goldwater called that an "off-the-cuff remark" and gave Percy his personal pledge of support if Percy should win the nomination. That sounded much like the reluctant pledge of support Percy gave candidate Goldwater prior to the 1964 national convention drive. Goldwater reflected the feelings of many others when he said that "85 percent of all Republicans are conservative, so we don't worry about the remaining 15 percent who are not." Percy responded to the Goldwater figures with a perspective of his own: "No figures I have seen indicate that. In fact, polls show that half of all Republicans see themselves as middle-of-the-roaders. I would say that if he was talking about the 1964 convention where [Nelson] Rockefeller was booed and where extremism was the symbol, his figures come close to accuracy but that was not a representative year." Exchanges such as this have sprinkled the Goldwater-Percy relationship over the years.

Alone, these hard-core Republican senators would not have much impact on national policy, but in coalition with Southern Democrats they are often the most potent force in the Senate. The coalition is a negative influence, voting not to change but to maintain the status quo or to thwart what others have labeled as reforms. The list of victories attributed to the coalition at the end of every session has been impressive when the total effort of the Senate is considered. The strength of the coalition has dwindled in recent years, but it remains a potent force.

One dimension of Percy's relationship with the traditional wing of his party can be viewed through his voting record with and against the coalition of Republicans and Southern Democrats. These records are compiled by Congressional Quarterly, an independent source of information gathered for clients. Through his first eight years in the Senate, Percy voted with the coalition about 35 percent of the time on issues, selected by Congressional Quarterly, in which there was coalition interest. Over the same period he voted against the coalition more than 40 percent of the time. For a point of comparison, during 1967 and 1968 Percy's

Illinois colleague Everett Dirksen supported the coalition 60 percent of the time and opposed it 34 percent. In the years starting 1969, Goldwater voted with the coalition about 50 percent of the time and opposed the coalition less than 5 percent.

There is no particular trend in the Percy voting figures. In his first two years the percentage of votes against the coalition (44) was markedly higher than in the second two years (31), but the figure rebounded in a third two-year period to 42 percent. In 1973–74 Percy opposed the coalition on 49 percent of the issues. In the years 1969–70 Percy supported the coalition a higher percentage of the time than he opposed it. The vote pattern was reversed in all other periods. Percy's record hardly qualifies him as a loyal member of the coalition.

Another benchmark in determining Percy's relationship to voting blocs is the number of times he joined other Republicans in voting on clearly partisan issues. These party-unity voting records, also compiled by Congressional Quarterly, are based on selected issues in which Democrat-Republican lines are clearly drawn. Through his first term Percy supported party-unity issues about 40 percent of the time. In the same period Goldwater averaged 50 percent. Percy opposed party-unity issues about 35 percent of the time, while Goldwater opposed party-line issues less than 5 percent. Also available from the same source is Percy's voting record on issues that gained broad bipartisan support in the Senate. In this category the comparison with Goldwater's voting record shows Percy to be far more bipartisan in his voting than the Arizonan. He supported bipartisan issues 69 percent of the time and opposed them only slightly more than 10. Goldwater's support averaged about 30 percent, and his opposition percentage was 15. Two points can be made from these statistics. One is that Percy agrees more frequently with the middle ground of Senate attitudes than with extreme points of view. Also it reflects a voting pattern with persons Percy often needs to pass his proposals, such as Democrats. While Percy's record on the number of roll calls is not the best among his Republican colleagues, it is not far from the top. During his first term the Republican average on roll calls was 82 percent. Percy averaged 78. There were some Republican senators who were present for 100 percent of the votes, and some who were present only 50 percent of the time.

Because of Percy's philosophical approach to some issues, particularly those in the social-services area, he often works closely with Senate Democrats and finds many of his supporting votes on the Democratic side of the aisle. One senator, a liberal Democrat, sees Percy as "genuinely concerned about the humanitarian aspects of public issues. He's more liberal toward individual needs than the more conservative Republicans, and I guess he probably finds it hard sledding in his party because his views are so much more liberal than his colleagues."

Percy has shown he can work with all factions toward a common goal, using his acquired talents as a legislator and the ability to work with an issue on which there is some desired unanimity. One such occasion occurred in 1971 and 1972 when the Drug Abuse Office and Treatment Act surfaced in the Senate. The act called for a comprehensive attack on the problem of drug abuse and authorized the spending of $1.7 million for federal and state drug programs. Percy's role in the passage of the measure is best described as a broker. Early in consideration, the Nixon administration approached Percy to sponsor its plan. The bill received consideration by the Government Operations Committee. Percy agreed, knowing that the Nixon proposal differed from those sponsored by Democrats, some of whom wanted to be the party's 1972 presidential nominee. Percy rewrote the Nixon plan and incorporated key information from the Democrats' proposals. From there Percy and staff assistants undertook to sell the package to Nixon and the Democrats. The relative success of the effort showed in the Senate's approval, 92 to 0 on a roll call. The House of Representatives later approved its version, and a compromise passed and became law in 1972.

Some of the tougher old-timers in the Senate take delight in trying to sidetrack a Percy project or punish the Illinoisan for some breach of conduct. The motivation behind this behavior is difficult to identify, because Percy is not the only target of these persons. Some of it must be laid to differences of opinion on specific issues and general disagreement on the broad spectrum of subjects as well. That seemed to be the case early in May, 1973, when Percy brought to the Senate floor a resolution calling for a Senate-approved Watergate special prosecutor. The resolution got little advance notice, and only a handful of senators were present when the voice vote was taken. "I didn't like it at all," a Republican senator high in seniority said. "I've always been resentful of legislation being enacted by a voice vote." Conservative Senator Carl Curtis of Nebraska was another who did not like the tactic. He attempted to have the matter reconsidered by the Senate but dropped the subject when there seemed to be little support for it. George Aiken openly criticized the Percy resolution, and according to the Vermont senator his comments apparently caused Percy some uneasiness: "When he felt badly about my comments about his actions on the floor, I said I'd go on one of his 15-minute programs [television]. He felt badly, and I didn't want it to linger." Apparently the TV appearance with Percy was supposed to settle the differences. Another senator who did not object to the specific resolution, said, "It's just not considered ethical to push legislation through like that." The small number of senators who objected must lead to the conclusion that the complaints were designed more to unsettle Percy than to get the matter reconsidered.

If Aiken's remarks upset Percy, it is an indication that he worries about what other senators think of him. In a controversy over a regional dam project in Illinois, Percy has defended his position—which made many residents near the proposed dam location unhappy—on the need to retain credibility with his Washington colleagues as opposed to currying favor with constituents. The situation involved a reservoir project called Springer Lake, in central Illinois, near Decatur. For years, while the project slowly moved through the planning stages, Percy remained a faithful supporter, along with other Republicans in the state and in Congress. Percy testified before Appropriations committees and did not hesitate to declare his support, even as opposition from environmentalists developed. Suddenly in 1974, Percy altered his total commitment position by raising environmental questions and asking for clarification before pushing the project further. The action stunned central Illinoisans, and many reacted with angry letters and telephone calls. Angry Republicans in the state accused Percy of switching his position because of his presidential ambitions and the need to satisfy environmentalists. Percy defended his position: "I can't continue to go back before that committee and ask for funds if they [the members] think I'm just blindly going along with something because it might benefit some voters. The committee members know of those environment reports, and if I ignored them, they would have a right to question my position. What would I do then, say they don't mean anything or that I don't care what the EPA [Environmental Protection Agency] says? No, I felt the questions were good ones, and that had to be reflected in my testimony. I'm sorry if the folks in central Illinois don't understand, but I have to be concerned about my credibility in Congress too." In political terms the decision to alter his support indicated that Percy felt his long-term support could be a liability to him if the project were dumped because of environmental objections.

In the final analysis Percy's actions must determine any answer to questions of his effectiveness in the Senate. Expressions by colleagues form only a small piece of the picture, and anger expressed at one time can be retracted at another. William L. Springer, a former congressman who later served as a member of the Federal Power Commission and in whose district the Springer Lake project was to have been developed, shed some light on Senate relationships: "These fellows on the Senate side are rather touchy. They have a rather clubby atmosphere, and it is hard to tell where real friendship begins and ends. I have heard them say unprintable things to each other in conferences between the House and the Senate—and then go out in the hallway and laugh and put their arms around each other."

When Percy ran for the Senate in 1966 an Illinois newspaper asked him, "Why do you feel you could better represent Illinois's interests in Washington than your opponent?" Percy said that he could represent the best interests of all Illinoisans because he was not tied to Chicago city hall; that by not being beholden to the Lyndon Johnson administration, he could act independently in behalf of Illinoisans; and with tenure and seniority in the Senate he could use committee assignments to the state's advantage. For a candidate trying to overtake an incumbent, those are predictable answers. His Senate record shows that he has not favored some interests over others. His independence of the Johnson and Nixon administrations kept him in hot water much of the time. There is a question as to whether the senator's committee assignments and seniority have paid off for Illinois. After shuffling committees in his early Senate years, he settled down with the Foreign Relations Committee; the Government Operations Committee, on which he is the ranking Republican; and the Joint Economic Committee. On some of the subcommittee work he has entered fields that benefit Illinois citizens, but no more than citizens in other states. It is hard to see the direct benefits to Illinois from Foreign Relations, Joint Economics, and Government Operations in the terms most persons have used to judge effectiveness. His opponents have been unsuccessful in building much of a case against his efforts in seeking pork barrel projects to benefit the state. When he switched from the Appropriations Committee, which determines where pork projects go, to Foreign Relations, he received as much criticism from Republicans as he did from Democrats.

Some Democrats observed early in 1972 that in order to give Percy any kind of run they would have to make an issue over his value to the state. Put in simpler terms: How much has Percy helped Illinois? Senator Stevenson raised the question briefly in February. Then, expecting to campaign with moderate vigor for Pucinski, Stevenson raised the question more directly in the spring of 1972. In a news release and a statement on the floor of the Senate, Stevenson contended that Illinois ranked 48th in overall per capita federal spending in the fiscal year of 1971. Stevenson could not be called to account for that relative position because his tenure began in 1970. Stevenson inferred that Percy had not done his duty in getting Illinois a better share of federal pork. In response to the specific charge that Illinois had not received its appropriate share of money for the Law Enforcement Assistance Administration, Percy countered that the problems were administrative in Illinois and Washington and were not because of any lack of effort by Illinois representatives in Congress. Beyond that Percy did not bother to refute any claims presented by Stevenson. When Stevenson ran for reelection in 1974, he contended that the state's position on federal funds had improved appreciably.

Under more normal conditions the Stevenson charge might have set the stage for a major issue, but Pucinski's inability to mount a campaign let the issue die. Had the Democrats struck at the issue, they would have encountered one major difficulty. It is hard to obtain figures that prove conclusively whether a senator has been faithful in his courting of federal cash. There inevitably are two sets of figures and at least two sides of the story. The campaign would have leaned heavily on the inference that with a Republican senator and a Republican president the state should have done better.

Percy believes in getting a reasonable share of federal pork barrel for Illinois but does not believe in using political influence to get projects the state does not need. Although others might disagree with Percy's determination of need, he sees his credibility with Senate colleagues at stake and so avoids seeking money for projects he does not feel are urgent. To claims that he might have received more for Illinois by being friendlier with the White House, Percy says that projects involving rivers, harbors, and dams are controlled mostly by congressional committee. However, experience has shown that Percy has had some encounters which indicate that the White House has gotten involved, despite protocol, when it was to its political advantage.

A measure of a senator's value to his home state is his responsiveness to state problems. During Percy's period in Congress, two of the state's more pressing concerns have related to financial problems. One situation concerned revenue sharing, which Republican officials in Illinois, particularly Ogilvie, felt would be the salvation of state finances for several years. Another had to do with rapidly increasing public aid payments and the pressures they brought on a tight state budget. Percy gets good marks for his Senate efforts in these two areas. Although they do not prove conclusively that he performs at peak efficiency at all times when state problems are at issue, it does give some insight into how he responds. In one case he succeeded. In another he failed to get what he sought.

With plenty of push from Illinois, Percy supported general revenue sharing when it came before Congress in the early years of the Nixon administration. The concept of returning federal money to the states and local governments started during the Johnson administration but never received President Johnson's favor. By the fall of 1972 the proposal, under support by Nixon, neared passage in both chambers. Each chamber had its own plan. The House plan favored the more-populated states, and the Senate proposal favored the less-populated states with a greater rural population. Over the five-year life of revenue sharing under the House plan, Illinois stood to receive $301,800,000. Under the Senate bill, the total would have been $250,900,000. The House bill, for example, favored states with an income tax in figuring the amount to be dispersed. Illinois enacted an income tax in 1969. Percy voted against the Senate proposal, although it passed the Senate 64 to 20. His vote brought an immediate outcry from Pucinski, who by that time desperately needed a major issue to turn the campaign around. Percy explained that he voted against the bill because it shortchanged Illinois. A vote against the bill, he said, meant more in parliamentary dealings than if he had gone along with the original proposal. The bill was to pass anyway, Percy said, and his protest vote meant the viewpoint of the more-populated states would be heard in conference committee.

The proposal went to conferees. Percy's strategy, along with the objections of senators from heavily populated states, had an effect. Many of the House conferees were from more-populated states, and none of the Senate conferees represented populous states. Whether the Percy strategy really had that much impact is hard to determine. The final conference bill, which both houses approved, gave Illinois $275,000,000, less than the House's proposed appropriation but more than the Senate's. Percy's explanation seemed to defuse the Pucinski claim that the senator had turned his back on the state. Senator Stevenson voted against the final bill because he objected to the concept of sending money to local and state governments. He continues to feel that local governments are not capable of handling this money efficiently.

The second concern in Illinois was the serious public aid financing problem that had developed in the state by late 1971. Illinois faced a deficit in the public aid fund, which would have to be met by an emergency appropriation of state funds before the end of the fiscal year. With the urging of Ogilvie, Percy introduced in 1971 what became known as the Percy amendment to the administration's national welfare reform and social security bill. Percy's plan would have the federal government reimburse the states for that portion of their welfare expenses that exceeded those incurred in the 1971 fiscal year, up to a total of 25 percent or more. The White House agreed to support the plan if Percy would adjust his figure to 20 percent, which he did. The Percy proposal, which was one of several amendments to the main administration bill (most of which failed) that had been proposed by senators, at one time had the backing of 20 governors whose states' welfare rolls had increased and who said their states were running into serious financial problems as a result. Percy's amendment was a stopgap measure designed to continue in effect only until a complete federal welfare system was enacted. Illinois Republicans testified before Senate committees and lobbied with congressmen on behalf of the plan. But the Senate turned down the amendment on a voice vote. When the bill finally passed late in 1972, it did not provide for any reform of the welfare system.

When Percy went to the Senate, the state's pork barrel benefits rested in the hands of Senator Dirksen. The two cooperated on projects and avoided any major clashes. Staffs of Stevenson and Percy have worked closely on many issues and state projects but usually without the direct involvement of Percy. As one of the Stevenson staff members expressed it: "Most of the Illinois project work is done through the staffs, and

Senator Percy really prefers to travel and concern himself with the larger questions." There is evidence that by early in the second Nixon term the relationship of Percy with chief aides in the administration had hurt the chances of some regional federal projects in Illinois. With Stevenson not likely to have entré to Nixon administrators and with a Democratic governor in Illinois, questions about Percy's effectiveness took on a serious tone. The pressure eased when Watergate problems occupied the time of Nixon aides and cabinet officers changed with increased regularity. It meant the projects were stymied, but at least they were not being scuttled by Nixon operatives.

All this would indicate that Percy is vulnerable on some questions concerning his interest in state affairs and the time and energy he devotes to getting federal projects for the state. He has taken the initiative on some big issues but never has represented himself as a cloakroom operator in the Senate or as a person whose sole interest is in building dams from one end of the state to another. He gladly leaves that to congressmen. As Percy assesses his standing in Illinois, it is unlikely he will attempt to pass himself off as attending only to the state flocks. It would not be believable on the one hand, and on another it does not fit Percy's image and visibility as a senator of broad interests. Important to building Percy's national image has been an ability to recognize issues that have an appeal and interest to the public. Through much of his political life Percy has been associated with critical national issues, giving him an opportunity to be heard publicly outside his own state and region. In contrast, many senators prefer to deal mainly with regional or state issues and remain out of the national spotlight. When it comes time for Percy to return to Illinois and appear before the voters, the important question will be whether the Illinois electorate sees Percy as an effective senator on issues that extend well beyond the state.

By virtue of the large population of Illinois, Percy receives almost the maximum in allowances for Senate office space and staff salaries. Only senators from New York and California receive more. Illinois senators receive essentially the same amount of money for office expenses as the senators from Texas, Michigan, Ohio, New Jersey, and Pennsylvania. In 1974 the allotment for Illinois totaled $589,950. Percy supplements the federal allowance with his own salary, which is $42,500 a year, and other personal funds as he feels is necessary. He also can utilize the staff associated with the Government Operations Committee.

On one occasion Percy's arrangements for funds to run his Senate office got him in minor hot water. In November, 1967, news stories revealed that home-state supporters were raising a $100,000 fund to help finance Percy's Senate office staff. The effort was headed by Richard Duchossois. Thomas Houser, Percy's campaign manager in 1964 and 1966 and a close associate and adviser in the years since, said at the time that Percy had spent nearly $70,000 of his own money during his first year in office to defray the costs of offices in Washington, Chicago, and Centralia, Illinois. Percy shared the Centralia office with Dirksen. Public pressure on Percy forced the money to be refunded. The cost of operating Percy's Senate offices has been considerable through the years.

Prior to the drive for the 1976 nomination, into midyear of 1974, the Washington staff totaled 30 to 35 persons. Another 15 were stationed in the Illinois offices at Springfield and Chicago. With Percy's increased committee responsibilities and seniority, he has acquired about 20 staffers, whose salaries are paid by the Senate committees and who do Percy's work on committee business. After Gerald Ford became president, Percy scaled down the size of his Illinois operation.

In 1969 Percy hired Joseph A. Farrell as his administrative assistant. To some extent the job is what one makes of it, although the administrative-assistant position on most Washington staffs is clearly the No. 1 job next to the officeholder. An administrative assistant's responsibilities are to oversee the entire staff operation and to coordinate the work on issues and deal with constituents. If an administrative assistant is skillful as well, part of the job becomes political strategy. Although Farrell did not join Percy until midway through the senator's first term, he worked his way quickly to the forefront of influence by gaining the confidence and respect of Percy. Farrell cemented his political position in 1972 by serving as Percy's campaign manager for the reelection effort. While some of Farrell's detractors contend that anyone could have managed such an easy reelection effort, Farrell nevertheless did it successfully and without major incident. After that, Farrell stood in the middle of the planning for the 1976 presidential-nomination effort while maintaining his involvement in staff subjects.

Farrell is the source of some mystery, which probably is the fate of most administrative assistants who labor in the shadow of the officeholder and often have to project the personality of the boss in order to accommodate his ego. The A.A., as they are called, must be anonymous most of the time and still maintain a position of strength in the internal affairs of the senator's office and political strategy councils. Farrell is viewed by Illinois supporters with skepticism. He has only infrequently visited the far reaches of the state. When the senator cannot meet or talk with Illinoisans, Farrell becomes a buffer. Having to work with an administrative assistant is irritating to longtime party workers.

In Washington, opinions vary about Farrell. He is a tough-minded person, who appears to give no quarter. He is not at ease with the press, so he frequently seems aloof. When interviewed, he often irritates the questioner by showing his impatience and a frequent unwillingness to discuss details of Percy's activities. A former staff member speaks with respect of Farrell's political and administrative skills but admits he is hard to know and like: "It's no secret that Chuck needs a strong man in that position just to run the operation, and Joe has done a remarkable job. He is not running a personal popularity contest." Farrell's philosophical leaning and his influence on Percy are harder to evaluate. Farrell is considered more conservative than many on the Percy staff. He tends to be more defensive of the moderate-to-conservative positions of the senator and less protective of the highly publicized liberal positions.

The Illinois congressmen's staff members who must deal with Farrell are mixed in their assessments. Few doubt Farrell's value to Percy or Farrell's political awareness. They mainly criticize Farrell's gruff manner. That part of his personality may reflect his military training. After attending Brown University for two years, he transferred to the U.S. Naval Academy, at Annapolis, where he graduated in 1952. He spent 12 years on submarines after that. During those years he accumulated a wife and seven children and ultimately gave up the military to be with his family more often. Farrell spent a tour in Honduras with the Peace Corps and upon his return headed the corps' volunteer-selection operation for three years in Washington. He met Percy through Thomas Houser, one of Percy's longtime political associates who spent some time working with the Peace Corps. Farrell has since divorced and remarried. His wife Claudia is a former Percy press secretary, who left that job in 1973 for work elsewhere in the Washington bureaucracy.

Farrell has developed an office organization that features a handful of key persons in speciality departments. All report to Farrell. Jerry McMahon, who joined Percy for the 1972 campaign, heads the Illinois operation, and Irish McRae in the Washington office deals with home-state support and works on federal loans and grants. Scott Cohen is Percy's foreign-policy adviser and military-affairs expert. His service to Percy predates that of all the other aides; he has been on Percy's staff since 1964. In charge of the legislative department is John Childers. The administrative-support department for Washington is headed by Alexis McMillan; and the press department, by Thomas Flaherty. The additions of McRae, Childers, and McMillan to the staff in 1969 reflect Farrell's influence on staff selections.

The addition of Thomas Flaherty as press secretary on April 23, 1973, is a good example of how the staff was upgraded during 1973 in anticipation of greater national exposure for Percy. As the exposure increased, it meant Percy had more frequent contact with the Washington press corps and writers and editors of the nation's larger newspapers and radio and television networks. The staff also anticipated that more members of the press corps would be traveling with the senator on campaign trips, so more of the staff's time would be required to make arrangements and handle the needs of the correspondents. Not only is Flaherty a friendly and engaging Irishman, he also has the media contacts. He last worked as a senior editor of *Life* magazine before joining Percy. From 1957 to 1972, Flaherty's variety of jobs on the magazine emphasized politics and Washington activities. He worked in the Washington bureau of *Life* from 1961 to 1964 and again in 1969. Flaherty has written several books and had a brief spell in television with a Chicago station. He lived in the Chicago suburbs through his high school years and attended Northwestern University, in Evanston. Although not one of Percy's intimate advisers and not necessarily one of Farrell's confidants, Flaherty would do nicely as a press secretary for either an important senator or a candidate for the presidency.

A member of Percy's staff with minimal exposure and visibility but maximum influence on the senator's personal schedule is his secretary, Nadine Jacobsen. She began with Percy in 1957 at Bell & Howell and has been with Percy ever since. Her job is to coordinate Percy's personal schedule and make sure all the conflicts of the schedule are resolved. As the person who can control access to the senator to a great extent, Mrs. Jacobsen enjoys a position of singular authority on the Washington staff.

It is through the work of his staff that Percy has been able to keep on top of the major issues before Congress and the nation. Additionally, strong staff work has made it possible in recent years for Percy to propose and pursue a list of high-priority personal subjects, on which his staff is constantly doing research. Percy's attention has been focused most recently on economic subjects, major activities involving the Government Operations Committee, and improvement of life for elderly persons. In these areas Percy has actively commented in public and has been at work in developing legislation.

As the national economy came upon hard times in the early 1970s, Percy put himself in the middle of major economic questions such as wage and price controls and the congressional budgeting process. In the midst of congressional and presidential efforts to control the economy, Percy made detailed proposals on long-term energy conservation. Percy's background in financial affairs and economics, his interest in foreign affairs, and his membership on the Joint Economic Committee gave him the various springboards from which to jump into the economic affairs of state.

In August, 1971, President Nixon imposed the first of his economic freezes on the economy. It came with suddenness, surprising members of Congress as well as citizens. By fall the president asked for broad powers to establish firm wage and price guidelines, and while some individual members of Congress were reluctant, Congress granted the president the authority he sought. Inflation was rising and the crisis seemed substantial. To some observers, this move gave Congress the ideal position from which to second-guess the president without having to share in the direct responsibility for controls that inevitably were to become unpopular with citizens in every walk of life.

Percy voted to extend the president's powers to control wages and prices. During the early discussions of economic freezes, Percy introduced to the public his proposal for productivity councils. Percy would pursue this idea through all discussions of wage and price guidelines until the presidential authority expired in 1974 and beyond into discussions of the economy under President Gerald Ford. As originally proposed, productivity councils had three objectives. One was to help Phase II wage and price control coordinating groups, such as the Pay Board, determine guidelines for industry wage and price performance. The second purpose was to identify the obstacles to increased goals in productivity in each major industry. Finally, the councils were to recommend the means of removing productivity bottlenecks in industry. Percy urged the creation of these councils by presidential executive order, but it never came. Percy said the theory supporting the councils "is that joint management-labor efforts to isolate the problems and expedite solutions is badly needed. First and most important is the need to recognize it as a national problem of top significance."

Labor and mangement initially reacted positively to Percy's proposal. Members of business and industry wrote Percy to explain their problems with productivity; and labor listened politely, without the negative reaction many thought it would have. But Congress did not take the proposal seriously, and that is one reason why the councils never were created during the period of economic controls. However, in time some industries adopted them voluntarily.

Percy's opposition to controls grew rapidly in 1973 after Nixon introduced Phase III and relaxed some enforcement aspects of the program. Phase III relied more on voluntary restraint by industry and business. In the summer of 1973, Congress, faced with a national shortage of meat and rising prices, implemented a freeze on meat prices. Percy opposed this freeze as being the wrong way to influence prices. Later, while debating the continuation of wage and price controls, Percy called all controls disastrous: "Look what happened when we tried to freeze meat prices. Look at the crippling impact on domestic supplies of raw materials. The effect of controls has been seriously to weaken the basic functioning of this economy. We should learn from experience." Shortages, reduced production, empty shelves in markets, and furious consumers were the result of the meat freeze Percy opposed, and generally speaking, by the time full controls were running out, the patience of the citizenry toward them had run out. Early in 1974 the question of whether to extend the president's authority on wage and price controls came before Congress. The authority was to end in April. Percy became one of the most vocal senators against extending any form of controls. His position put him in conflict with Adlai Stevenson, who favored putting the question of controls in the lap of the president. On national television in March, Percy declared the controls unsuccessful in dealing with inflation and added, "Let's do away with wage and price controls." He said labor and management both agreed with that conclusion.

Percy also fought consideration of a tax cut, which had been proposed as a means of pumping more money into the economy in the mid-1970s. With quarterly economic reports gloomy, some economists said that technically speaking a recession had hit the nation. Percy opposed a cut and appealed for "a total national commitment to restraint and responsible action." He said putting more money into the economy through a tax cut would only feed the "fires of inflation." The tax-cut proposal kicked around Congress much of that session but never got far because of substantial Republican opposition. When a tax-cut plan surfaced in 1975, Percy remained silent but proposed a tax increase of his own on tobacco and liquor.

Percy carried the restraint theme into his fight against controls. This position reaffirmed his advocacy of free marketing and individual action rather than total governmental control of the economy. In a Senate speech he said, "If we put controls aside and rely on labor and management to exercise restraint—restraint by Congress as well as by labor and management—we can return to stability and a free market." Integral to his appeal for restraint by labor and management was a renewal of his plea for productivity councils: "I call on American business and labor to join now in creating productivity councils to operate on the plant floor, in plant after plant, throughout American industry to increase efficiency, productivity, and innovation." Percy felt that the voluntary-restraint idea would appeal to the public, thus restoring credibility and faith in Congress and government. He spoke of a lack of buyer confidence and viewed the role of Congress as seeing "what we can do to settle these matters as quickly as possible so that there can be a national and international restoration of confidence in our leadership. Certainly Congress has a great obligation to act responsibly in the light of the given facts, and I trust we will face up to that responsibility, just as we expect labor, management, and the executive to act responsibly in these critical times." Later in the year Percy proposed cutting $10 billion from the federal budget as a curb to inflation.

If Percy wanted to build a reputation for expertise in economic affairs, he got his chance during debate over federal controls. At one point in Percy's discourse on economic matters, Senator Mike J. Mansfield of Montana, the majority leader, thanked Percy for his comments, adding, "I think they carry a lot of weight because of the business experience which the senator from Illinois has had as president of Bell & Howell, one of the big business concerns in this country..." Congress dropped any effort to continue the authority for wage and price controls, putting an end to one of the more perplexing chapters in the nation's economic history but not ending the struggle with inflation.

While economic subjects were interests of Percy during the early 1970s, they did not occupy a large share of his visible concern. The war in Indochina, Watergate, and impeachment were the issues of those days, and Percy stayed in the middle of them. If Percy watchers wondered what issues he would develop with the passing of Watergate and impeachment in 1974, they did not have long to wait. By late fall Percy was into economic matters with a fury. His major emphasis was on energy conservation and its application to the nation's general economic woes. In his annual printed message to Illinois constituents, Percy sounded the call: "We are seeking and suggesting answers to the serious economic and energy problems now confronting our country—problems that have now assumed the number-one priority in my office." His efforts were subject to some skepticism. Those who had been in the energy battle much longer suggested cynically that Percy reacted only because it had become a public issue and that he had no background of activity in this area. Before 1975 had progressed far, Percy presented Congress and the public with a detailed program for energy conservation that included an increase in the federal tax on gasoline at a time when such a tax was not a very popular idea. Trying to leave the impression that he was filling a void in the public discussion, Percy said in a December, 1974, speech to the chairmen and deputy chairmen of the Federal Reserve Board: "Neither Congress nor the administration seem willing to set tough policies to help cure our unstable economy. . . . I have no doubt that the people will respond to leadership that calls for sacrifice. The question now is whether their leaders will have the will to make tough decisions." A month later President Ford offered his first concrete energy and economic proposals, overshadowing those made by Percy.

When Percy was not occupied with the nation's economic and energy problems, he worked hard at getting Congress more deeply involved in other concerns, namely, better care for senior citizens and a budgeting system that would make the executive and legislative branches partners in establishing economic and financial priorities for the nation. Percy also took part in another attempt to create a consumer protection agency and in hearings on the effectiveness of the Drug Enforcement Administration.

One of Percy's Senate activities in 1972 concerned the development of an independent consumer protection agency for the federal government. The bill would have created a federal advocacy unit to represent the interests of American consumers before other federal agencies and the federal courts. Senator Jacob Javits of New York, Senator Abraham

Ribicoff of Connecticut, and Percy sponsored the bill. Percy's support brought him in conflict with the Illinois Chamber of Commerce, one of the state's largest lobby groups, as well as with the U.S. Chamber of Commerce. The battle could have cost Percy, involved in a reelection campaign, important support in a tighter election race, but it had virtually no impact on the Pucinski-Percy confrontation. The business community in Illinois is strongly influenced by the state chamber of commerce, which has a reputation for thoroughly researching its point of view on federal and state legislation. It has a large staff and an active membership. One of Percy's supporters believes that the sponsorship of the consumer affairs bill did hurt the senator in the business community, and politically speaking it was not a good issue to champion.

Percy had been an outspoken advocate of a consumer protection agency since the measure first came to the Senate in 1970. At that time President Nixon said he opposed an independent agency, and in his February 24, 1971, consumer message, Nixon asked Congress to postpone action on the measure until after further White House study of the recommendations of the advisory council on executive reorganization. So early in the consumer affairs story Nixon opposed the idea that again came to the Senate in 1972.

One version of the consumer legislation passed the House of Representatives in 1971, but the bill's weaknesses were apparent. Early in consideration of the Senate bill, the administration publicly supported the House version, which would not have permitted the consumer protection agency to participate in as many kinds of proceedings and activities as outlined in the Percy bill. The Senate bill was hotly debated in the fall of 1972. As Senate and House action neared on February 3, 1972, the Illinois Chamber of Commerce, through its president, Lester W. Brann, Jr., made a public statement. He said consumer protection legislation was dangerous to the interests of business mainly because of its investigatory powers and the authority it would have to lobby on behalf of consumer protection laws. Viewing the threat as pervasive, Brann called for a "grass-roots response indicating opposition. Illinois congressmen and senators need to hear from you now, particularly Senator Charles Percy who favors the bill."

Percy, in a speech on the Senate floor, called the Brann letter "a disservice ... to the citizenry and business community of Illinois and to my office." In striking back at the state chamber of commerce, Percy said, "Our [the Senate's] deliberations have been impeded by unwarranted and impassioned attacks on the legislation from segments of the business community which have, in the past, assisted our efforts in the consumer area through rational articulation of the issues and concrete suggestions for improvement. Now instead, my office and other Senate offices are being deluged with mail directly traceable to a blunderbuss blast . . . by local and state chambers of commerce and by the U.S. Chamber of Commerce."

After three cloture votes (proposals to end debate) failed, the leadership of Congress shelved the measure. A filibuster had won the day. None of the three cloture votes had failed by more than four votes. Almost the same scenario took place when the proposal for a consumer protection agency surfaced two years later in 1974. Again a filibuster, this one led by Senator Sam Ervin of North Carolina, finally prevented consideration by the Senate after cloture votes failed.

One difference in Senate consideration of a consumer affairs bill in these two years was the involvement of Nixon and his aides in 1972. Although the administration reaffirmed its opposition to the plan, Percy persisted in trying to lure them to his side. After the second cloture vote Percy called on the administration "to join in a bipartisan effort" to stop the filibuster. "The administration is said to support this stall as a means of getting greater consideration for the five amendments it has put forward. Those amendments will get no consideration so long as this filibuster continues because those who are responsible for it . . . refuse to permit a vote on any of their amendments or the amendments of other senators. . . . If the administration will take the first step, I will make sure that the amendments that it intends to offer will get every reasonable consideration with a view toward reconciling what differences we may have." Percy's plea did not have any effect because behind the filibuster and behind the administration's reluctance to swing over to Percy and others was a major lobbying effort by the nation's business community. Finally, the lobbying became so intense that President Nixon not only refused to support the Senate bill but also withdrew his support of the House version. Percy received no response from the White House when he asked the president for a personal meeting on the consumer question. As consumer protection continued to be a congressional issue beyond 1972, the administration still opposed it. In one of the more pointed comments Gerald Ford, then vice-president, labeled the proposal a "liberal" program that could be expected to pass with Democrats firmly in control of Congress.

Percy made no converts on the consumer affairs issue. The national and state chambers of commerce remained opposed to the idea and continued their opposition through subsequent revivals of the proposal. And their continued opposition led to the failure of the consumer protection agency in 1974.

In April, 1973, an incident occurred that caused concern beyond its immediate locale and eventually involved Percy. Members of a federal narcotics task force forced their way into the homes of two families in Collinsville, Illinois. The uproar created by the entry, the alleged abuse of the families, and the subsequent court cases kept the subject alive for nearly a year. Damage suits were filed after that. One of the least likely persons to become involved was Percy.

The immediate outcry from the raids centered around the alleged physical and mental abuse of the two families. Newspapers in the St. Louis area, where Collinsville is located, carried frequent stories relating tales of the raids and quoting the families. Within a month several grand jury investigations were under way. Percy became involved through a subcommittee hearing in Chicago to gather information on whether a single agency, the Drug Enforcement Administration, could effectively combine the enforcement functions of four other federal agencies.

The hearings focused on the Collinsville raids, and one of the families came to Chicago to tell its story. They told of being insulted, threatened, and terrorized by the federal agents. At the hearings Percy said that if the lesson of the Collinsville raids is that "being a narc means never having to say you're sorry, then I pledge here and now to do everything in my power to change that." Agents did not appear at the hearings because of the grand jury investigations, Percy said.

As Percy conducted hearings across the nation on the drug agency, he referred to the Collinsville raids, thus giving them notoriety. A major national survey by the New York Times later confirmed that the Collinsville raids were not an isolated occurrence and that similar drug raids had happened as part of a nationwide federal crackdown. Those debating the issue also raised questions as to the methods that are most effective in actually reducing the illegal sale of drugs. A month after the hearings in Chicago, Percy held hearings in Atlanta. He said, "We should not lose sight of the festering sore of drug abuse, but at the same time ... we cannot forfeit the underlying values of free America to the extent that we permit police state indignities." Percy stopped short of pointing a finger at specific persons, but his audiences could tell he placed the blame squarely on federal authorities.

In a federal court trial that ended almost a year to the day after the raids, members of the narcotics task force were acquitted of any wrongdoing. At the trial, defense attorneys for the agents accused Percy of using the issue to further his presidential ambitions. One attorney said that Percy pressured the Department of Justice to bring indictments against the agents. Percy did not reply to the specific charges, but he warned that acquittals should "not give impetus to any future actions which would violate constitutional rights." Attorney General William B. Saxbe pledged that care would be taken in future raids.

Percy's involvement in the drug-raid issue is partially explained by acknowledging his opportunism. He took an issue that had great emotional impact in Illinois and tied it in neatly with Senate business that he was conducting on the use of drugs and an agency to control them. The cries of "politics" cannot be ignored, considering the nationwide campaigning Percy was conducting at the time.

An area of intense Percy interest, and one with which he has had minimal success in recent years, results from his membership on the Senate Special Committee on Aging, with three subcommittee assignments on senior citizens—their consumer interests, their health, and their long-term care, respectively. In each session of Congress beginning in 1971, Percy proposed legislation that covered broad assistance for the elderly, including nursing home care and income security. He also made proposals in the field of housing for the elderly. Most of the plans were Percy-only proposals. Experience has shown that measures Percy alone sponsors or promotes without the added push of other Senate colleagues often do not fare well. There is interest among some senators for greater aid to the elderly, but apparently it is not the time for concerted action in Congress on this subject.

When Percy began showing an interest in the elderly, the question asked most frequently had to do with his sincerity. It had not been a major concern of the senator's in the early years of his Senate service. A former aide added one piece of the answer: "Percy really didn't feel it—I mean deep down—until he visited an old folks' home. Then he got the spirit and thought it was all his idea." Cynical as that may be, it does explain the intensity of Percy's feelings on the subject. During 1971 hearings on nursing home care, his sympathy showed as he said, "An inordinately large number of [nursing] homes [are] unfit for anyone—let alone helpless and chronically ill elderly people."

In 1971 Percy and Senator George McGovern, who then was chairman of the Senate's Select Committee on Nutrition and Human Needs, toured parts of Illinois. From this trip Percy got a feel for the problems of the aged as they relate to food. It is easy to see how the senator could have been affected. While visiting in East St. Louis, Illinois, on the tour, Percy remembers talking with an 87-year-old woman. He asked how frequently she ate meat. She replied, "Meat? Why senator, I can't remember when I have been able to afford meat. We have chicken wings a couple of times a week, and that's it." On another occasion during the hearings, Percy remembers a witness saying, "We do not buy the most nutritious food. We buy the kind we can afford. Dog food is not poison. It tastes good. It has a lot of protein and costs about 39¢ a can. Go into any supermarket in poor areas and ask an old woman, as I did, why she is buying 10 cans of dog food. She replied, 'I feed my dog.' I told her that it doesn't taste bad. She hesitated, then agreed. That was the giveaway that she was eating it." Percy told both of those stories in his book *Growing Old in the Country of the Young* (published in 1974), which outlined his thoughts and his work on programs for the elderly. Percy believes his activity on behalf of improved benefits for the aged is a major contribution to the total field of civil rights for persons who need the assistance of government.

While the Senate through the years has increased social security benefits, usually at the most politically expedient times, no specific reform proposed by Percy has been adopted. He has voiced disappointment in the Senate's inaction. In 1972 he told colleagues, "Our elderly is the only minority group in America today where conditions are getting worse rather than better, where the incidence of poverty is increasing rather than decreasing for them. . . . The elderly are among our neediest." While willing to chastize the Senate for its failure to aid the elderly, Percy proposed programs that seemed designed to only awaken the Senate to the need, without expecting any action. In remarks on the Senate floor in 1974, after introducing a package of bills designed to give the elderly increased income security, Percy said, "I do not pretend to have all the answers. I do not pretend to be able to solve the income problems of the elderly overnight, but I believe we must set ourselves a specific goal and begin to analyze the alternative ways of achieving that goal." At the 1973 National Council on the Aging in Chicago, Percy acknowledged that his proposals were costly and "to enact them all might be more of a drain on the budget than the Congress would be willing to accept." He said his intention was to "generate the necessary debate within Congress" that might lead to passage later.

Percy backed up charges about substandard nursing homes with a legislative package in 1974. A feature of the legislation was low-interest government-insured loans to nursing homes that would permit quick improvements without risk to the health and safety of residents. Other facilities that cannot be so quickly improved should be closed, he said, adding, "To cite one chilling statistic, 59 percent of all certified skilled nursing facilities—some 4,300 out of a total of 7,300—are not in full compliance with the Life Safety Code prepared by the National Fire Protection Association." Another bill in the package would have amended the Social Security Act to impose restrictions on the discharge or transfer of patients from nursing homes. The plan would have reduced premature or unnecessary discharges of patients who might not have other places to go or might still require nursing home care.

One of Percy's earliest proposals in the field of housing for the elderly would have created the office of assistant secretary of housing for the elderly in the Department of Housing and Urban Development. The plan, in the form of an amendment to a housing bill in 1972, received Senate approval but died later. The department opposed the plan.

One of Percy's most complete legislative packages for the elderly came in 1974 and dealt with a number of questions related to income security.

In introducing the proposal Percy said, "Let there be no mistake: By introducing this legislation I am not suggesting that the Treasury of the United States assume the responsibility of issuing monthly checks to every retired person in order to maintain his income at preretirement levels. I am suggesting that more can be done to facilitate an individual person's effort to obtain a decent retirement income or to take care during his productive years to provide for his own financial well-being during retirement." The eight bills in the package included one to establish a National Commission on Retirement Income to study means of assuring retired persons of an adequate income. One bill asked for more consideration of older workers by creating an affirmative-action hiring program at the federal level. He asked for a special program of counseling and placement services for the elderly. Several bills proposed tax breaks for the elderly by revising laws dealing with deductions and earning limitations. One bill suggested equal treatment of men and women under Social Security. Although Percy would like to see his proposals for the elderly enacted, he has said that the short-term answer might simply be to insure effective implementation of existing programs. He said it is a truism that enacting well-conceived and good-intentioned legislation helps no one unless it is effectively administered.

Percy has grown increasingly critical of the Medicare program. He has recognized publicly that many elderly persons misunderstood the purpose of Medicare when it passed Congress and became law during the Johnson administration. First of all there was no assurance of quality medical care, Percy noted. Second, as inflation caused rapidly rising medical-care costs, the elderly found Medicare paying a smaller and smaller percentage of total costs, thus placing an increasing financial burden on the beneficiaries. Percy believes the major oversight in Medicare is that it does not pay drug costs. Although Percy has pointed out the problems with Medicare, he is also quick to reflect that correcting the flaws in the law will be expensive and therefore may never receive the consideration of Congress. During 1974 Percy estimated that one proposal to expand Medicare benefits and have the federal government pick up all the costs would add $17 billion to the federal budget.

Although Percy's intentions on behalf of the elderly seem well directed, he has faced some angry protesters. While visiting in Chicago in 1974, Percy was confronted by angry senior citizens, who charged that he had received large sums of money in the 1972 election from drug-company interests and had "sold out" to them. They specifically sought his support for bills in the Illinois legislature to lower drug prices for the elderly. Percy pointed out, correctly, that he had sponsored federal legislation in the drug-price field similar to that before the state legislature and let the group know that he resented the implications of misdeeds. He also criticized the group for "trying to malign the motives of the drug industry." On another visit to Chicago a small group of elderly persons picketed Percy in opposition to a federal mortgage policy they contended hurt the elderly. The picketers accused Percy of not being willing to set up a meeting on the subject with officials of the Department of Housing and Urban Development. He met with the group and promised to arrange the meeting.

Percy sees eliminating poverty for the elderly as one of the national challenges in the years ahead. "The time has come for the nation, working through the Congress, to set as a goal the elimination of poverty among our elder citizens. The time has come for Congress to take some significant steps toward achieving this goal," Percy has said. Action by Congress has been slow, and with increasing pressures on the federal budget, achievements will likely come in small pieces.

At the same time that Percy was working on legislation to improve conditions for the elderly, he was involved in a two-year battle that led to the passage of the Congressional Budget Act, which in Percy's view is the most important piece of legislation enacted in his years in the Senate. The implementation of the act probably is destined to receive little public attention, but that does not detract from its importance.

The roots of congressional budget reform were in a presidential power play with Congress in the fall of 1972 that nearly cost the legislative branch a slice of its authority to determine federal spending levels. The power play began with a White House proposal, tied to a bill to extend the federal debt limit, that would give President Nixon the authority to impound funds as necessary to enforce a $250 billion spending ceiling in the fiscal year of 1973. The House, seeing some advantages to establishing spending levels in an election year, passed the Nixon proposal, thus giving him unlimited discretion in trimming federal outlays. The Senate balked, although there was substantial support among those up for re-election to follow the House's lead. Finally, after a conference-committee hassle, the presidential authority was removed from the final bill, which was approved on a voice vote in each house of Congress. The elimination of the powers he wanted caused Nixon to retaliate by vetoing other spending bills. Congress overrode some of those vetoes.

When some members of Congress began to see that granting the president this authority very nearly cost them a large measure of budgetary control, they were inspired to begin drafting legislation that would increase the responsibility of Congress and give it a mechanism within which to maintain control.

Before the reform measure was drafted, Congress had completely abdicated to the executive branch whatever involvement it should have had in budget making. The budget originated with the executive, and it came to Congress with the supporting documents and facts gathered and presented expertly by persons from the Office of Management and

Budget, an arm of the executive. Usually by the time Congress received the budget, in all its weight and detail, and began hearings on appropriations, the fiscal year was at hand. Delay in approving appropriations meant that agencies and departments of government operated on an extension of the previous year's budget. Oftentimes the new budget did not receive congressional approval before time arrived to work on yet another. It often happened that an agency of government dealt with three separate budgets at one time as a result of the delays. Percy commented on the budgeting process: "I had a better budget department at Bell & Howell than Congress has." In addition to the lack of time for adequate consideration of the executive budget, there was no single congressional body to act as overseer. Congress normally passed 14 separate appropriations bills on a willy-nilly basis, and the only time anyone knew what the total fiscal-year expenditure would be was when all the appropriations were made and the totals were added together.

As ranking Republican on the Government Operations Committee, Percy, with Senator Edmund Muskie of Maine, cosponsored the Congressional Budget Act with Sam Ervin of North Carolina, the chairman of the committee. Passage of the bill and approval by the president occurred only a few months before Ervin's retirement from Congress. Percy's role in shaping the legislation included speaking frequently on its behalf, debating its virtues in committee, proposing certain additions and changes as the process developed, and rallying support from interests in and out of Congress. He remained an advocate even when some of his ideas and criticisms were ignored and other committees riddled the original bill with changes. His efforts gained him recognition in the media, notably *Time* magazine and the *Washington Post*. Ervin acknowledged the Percy involvement by saying to the Senate that Percy "had made contributions to the development of this legislation which are impossible for me to overmagnify."

Opposition arose immediately in Congress when the initial reform was proposed in 1973. Percy said the opposition came from "vested interests" and "lobbyists" who feared the new process would eliminate their influence in budgeting and appropriations. The "vested interests" were chairmen of the Appropriations committees and other legislators who did not want anything to upset the cozy process for funding projects. Some opposition came from persons who thought the new plan, with its permanent Budget committees, would erode the authority of established committees such as House and Senate Appropriations, House Ways and Means, and Senate Finance. Before the bill came to the full Senate for consideration, it had undergone significant changes, resulting mainly from alterations by the Rules and Administration Committee, whose major spokesmen were Chairman Howard W. Cannon of Nevada and Robert C. Byrd of West Virginia. Rules and Administration eliminated or reduced much of the reform aspect of the bill.

As approved by both houses of Congress and signed by Nixon, the law goes into effect in 1976. Its main features include the establishment of a Congressional Budget Office, with powers to obtain information and background that will be helpful in understanding and probing the executive budget. It also creates a budget committee for the House and one for the Senate. The committees' job will be to gather budgetary items from other committees and propose spending ceilings. In each house, the committee has the authority and responsibility for much of the budgeting procedure. To eliminate fears that the new committees might conflict with established Senate and House committees that deal with appropriations, Ervin said they "would not infringe on the jurisdiction or operation of the now-existing committees." Ervin added further justification for the committees: "Neither Finance nor Appropriations alone can bring together tax and spending policy, and for this reason a new Budget Committee is a necessary step in budget reform."

The most important aspect of the bill is its timetable for budget consideration. The bill begins by establishing a new fiscal year starting October 1 instead of July 1. A current services budget is to be submitted by November 10 and reviewed. The president's formal budget is to come to Congress 15 days after the legislature convenes early in January. By March 15 all committees in the House and the Senate are to report to their Budget Committee. The Budget Committee reports its first budget resolution to the floor by April 15. This is really the first major step in establishing spending control. The bill provides that this first resolution would establish "appropriate levels of spending" as a "guide" to Congress. It would put a tentative ceiling on the federal budget—not only expenditures and revenues but also the national debt.

The provision to set up tentative spending levels resulted from a major compromise on the question of how rigid the budget ceiling should be. In committee and subcommittee deliberations, Percy, one of the bill's sponsors, supported a version of the bill that would have established firm ceilings on the budget early in the process. Then as committees determined specific appropriations, they would be guided and limited by the ceilings. During the Government Operations Committee's work on the budget act, substantial opposition to Percy's plan developed. Chief among those senators who wanted more flexibility was Edmund S. Muskie, another sponsor of the bill, who in 1975 became chairman of the Senate Government Operations Committee. Muskie and his supporters wanted "target" figures developed in the early stages of budgeting. The target would not bind the committees in the appropriations process, and any differences between the target figure and the amount requested by the committees would be reconciled by a final budget resolution.

Senator Ervin, the third sponsor of the budget reform bill, agreed with Percy that firm ceilings should be established. When he introduced the bill in the Senate, Ervin said, "Long and serious consideration was given to the possibility of setting a firm limit on total expenditures in the first budget resolution. I believe that such a limitation, if it were feasible, would offer the most effective path to budget control." But the conference committee did not feel as Ervin did, and the final bill called for flexible ceilings. Supporters and opponents cautioned that such flexibility meant the success of the reform would rest squarely on the shoulders of Congress and not in the law.

After the first budget resolution is approved—according to the timetable this must occur by May 15—the appropriations process begins. A second budget resolution is passed by Congress on September 15, either reaffirming the original budget targets or reconciling any differences between them and any resolutions that occurred in the interim. At this point, binding totals that could not be exceeded by any appropriation at a later date would be established for expenditures. The deadline for budget action is September 25.

When the final bill came before the Senate, Percy defended it despite his earlier stand for strict rather than flexible budget ceilings: "I will now have to counter my esteemed colleagues' arguments with my own conviction that this bill creates a workable new process that will prove to be useful and effective precisely because it does permit latitude for flexible responses to changing situations." That seemed about as good a way as any to say that if they did not take the bill as changed, they would not get any bill.

In the *Washington Post*, columnist Clayton Fritchey questioned whether after all the work there was really any reform in the process. He said that the unanimous approval of the bill in the Senate—the vote was 80 to 0—indicated that the reforms really did not amount to much. If the bill had any teeth in it, Fritchey suggested, it would have drawn some negative votes. Senators Ervin, Percy, and Muskie wrote a letter to the *Post* defending the bill. In referring to Fritchey's comment about the unanimous vote, the senators wrote: "Rather, we believe that the reason for the overwhelming support budget reform received in the Senate was that the bill was carefully worked out in three different committees over a period of more than a year. There is no doubt in our minds that the reforms in this bill are meaningful and that they will force Congress to change the way it now operates. . . . It will work if members of the Congress exhibit the same kind of determination to implement this bill that they did to draft it."

Establishment of a mechanism such as the Congressional Budget Office, with a central staff for gathering information, struck at the heart of one of Percy's major frustrations as a member of the Appropriations Committee earlier in his Senate career. During that time he found it exasperating never to have sufficient information at hand to rebut documents from executive-branch departments and agencies. He felt that the senators were put on the defensive because they found it nearly impossible to contest the appropriations requests without exposing themselves as ill-informed. With budget reform, even considering that its flexibility could make it little more than a procedure, Congress will have the resources to modify the budget rather than having to swallow it whole.

Percy's dedication to budgetary reform never waivered during the lengthy negotiations. On some occasions he called it "one of the historic turning points in the evolution of our institution, a reversal of the accelerating erosion of the congressional purse power, a reassertion of our correct role in the American plan of government." Ervin echoed the comments with his own declaration that it was "one of the most important pieces of legislation considered during my service in the Senate." While other members of the Senate were less verbal in their enthusiasm, the new law obviously appealed to conservatives and liberals, who saw in it a means for Congress to gain greater control over the budget. For Percy the passage of this bill may have been his greatest Senate achievement.

CHAPTER IX

PERCY, DIRKSEN, AND STEVENSON

Much has been made in Illinois and Washington of the differences between Charles Percy and Everett M. Dirksen when the two served in the
U.S. Senate from 1967 until Dirksen's death in 1969. Those in Illinois
who magnified the disagreements were Republicans who admired Dirksen,
even worshipped him, and could not tolerate Percy. United States
senators who remember the days when the two were in Congress recall
some clashes between them but doubt that they have political implications for Percy among Illinois Republicans.

Some of the more conservative congressmen in the Illinois delegation
who served then and now were longtime associates of Dirksen, and they
have long memories. One of those was former congressman Leslie Arends.
When Dirksen served as minority leader of the Senate and Arends held
party leadership in the House, Illinois had a strong and influential one-
two Republican punch. Pork barrel favors, committee assignments, and
other fringe benefits were available to Illinois congressmen who kept peace
with the pair. When Dirksen died and Percy became the senior senator,
Arends refused to recognize any leadership that Percy offered. Arends and
his followers had disapproved of Percy's Republicanism and his Senate
style before Dirksen's death and even more so afterward. In the name of
Dirksen they carried on a feud with Percy as if that would ultimately
pressure Percy into becoming Dirksen incarnate.

Dirksen served eight consecutive terms as congressman from Illinois
from 1933 to 1949, representing his hometown area near Pekin. In 1949
Dirksen voluntarily "retired" from public life due to an eye ailment that
many feared would cause him to be blinded. It turned out that the
retirement was temporary, to say the least.

In his 16 years in the House, Dirksen's voting record was moderate on
most issues. He avoided associating himself with isolationists, and he
supported many Democratic administration programs such as the Marshall
Plan. In Illinois political circles, Dirksen took a different road than one
of the party's most influential persons Colonel Robert McCormick,
publisher of the *Chicago Tribune*. Contrary to the association that later
developed between the two, in Dirksen's days in the House he often

found himself at odds with Illinois Republican strategy as outlined by the powerful McCormick and his newspaper, which was the voice of mid-western conservatism. Dirksen's congressional district was far enough from Chicago to give him a degree of independence, although the Pekin-Peoria area was hardly a bastion of liberalism. If anything, in those years Dirksen had more in common with Marshall Field III and his *Chicago Sun* than with the *Tribune* and McCormick.

The picture began to change after Dirksen left Congress in 1949. When his eye ailment began to ease, and after he returned from a world tour financed by contributions to his campaigns, Dirksen decided to run against his friend Senator Scott W. Lucas in the 1950 senatorial election. Dirksen realized he needed more statewide appeal, and he actively began courting McCormick by changing positions he had taken on issues as a congressman. By the time of the Senate campaign Dirksen had swung noticeably to the right. He reversed his stand on the Marshall Plan, and he talked increasingly of isolationism and the Communist menace. These changes earned him a reputation among friends and colleagues as Mc-Cormick's errand boy. There is nothing on the record to indicate that Dirksen disliked the tag.

Lucas had been the Democratic senator from Illinois since 1939. His work in the Senate had earned him the job of majority leader. The demands of the work in Washington meant that he could not spend much time campaigning in the state. An unforeseen element in the contest was the appearance of a fellow Democratic senator, Estes Kefauver of Tennessee, who brought his investigating-committee hearings on crime and corruption to Chicago in 1950. The revelations elicited from the witnesses during the hearings so angered the citizenry that thousands turned out for Republican candidates in Cook County. The rebellion in Democratic ranks injured Lucas. Dirksen took advantage of that, along with Lucas's failure to campaign in Illinois. With the strong support of Illinois Republican traditionalists, newspapers, and party workers, Dirksen won handily. Thus began a Senate career that would eventually rival Lyndon Johnson's in influence and power during the years they both served in the Senate and the years Johnson served as president; it also brought a lasting friendship between Dirksen and *Tribune* publisher McCormick. After the publisher's death in 1955, his lieutenants—including W. Don Maxwell, the paper's editor, and George Tagge, its political editor—continued McCormick's warm relationship with Dirksen.

One of Dirksen's greatest efforts for McCormick occurred at the 1952 Republican National Convention. McCormick made no secret of the fact that he favored the candidacy of Senator Robert A. Taft of Ohio over that of Dwight D. Eisenhower. As a gesture of faith to Taft and McCormick, Dirksen served as the Ohio senator's Illinois campaign manager as well as serving as chairman of the state delegation to the convention. Amid rumors that if Taft were nominated he would choose Dirksen as his vice-presidential candidate, the Illinois delegation voted 59 to 1 for Taft. After the nomination was secured for Eisenhower, the convention offered its voice acclamation, but the Illinois vote, 59 to 1 for Taft, remained on the record. Dirksen said to a fellow delegate on the floor, "Let the record stand. It represents our convictions." In anger at Eisenhower's nomination, McCormick's advice to voters was for all "good Republicans" to remain home on election day. Eventually, however, the *Tribune* gave its support to Eisenhower's candidacy, if not his policies.

At his death Dirksen held positions on the Judiciary and Finance committees of the Senate and was Republican minority leader. Dirksen served 12 years as a member of the National Republican Congressional Campaign Committee, eight of them as vice-chairman. He served as a delegate to Republican National Conventions in 1944, 1948, 1952, 1956, 1960, 1964, and 1968. He served as chairman of the National Republican Senatorial Committee from 1951 through 1954, and in 1957 he became assistant minority leader in the Senate. In 1959 he became minority leader, a post he held until his death. He used this position to help him in taking over the leadership of the national party in the early 1960s. At the 1968 National Convention, Dirksen served as chairman of the party's platform committee.

Dirksen gained strength in the Senate during the Eisenhower days of the 1950s, although he often contested administration programs. By the time a Democrat returned to the presidency in 1961, Dirksen had maneuvered himself into a position of power in the party. Richard Nixon might have provided party leadership but he decided to seek political office in California after his loss to John F. Kennedy and did not have time for national party affairs. Republicans in Congress were a distinct minority in both houses, but by combining with conservative Southern Democrats they had a strength beyond their numbers. Many Washington observers look upon the early 1960s as a personal ego trip for Dirksen, a point loudly contested by his followers. These years were also a time of declining impact for the Republican party. David Broder, *Washington Post* columnist and political observer in the capital for several years, wrote in his book *The Party's Over:* "They [Dirksen and company] became a classic party of lost causes, symbolized by Dirksen's dogged efforts to reinstate prayer in public schools . . . and his equally futile effort to reverse the one-man-one-vote ruling." Dirksen milked these two issues for publicity and sympathy through much of his service in the 1960s. Percy opposed Dirksen's attempt to call a federal constitutional convention for the sole purpose of including a prayer statement in the constitution. After some delay Percy finally supported the one-man-one-vote effort.

Although Dirksen and Percy had worked together in party affairs at the state and national levels for several years, Percy did not live in awe or fear of the eloquent and crafty senator. Before Dirksen's second term expired in 1962, Percy canvassed the state to test how much support he would have in a primary contest against Dirksen. Percy's brashness irked Dirksen. Stories have persisted of Dirksen's efforts to belittle Percy in private conversations during those years. According to one story, Dirksen told President Kennedy that Percy's ambition was to sit in the White House. Whether or not this was true at that point in time, Percy had given more than a passing thought to battling Dirksen in the 1962 primary. He said later, "It was not an unthinkable thing for me to run against him in the primary. In the late 1950s the view was not nearly as unanimous as it is now that Everett Dirksen was invaluable." Percy claims to have been dissuaded from the primary contest by Senate moderates, who felt it would have been a disservice to the party to challenge Dirksen. Realistically, Dirksen's party strength at the time had to be a factor too. Dirksen worked for Percy's election as governor in the 1964 contest but often seemed preoccupied with activities on the national level. The same year he served as cochairman of the Illinois delegation to the national convention and worked hard for the nomination and election of Barry Goldwater, with whom Dirksen felt a kinship.

The preliminaries of the Dirksen-Percy Senate relationship began in 1965, after Percy's gubernatorial defeat and before he committed himself publicly to run against Paul Douglas. Percy says that Dirksen and 15 other Illinois Republicans insisted that he challenge Douglas, though there seemed little doubt in people's minds that Percy would run anyway. As some of Percy's aides believed at the time, Illinois conservatives could have been giving their support to Percy in an attempt to push him into an impossible situation against Douglas and thus ruin his political career. Perhaps sensing this, Percy extracted a promise from Dirksen and other Illinois Republicans that if he lost to Douglas there would not be any opposition to a Percy campaign for governor in 1968. Dirksen made that promise, and Percy ran in 1966. Also about that time Percy obtained in writing from Dirksen an unusual pledge that gave Percy the right to go his own way on Senate issues if he were elected. In that statement, Dirksen said, "From time to time we may feel differently on some issues and I respect this right on his part."

Percy later elaborated on the deliberations that led to the Dirksen letter: "I said I'm not about to come down here [Washington], leaving a great job, a wonderful company [Bell & Howell], and a wonderful association that I've had for several decades and ... every time I cast an 'aye' vote and you cast a 'nay' vote find myself criticized. I said I don't mind a difference of opinion, but I just don't want a lot of nit-picking on this, and I'm not going to take it." Percy said he did not like the idea of being a "junior senator" when it came to casting a vote: "Once you're a senator, you're a senator; there's no junior thing about it. When it comes to your vote you don't subordinate your vote.... I said, 'Everett, I'm not about to subordinate myself to you.' "

Percy said he told Dirksen that they saw the world differently and that while he respected Dirksen's political abilities, "I don't want to be down here being chewed up." Percy said unless there was an understanding, he would not run for the Senate. Percy remembers that Dirksen said, "I'll not only have an understanding, I'll give it to you in writing." "He never broke that," Percy said. Demonstrating an ability to make something of most any situation, Dirksen ended his statement to Percy: "I know that we're all in accord on the historic progressive principles of Republicanism." At another time Dirksen said, "Surely it is better to have a senator who disagrees with me on a few things than to have a flaming liberal with whom I disagree on everything."

That "flaming liberal" comment might have been made for the benefit of Paul Douglas, with whom he seldom agreed in the years they served together from Illinois. There was a feeling of some warmth and respect between the two, but it did not surface publicly during the 1966 contest. After Douglas's defeat, Dirksen said only that he would miss the Democrat's debating skill in the Senate. Douglas treated Dirksen matter-of-factly in his memoirs.

On the surface there was every reason to believe that Dirksen and Percy could not possibly coexist in the same room, let alone in the same party. If their relationship was amiable, as Percy insists, it may have been because of Dirksen's flexible manner rather than because Percy was willing to see things Dirksen's way or to accept his leadership. When Percy entered the Senate, Dirksen was enjoying his greatest influence in Congress. Much of that influence can be attributed to his work with President Johnson. Dirksen liked being the center of attention, and Johnson lavished praise and respect on the Illinoisan. Dirksen stood less firm on major issues in those days, partly in an attempt to maintain his hold on the party leadership. Dirksen wanted to be involved in the passage of the many major bills that came before Congress as part of Johnson's Great Society program. And Dirksen was instrumental in achieving the necessary compromises between Democrats and Republicans and between Congress and the White House that made key legislation possible. These compromises earned him some respect, but no one accused Dirksen of standing on principle very long. Dirksen explained his pragmatism in such a disarming manner that most of his detractors were kept off-balance.

Percy calls his relationship with Dirksen "quite good" and notes that Dirksen helped him in several ways. In 1967 Percy wanted to push for a federal housing plan, and the appropriate committee from which to do this was Banking and Currency. Dirksen used his influence to get Percy that assignment. Also, Dirksen, aware of Percy's interest in the arts, was responsible for getting him on the board of the Kennedy Center for the

Performing Arts in Washington. Percy later served as a vice-president of the center, and this association brought him in touch with an influential segment of the Washington community.

The two senators seldom disagreed on Illinois projects, although political dealings in Illinois by Dirksen partisans and staff members often irritated Percy. Harold Rainville, Dirksen's Illinois operative, was Percy's chief problem in Illinois. Rainville told anti-Percy stories from one end of Illinois to the other. Percy first encountered Rainville in 1959 when Rainville represented Senator Dirksen at most meetings of the Republican Committee on Program and Progress. One observer of those meetings said that when "Rainville spoke, he was listened to with patience and sometimes tolerance because he represented Everett Dirksen." Rainville did what he could in Illinois to keep Percy from establishing a political base that would threaten Dirksen. All during the 1967 warm-up to the 1968 presidential year, Rainville fought a rear-guard action in Illinois. As Percy traveled across the nation establishing himself as a national figure, Rainville reminded Illinois Republicans that Percy's speeches were not being made in his home state. When rumors of Percy as a vice-presidential nominee began, Rainville said, "What president would be happy with Chuck warming up behind him?"

The major area of disagreement between the two senators occurred over the appointment of federal judges in Illinois. Dirksen preferred to recognize loyalty to the party and to his campaigns as chief requirements for the job. Percy, who ultimately earned a reputation for appointing well-qualified federal judges, disagreed with Dirksen's political approach. This difference of opinion caused more than one impasse over an appointment. A federal judge cannot be approved without both senators agreeing and signing the appropriate documents. Percy recalls refusing to sign more than once. One case involved an attorney he "knew quite well," and he said that this man was one "whose ethics I thoroughly disagreed with. I would not appoint him." Percy explained how he and Dirksen worked out disagreements: "We argued about them privately—I won't even use the word argue—and he said, 'I'd like this person to be appointed,' and he told me why and I told him my analysis. . . . He was really a very good colleague to work with."

Social issues were particularly controversial ground for Dirksen and Percy. Dirksen adamantly refused to support the busing of schoolchildren for purposes of desegregation, and his opposition to open housing was made clear in the summer of 1967 during a floor debate on an amendment to the civil rights bill. This amendment would have deleted appropriations for a federal nuclear accelerator station in Weston, Illinois. Opponents of the appropriation said that because there were no open-housing guarantees for blacks in Illinois, the state should not benefit from the federal project that was part of the civil rights bill. Senator John O.

Pastore of Rhode Island spoke on behalf of the amendment. Dirksen, rising to the occasion with a definite patronizing attitude, said the arguments were "about the airiest nonsense and persiflage...that I have heard on this floor for a long time." He said Illinois had "more Negroes than the entire population of Rhode Island," and "we look after them pretty well." He admitted that housing was a problem in Illinois but added, "We deal with it rather competently and rather efficiently." Percy also called the criticism by Pastore and other senators unfounded but for a different reason. He did not believe the Senate had any business standing in judgment of Illinois if it could not meet the national need. Percy said, "We in this body...in 1967, have not brought forth from committee...an open occupancy bill or civil rights bill to redress many wrongs...in our country."

Despite his feelings on open housing, Dirksen helped pass the Civil Rights Act of 1968, which contained an open-housing provision. Dirksen saw no advantage to his stand against open housing in the changed circumstances of 1968, and so he switched his position. He explained, "One would be a strange creature indeed in this world of mutation if in the face of reality he did not change his mind." However, reports persisted that Dirksen had made a deal with President Johnson. In exchange for Dirksen's vote on the 1968 civil rights bill the Democrats were to choose a weak candidate to run against Dirksen in the 1968 Illinois senatorial contest. Both Johnson and Dirksen denied this allegation. Writing in his memoir The Vantage Point, Johnson said, "I never once discussed supporting Dirksen's 1968 Illinois election with him. No President could 'force' a strong local party, headed by as forceful a person as Mayor Richard Daley of Chicago, to commit political hara-kiri—especially over a bill that most of his constituents did not want anyway."

In 1967 Percy and Dirksen opened a "nonpartisan" office in Centralia, in the southern part of Illinois. The press speculated that the office would be used to promote Percy as a candidate for the 1968 presidential nomination, because virtually everything Percy did in those days seemed directed toward such an effort, or so it often seemed to a curious media. During the 1966 campaign, Percy had promised to open the office. Dirksen seldom visited the office, and Percy did not have Centralia on his list of priority places to visit. The office closed in 1969 with little fanfare.

The national issue that most divided the two senators was Vietnam. Dirksen's position is best explained in a statement he made on January 17, 1966: "Let us be crystal clear. Vietnam is not our war, but we pledged ourselves to help a small nation. Our word was given. We are there to keep our word...to retreat and get out would be deemed a confession that we are a paper tiger....To forsake our pledges would shatter confidence in us and further diminish our prestige." Dirksen spoke the party line, or more appropriately the administration line, during the Johnson years. Dirksen remained one of President Johnson's staunchest Senate allies, and although he hedged some bets as the war became more unpopular and Republicans increasingly criticized its conduct, Dirksen never veered far from justifying the pursuit of victory.

One of the first times the two senators openly differed on the Vietnam war occurred during Percy's Senate contest in 1966. Percy proposed a conference of Asian nations to settle the conflict or to seek ways of settling it. Many Republicans, looking for some alternative to the Johnson program, seized upon this idea. Actually, the idea did not originate with Percy, but his name was linked with it from the beginning. Dirksen looked for any way to deny credit to Percy. At one point on the Senate floor, Dirksen attempted to credit Senator Jack R. Miller of Iowa with the idea, but it never caught on. The champion of Percy's plan was Senator Thruston B. Morton of Kentucky, a strong voice on the Senate Foreign Relations Committee. He undertook the chore of convincing Dirksen to support the plan. Dirksen supposedly said in private, "It's not going to amount to a god-damn. It's like being against sin." Republicans— including Richard Nixon, whose previous statements had been hawkish; Dwight Eisenhower; and Gerald Ford—turned to the all-Asian idea. Thanks mainly to Morton's efforts, the Republican Coordinating Committee, a key party-policy group, pledged its support of an all-Asian conference. Dirksen, because of his seniority on the committee, had to announce the endorsement. In his skillful manner Dirksen gave credit for the idea to the foreign minister of Thailand. This snub to Percy went unnoticed by the public but not by those who had worked hard to give the plan united Republican approval.

Well into 1967 Dirksen carried the administration banner on Vietnam. In May he left a hospital bed to ask a luncheon conference for "four-square" support of the president. Meanwhile, Percy joined Senator Javits, Senator Hugh D. Scott, Jr., of Pennsylvania, and other senators in pleading with Johnson for a negotiated settlement of the war.

For all their differences, and their philosophical separation, Percy and Dirksen seldom aired their disagreements publicly. Each suppressed the temptation to publicly rip the other, but each had his own way of gouging the other subtly. At a commencement speech in June, 1968, less than two months before the Republican National Convention, Percy told graduating seniors why Dirksen's hair was thinning: "His hair got that way when he first heard I had been proposed for national office."

For the first three years of his Senate term, Percy lived with what literally grew to be a legend about Dirksen and his romance with hard-line Republicans in Illinois and across the nation. Dirksen knew their language, said the right things at the right time, spoke eloquently, and by virtue of such actions as supporting the marigold as the national flower and cutting a record of patriotic statements, earned a special place in their hearts.

Percy's appeal is entirely different, and in contrast he does not like to engage county-level politicians in small talk. They correctly feel he does not talk their style of politics, although they incorrectly assume that this means he is disinterested in their concerns. In retrospect at least, Percy recognized the differences between his and Dirksen's appeal: "It's true that to the regular Republican organization Everett Dirksen was more their kind of Republican. They took him to heart much more and had a much deeper affection for him." Percy said this attitude never bothered him: "He was Everett Dirksen, and I was Chuck Percy; he accepted the differences, and I accepted the differences. Neither one of us would have wanted to change shoes and been each other's person."

Despite Percy's rational assessment of the feeling for Dirksen in Illinois, the reverence shown Dirksen rankled at times. Percy did not want the impression left that Dirksen's apparent popularity among Republicans had made him a landslide winner in state elections. Percy compared his vote-getting ability in Illinois with Dirksen's as a means of measuring popularity. "I've never felt I suffered by that comparison," Percy has said.

The vote totals do give some insight. In 1950 against Scott Lucas, Dirksen won with 54 percent of the vote and a margin of 294,354 votes. In 1956 against Democrat Richard Stengel, Dirksen again polled 54 percent of the vote—this time in a Republican presidential year—and the victory margin reached 357,469 votes. Against Congressman Sidney R. Yates in 1962, Dirksen won with 52.7 percent of the vote. Yates, a popular Cook County Democrat and friend of the Richard J. Daley political organization, did not campaign with vigor Downstate, but even so his showing was substantial. Dirksen won by 213,195 votes. In Dirksen's last campaign he battled Illinois Attorney General William G. Clark, a dedicated dove on Vietnam at a time (1968) when Dirksen still held closely to the administration line. The percentage for the senator was 53.2, and he won by 280,705 votes. Against the field in his senatorial contests, Dirksen's best showing came against Stengel, the man who had the least going for him in terms of statewide appeal. Many Illinoisans felt that Clark might have beaten Dirksen in 1968 if he had received stronger backing from the mayor of Chicago. Daley's support of Lyndon Johnson's war policy influenced the amount of help he gave Clark. Dirksen beat Clark even though he did not campaign vigorously, and rumors spread that his health was failing.

In comparison Percy's vote-getting record includes one defeat, in 1964 to Otto Kerner. In his winning campaigns, Percy rolled up impressive victories. He defeated Douglas with 55.6 percent of the votes in 1966. His vote margin was 422,302. He overwhelmed Roman Pucinski in 1972 with 62.2 percent of the vote. The vote margin was 1,146,047, the largest plurality in any Senate contest in Illinois political history.

On September 7, 1969, Everett McKinley Dirksen died. He was accorded highest national honors in Washington and Illinois, and literally dozens of colleagues in the House and Senate made speeches extolling his virtues and praising his accomplishments. Percy spoke on the floor of the Senate. He did the best job of all the congressmen in explaining the Dirksen flair, his way with friends and foes, and his appeal to courthouse politicians.

"I think I shall always remember him most vividly in the setting where I first got to know him years ago—at innumerable political dinners in our State of Illinois. Usually their intent was to raise funds, and their theme was invariably partisan. Their flavor, however, was pure Dirksen.

"Following a version of the National Anthem—during which the assembled audience would grope for the key—the group would sit through an all-too-frequent meal of chicken and peas and then through perhaps a dozen 'brief' preliminary speeches, each of them viewing with alarm the latest outrage perpetrated by the Democrats. Hundreds, occasionally thousands of people, would patiently sit through these evenings without complaint only because of the promised finale: An address by the Honorable Everett McKinley Dirksen. A political audience would pay any price, bear any burden, to hear him speak. They were seldom, if ever, disappointed.

"He would talk glowingly of the Republican party: 'Jerry Ford—before that it was Charlie Halleck—and I need more troops in Washington,' he would say, and then predict an unquestioned Republican majority, if not in the next Congress, then most assuredly in the one just just after it.

"When I came to the Senate three years ago, I soon realized that the respect and affection he kindled at these Illinois dinners was shared by those who know him best—his colleagues in this body. And here, as in Illinois, he returned that respect and affection in full measure.

"Everett Dirksen's political prowess at home was more than matched by his legislative skill in Washington. His secret perhaps was that, while a master of the reasonable compromise, he would never compromise a principle—and he would never ask another man to do so. It would have been easy enough for Ev Dirksen as the the leader of my party in the Senate, and as the famed senior Senator from my own state, to ask me to go his way on many an issue, even when he knew my inclination was in another direction—and it would have put me in a difficult position to refuse. But he never once did. Before I came to Washington, he said that, whenever conscience dictated, we should simply agree to disagree, and he always honored that principle between us."

After Dirksen's death Governor Richard B. Ogilvie fulfilled a political promise by appointing Speaker of the House Ralph T. Smith of Alton to fill the Dirksen term until the election of 1970. Smith, a Downstate Republican, was one of a few party leaders in the southern half of the state who had supported Ogilvie's candidacy for governor through the primary and general elections in 1968. That support got him the senatorial appointment. Smith, whose voting record during his state House tenure reflected parochial and regional concerns, tried to emulate Dirksen in the year before the election. If some of the Dirksen glow could have stayed with Smith, his chances in 1970 would have been markedly improved. But Smith was in over his head, intellectually and in terms of the savvy needed to build a quick record on which to run. When Smith did vote in the Senate, he usually took the straight Nixon line, and consequently Smith and Percy often found themselves on opposite sides. Smith had little chance to establish a relationship with Percy in the Senate, although they knew each other from Illinois political contests. Smith played to the conservative interests of the Illinois party because he realized that he needed their money and their aid in 1970. That strategy led Smith to be coy in 1970 when reporters asked if he would support Percy for reelection in 1972. Assuming that open support of Percy at that time was a liability, Smith put off answering the question directly until well into the year. Finally he gave his support to Percy's reelection bid. Percy campaigned for Smith in his 1970 contest against Adlai E. Stevenson III, whose single term as state treasurer of Illinois ended that year. Percy worked for Smith as much as he had for Republican Senate candidates in other states, even though he differed with the candidates philosophically. He looked for safe issues and party matters and avoided controversial and difficult questions of principle. Percy's work for the Smith campaign included throwing a "vote fest" in Springfield that attracted 7,000 persons. But nothing could help Smith against Stevenson. In desperation Smith undertook a last-ditch television advertising campaign in which he emphasized Stevenson's "liberal-radical" leanings and attempted to associate Stevenson with radicals and campus riots and lawlessness. Percy stayed clear of the campaign and its implications. The attempted smear campaign failed to ignite the public. In a television appearance after the 1970 election, Percy blamed Smith's managers for misgauging the electorate: "They continued to feel that law and order was the major issue and the television commercials that I saw emphasized this as the prime issue. It long had ceased to be the main issue. Economics became the major issue in the final three or four weeks of the campaign."

Adlai E. Stevenson III, great-grandson of a U.S. vice-president and son of a two-time nominee for president and U.S. ambassador to the United Nations, served a term in the Illinois House of Representatives before being elected state treasurer in 1966. He learned of Dirksen's death while holding a huge Democratic picnic at his family's farm near Libertyville, Illinois, not far from Chicago. Speculation had been rampant about Stevenson's interest in running against Dirksen in the future or even against Percy in 1972. There always was the possibility that Stevenson might have to seek reelection to the uninteresting treasurer's job just to keep his name before the public. From the time of Dirksen's death, few doubted that Stevenson would be his party's choice for the Dirksen seat, though other Democrats privately, and occasionally publicly, pined for the role. Stevenson first had to make peace with Richard J. Daley and the organization Democrats. Two years before, when Stevenson had sought the opportunity to run against Dirksen, the Chicago Democratic organization denied him the chance, apparently because he did not support the administration's Vietnam position. While Stevenson took issue with much of President Johnson's war policy, he never stood as far to the left as many Democratic leaders thought he did. In any case, Stevenson did not get the party nod in 1967. It was different in 1970. The party rallied to Stevenson, and the rifts of the past seemed to have been forgotten.

It would have been easy for Stevenson to come to Washington on the crest of a large publicity campaign, for he bears a famous political name. Instead, Stevenson's entry into the halls of Congress went almost unnoticed. In the early years of his term, he served quietly, avoiding national publicity and choosing to establish his credentials internally with various factions of the party leadership. Had Senator Edmund S. Muskie of Maine received more serious consideration at the 1972 Democratic National Convention, Stevenson might have been thrust into the national limelight. Stevenson did not fit comfortably with Senator George McGovern, the 1972 Democratic nominee, on many issues, and Stevenson had remained a Muskie loyalist through the national primaries and the convention. As a result McGovern forces virtually ignored Stevenson, which made the Illinoisan happy. Stevenson considered the McGovern nomination a critical mistake for the Democratic party.

For much of the first few years of Stevenson's term, Percy and his colleague shared similar feelings about the Vietnam war. They were reluctant to accept the idea of a fixed deadline for the withdrawal of U.S. troops from Vietnam, but finally both came to that conclusion. Stevenson arrived there earlier than Percy. Although Stevenson's war position often sounded more partisan, there never appeared to be a marked difference in the approach of the two Illinois senators toward ending the conflict. And so, before very long, it became clear that two dedicated doves represented Illinois in the Senate. After the war, but before a program of conditional amnesty had been proposed by President Gerald Ford, the two senators opposed any effort to pass an amnesty proposal through Congress.

A former aide of Percy's described Stevenson and Percy as "friends for some time, but not intimates. They feel comfortable socially, and Percy has always thought it was nice he didn't have to run against Stevenson. I think the feeling is mutual." Stevenson helps Percy by being a "liberal lightning rod" for the anti-Percy elements in the Republican party. Stevenson has given these critics, such as the *Chicago Tribune*, more than Percy at which to level their guns. The two senators also share some of the same power base, which would give them something to worry about if they had to run against each other—a possibility they will never have to face. In his election victories for the Senate in 1970 and 1974, Stevenson attracted strong voter support in the Chicago suburbs, where Republicans were thought to have an upper hand. Democrats from the city of Chicago have moved to the suburbs in great numbers, and although they often register as Republicans, they retain strong identification with some Democratic names. Stevenson's drawing ability in the suburbs prompted a television interviewer to ask Percy if he and Stevenson had "overlapping constituencies." Percy said the Stevenson success in the suburbs only proved that the "challenge that the Republican party faces now [is] to have candidates that have a broad-based appeal and to recognize that people are less inclined toward party orientation now." Percy recognized the fact, acknowledged by many political scientists, that it is dangerous to assume the suburbs will be Republican strongholds in the future. Percy admitted that there is some overlapping of his and Stevenson's constituencies and that the two of them have similar philosophies on some national issues. Many Illinois voters share this feeling.

After Dirksen's death Percy became the senior senator from Illinois, and with that distinction came the right to name U.S. marshals and sponsor judges for the federal bench. This includes the U.S. District Court in Chicago and the U.S. Court of Appeals. In Chicago, politics has been hard to separate from the legal process at the judicial level, from local judges to the federal bench. Percy's immediate predecessors, Dirksen and Paul Douglas, leaned heavily toward judges who had considerable political activity in their backgrounds. Some professional legal organizations in Illinois—such as the Chicago Council of Lawyers, which periodically ranks the judges—have felt that in some cases judicial quality was sacrificed for political loyalty. In the first five years after he became senior senator, Percy named six men to the federal bench. Almost to a man they are considered the cream of the U.S. District Court, according to the lawyers' council and legal scholars. That does not mean politics played no role in the Percy selections; politics almost always is involved. But it does signify that involvement in Republican politics was not the primary consideration. Percy's approach had meaning for the Chicago Democratic organization, which, until Percy began making appointments to the bench, had a measure of control over judges, many of whom were selected as a reward for their past political activity in the party.

Percy's emphasis on a prospective judge's qualifications has changed the judiciary, especially regarding patronage. The change came about quietly and without fanfare with one exception. In 1973 the selection of Prentice H. Marshall, a law professor at the University of Illinois, rattled the political cages of the Republican party throughout Illinois because Marshall is a Democrat. All of Percy's previous appointees were Republicans. The Marshall appointment gave Percy's foes in Illinois, particularly those who had challenged his loyalty to the party before, an opportunity to sound off. John C. Hirschfeld, a state legislator from Champaign, cried the loudest of all and attempted to have Percy censured in the state legislature for his action. Hirschfeld, an attorney, has been one of Percy's most vocal critics. Despite the noise from Hirschfeld, Marshall's nomination breezed through the Senate without hesitation, and the state party quickly forgot the incident.

Percy has applied a "no deals" approach to those in the judiciary who might be potential nominees to the U.S. District Court bench. Some years ago Percy asked William Bauer, a state circuit judge in a suburb of Chicago, to serve a two-year stint as U.S. attorney. He told the judge that if an opening should occur on the district-court bench Percy would consider naming Bauer to it, providing he had served well as U.S. attorney. Percy then made his pledge to the judge public. "That is a principle I insist on in making any promises," Percy said. Bauer was later named to the district court. Apparently the Stevenson and Percy attitudes toward appointments to the courts have meshed. Stevenson has agreed with Percy's judicial and U.S. marshal appointments.

The major areas of disagreement between Percy and Stevenson reflect their partisan philosophies for the most part. Stevenson generally holds to the liberal Democratic view, which sees the federal government as the solution to the nation's great common problems. Percy, while agreeing with that concept on some questions of social services, has supported efforts by Congress and the Republican administration to return some of the federal government's authority to state and local governments. For example, Stevenson led the fight on the Senate floor to have federal price and wage controls extended in 1974, and Percy worked just as hard to let the controls expire, which they ultimately were permitted to do. During the energy crisis of the mid-1970s, Stevenson proposed the establishment of a federal oil and gas company, which in effect would begin a greater degree of federalization of the domestic oil industry. Percy balked, claiming that the government had no better efficiency record than private industry had. He said that the government has "regulated the railroads right out of business" and that the government would be no more efficient "pumping oil than delivering the mail." But Stevenson persisted in his efforts to gain greater federal control of the oil industry.

A long-standing disagreement between the two senators on an economic issue of importance is over federal revenue sharing. Stevenson remains one of the Senate's most devout opponents of the system of returning federal money to local and state governments. When the program started in 1972, Stevenson voted against it. He cited revenue sharing as a case of "the camel getting its nose under the tent." Stevenson believes it is a waste of tax money to give large sums of federal funds virtually without restrictions to governments that often are poorly managed. Stevenson's answer is a direct-grant program controlled by the federal government with incentives for reform built in. Percy originally saw revenue sharing as an answer to hard-pressed state and local governments and as a means of relieving the pressures on local property taxes. In 1972 he also supported the theory, advanced by Nixon, that revenue sharing formed a keystone in a program to give local governments more opportunity to determine their own destinies. Nixon promoted revenue sharing as part of a plan to decentralize federal government spending programs, particularly in the social services.

Stevenson and Percy also have differed over defense-department appropriations. Stevenson has consistently voted for reduction in the defense-department budgets, particularly the expenditures for arms and new weapons systems. Percy believes a strong defense system is necessary to back up the nation's foreign policy, and throughout his Senate years he has voted to maintain defense-spending levels. In 1974, when spending proposals for the Department of Defense came to the Senate, the two Illinois senators disagreed over such specific defense expenditures as a study to find alternatives to a new Air Force bomber; a reduction in research and development funds for combat-support aircraft; a ceiling on fiscal 1974 spending; and a deletion of funds for researching, developing, testing, and evaluating a missile. In all cases Stevenson voted for the proposals; and Percy, against. A Percy aide explained the votes: "Percy has always voted for strong defense. Don't get his Southeast Asia positions during the war confused with his posture on defense." Percy opposed escalation of the war and pressed the president for a quick end to the conflict. Percy's voting record does show a willingness to support U.S. arms and weapons sales to such countries as Greece, where an oppressive military junta existed. In 1972 he opposed a plan proposed by Senator J. William Fulbright of Arkansas to end U.S. financing of foreign police and weaponry. At times Percy has urged Congress to use its control of the purse strings to deal with the executive branch on foreign matters, but his voting record shows he does not support an across-the-board spending curtailment or a substantive reduction in military spending.

On foreign affairs matters Percy and Stevenson have agreed more often than not. However, a growing difference of opinion began to surface early in 1974 over the role and activities of Secretary of State Henry Kissinger. Percy has remained a staunch supporter of Kissinger and his diplomatic efforts. Stevenson began by criticizing Kissinger's methods in private, preferring, he said, to remain out of the public eye because of Kissinger's successes in foreign affairs and the delicate nature of negotiations. An episode late in 1974 changed Stevenson's attitude. It had to do with a critical measure—a trade bill with Russia—that was before Congress. One of the bill's provisions, by Senator Henry M. Jackson of Washington State, established specific numbers of Russian Jews who were to be permitted to leave the Soviet Union. At the same time Stevenson submitted an amendment that restricted Soviet Union export-import credits with the United States to $300 million instead of the $1.2 billion Kissinger reportedly had promised Soviet officials. When the trade agreement was rejected by Russia early in 1975, Kissinger openly blamed Jackson but privately lay a good share of the blame on Stevenson's amendment. Sensing an effort to undercut him with Democrats, Stevenson made a blistering public attack on Kissinger. He said Kissinger used "bribes" to gain favors with other countries and called the secretary of state's methods "egocentric."

Percy kept silent, preferring to stay out of any brawl between the two men. In private he said he was particularly disappointed in Stevenson's public criticism at a time when Kissinger was preparing to visit the Middle East and make another attempt to arrange a settlement there. Percy called Stevenson's remarks "politics as usual." Percy may have smarted some from inferences that members of Congress, and particularly the Senate Foreign Relations Committee, had become too cozy with Kissinger and the foreign-affairs establishment of the Nixon-Ford administrations.

One of Percy and Stevenson's cooperative ventures has been the filming of a television program for dissemination in Illinois and adjacent states. The program started at the request of Chicago's WGN-TV, the broadcasting arm of the *Chicago Tribune*. The shows were filmed throughout 1971 but were discontinued in 1972 when Percy sought reelection. They resumed again in 1973 but were halted when Stevenson sought reelection in 1974.

On the 15-minute-long shows, the senators are questioned by a newsman, often someone from a Washington news bureau. Occasionally, correspondents from Illinois newspapers participate. Sometimes the senators interview their own guests. The films are made in the Senate recording studio, which is staffed by employees of the Office of the Sergeant at Arms of the Senate. The production fee for each week's taping is paid by WGN. If a local station chooses to use the program, it pays for shipping costs, but the senators pay the cost of duplicating the tape for each of the participating stations. The show, called "Your Senators Report," produces some mild debate, but its time restriction hardly accommodates a detailed discussion of issues. Illinois TV stations use the program for filling their public-service requirement, and consequently the show often appears at odd hours.

The relationship between Percy and Stevenson is free of the tension that existed between Percy and his first Senate colleague from Illinois. Percy's public remembrances of Everett McKinley Dirksen notwithstanding, the two often found it difficult to suffer each other. Much of the trouble was unavoidable and probably predictable, given the stages of their respective careers. Dirksen, slower and ailing, was showing signs of the pressures that work on a man who has been in Washington more than 35 years. Although he held high office and commanded respect among his Senate peers and in the national party, his influence fluctuated, depending on the issue and his stamina. New Republican faces were on the scene, and one of them was Percy, who was just beginning a career that seemed to have no end other than the White House. Resentment by Dirksen seemed natural. The two senators grinned and managed to make the most of it in spite of their personal feelings and the issues between them. Percy's optimistic attitude about almost everything and his unwillingness to resort to petty backbiting helped make the relationship work. Dirksen was not about to be driven to public criticism of a junior colleague. Stevenson and Percy, on the other hand, have managed to find a variety of ways to cooperate on Illinois projects. Members of their respective staffs snipe at each other occasionally, but no permanent damage is done. Usually, the two senators meet only when a problem is of such importance that it needs their face-to-face consultation. Their different life-styles mean their social paths seldom cross.

The result of this more amiable relationship with a colleague, despite some major differences on national issues and the fact that they are not members of the same political party, is a working atmosphere that does not consume their personal time, except when they want it to. Each of the senators can go his own way and say what he wants without feeling that the other is dealing behind his back. They respect each other, and from that respect comes a certain tolerance of the minor irritations that can plague any relationship. Each has been able to nourish his own private dreams about the presidency without having nightmares about the other's ambition.

CHAPTER X

PERCY AND NIXON

Political life for Charles Percy changed dramatically with the resignation of Richard Nixon from the presidency. This was the first time in Percy's political career that the specter of Nixon did not rest somewhere on the horizon as either a political associate, rival, adversary, leader, foe, or, in light of Percy's presidential ambitions, a future executioner. As the two men's paths crossed dozens of times from the 1950s to the mid-1970s, Nixon was at one time or another all of these to Percy. The freshest memories are of Nixon as a threat to Percy's career and Percy as a challenger to the goals of the Nixon administration. But before this adversary relationship developed, there was a time when they worked together in the Republican party, although each saw it through different philosophical glasses. There were any number of times in the years since 1959 when the two could have cemented a lasting political relationship. It could have happened in 1960 at the Republican National Convention, but it didn't. It could have happened in 1967 and 1968 when Percy got within inches of the vice-presidential nomination, but it didn't. A bond might have developed during Nixon's presidency because they shared common goals in foreign affairs, but it didn't. No matter how hard they tried, they could not avoid each other. No matter how many opportunities there were to work as a team, they could not get together.

Much of the story of Percy's political career must be told as it relates to Nixon. Before Nixon's resignation, he and Percy seemed on an unalterable collision course leading to the presidential nomination process in 1976. No matter how neutral Nixon appeared, many political observers felt he was waiting for the opportunity to scuttle Percy's presidential effort. Percy, on the other hand, planned much of his strategy to neutralize Nixon's influence until it could not do him any damage. The irony is that Nixon had the final word when he turned the presidency over to Gerald R. Ford, ending, at least temporarily, Percy's pursuit of the party nomination.

Some insight into the relationship of Nixon and Percy can be gained by looking at Senate voting records, particularly during the critical first few years of the Nixon administration. Statistics do not tell the whole tale, but the data may provide some answers to an important question: Was Percy anti-Nixon? The information was gathered by Congressional Quarterly, the nonpartisan service for news organizations. During the first two sessions of the 91st Congress, 1969 and 1970, Percy voted with Nixon 63 percent of the time and against the administration position 15 percent of the time. The votes were on 163 issues identified as being sponsored or favored by the president. By comparison, Senator Edward J. Gurney, a Florida Republican who was considered a strong ally of the president, voted with the administration 64 percent of the time and against it 26 percent. Senator Mark Hatfield of Oregon, considered more liberal than Percy on many issues, voted with the president 48 percent of the time and against him 37 percent. On the basis of these figures Percy's voting record puts him in the pro-Nixon camp during the first two years of Nixon's administration. Of greater significance than the percentages is the fact that during 1969 and 1970 Percy voted against the president on such major administration issues as the antiballistic-missile (ABM) program, the confirmation of Judges Clement F. Haynsworth, Jr., and G. Harrold Carswell, and the supersonic-transport (SST) program. Because of his negative votes on these particular issues, Percy was accused of abandoning the president. Also during these two years Percy voted against several administration proposals related to ending the Vietnam war.

In the 92nd Congress, the second two years of the Nixon administration, the picture changed. On 128 Nixon issues, Percy supported the president only 48 percent of the time, a sharply lower percentage than for the 1969–70 period. He opposed Nixon 37 percent of the time, slightly more than he had in the 91st Congress. For the years 1971 and 1972 the difference between Percy's and Gurney's records was greater. The Florida Republican voted with Nixon 86 percent of the time and against him 13 percent. Hatfield's record was for the president 27 percent and against him 50 percent.

In 1972 Percy voted with the president less than in previous years: with Nixon 46 percent of the time and against 48 percent. This 1972 record placed Percy in a fifth-place tie with Richard S. Schweiker of Pennsylvania on the list of Senate Republicans who voted most often against the administration. Those senators ahead of Percy and Schweiker and their percentages were Clifford P. Case of New Jersey (54); Jacob K. Javits of New York (54); Edward W. Brooke of Massachusetts (52); Charles McC. Mathias, Jr., of Maryland (50).

The figures reveal that Percy's voting record in relation to the president was fairly supportive in the first years, then moved to the middle ground for a short time. Percy's more negative direction in relation to Nixon programs in the later years of the administration paralleled a trend in Congress. In 1972, for example, Nixon won 66 percent of the congressional votes that involved a test of support for his views. This year was the lowest in percentage of victories in Nixon's first administration; it was also the lowest for any president since 1960, Dwight Eisenhower's last year in office.

While voting records from the first three years of the Nixon administration may not make Percy out to be totally anti-Nixon, some of his more celebrated Senate votes established such an image. Even now the issues have a familiar ring: Haynsworth, Carswell, ABM, SST. In the eyes of many conservative Republicans and those who steadfastly supported Nixon at the time, the fact that Percy agreed with almost two-thirds of all Nixon issues during this period was of no consequence. He could not be counted on for the big ones. Percy answered critics of his voting record in an article that had been published in the May, 1971, issue of *Today's Education* magazine. Percy told of receiving a letter from an Illinois constituent who had criticized a wide range of Percy's votes. The writer said: "How can you possibly justify your votes against Judge Haynsworth, Judge Carswell, and the SST when President Nixon supported all of them? Why did you support the Cooper-Church Amendment? Wake up and support the President. That's what we sent you to Washington for." Percy explained that the executive and legislative branches of government are independent of each other and then said, "I have an obligation to my constituents to do more than rubber-stamp every idea that comes to Capitol Hill from the White House."

Not all of Percy's advisers believed his posture toward Nixon made good sense. Some of the more politically inclined staff members who were more concerned about Republican acceptability of Percy felt the senator needlessly criticized Nixon and went out of his way to be difficult, particularly when the issue was not a matter of principle to the senator. One staff member blamed Percy's habit of letting reporters' questions needle him until he leveled a blast at the president. As one aide said, "Politically, Percy's relationship with Nixon . . . made him one of the most popular people in the country, but not with rock-ribbed Republicans. It was not the thing to do politically."

The issues of Haynsworth, Carswell, and the ABM and SST all had significant common characteristics in a political sense. The media knew that the Senate votes on these issues, or amendments to them, would be close, and so a great deal of attention was focused on the outcome. The Haynsworth voting, for example, received virtual blow-by-blow coverage. The congressional decisions on all these issues were major setbacks for Nixon, and he fought back, personally and through his staff. The era of secret warfare, fear of retribution, and emphasis on loyalty to a president had begun. Pressure on senators mounted as the votes drew near, and one thing was clear: Those who jumped the Nixon ship would be subject to retaliation in the years to come. This would be particularly true for Republicans. If the president could have kept his own party in line, he would have won on all the controversial issues.

On August 18, 1969, President Nixon sent to the Senate for confirmation the name of Clement F. Haynsworth, Jr., of Greenville, South Carolina, to fill the Supreme Court seat vacated by Associate Justice Abe Fortas, who had resigned three months earlier as a result of a conflict-of-interest affair. Democratic senators still smarted from the Fortas matter, and when labor unions and civil rights organizations began to zero in on Haynsworth's record, they joined the hunt. Added to this atmosphere of revenge were concerns over the judge's propriety in conflict of interest matters and his stand on civil rights questions. As chief judge of the U.S. Court of Appeals for the Fourth Circuit, Haynsworth voted against a ruling that Prince Edward County, Virginia, had to begin school desegregation efforts. On another occasion, he ruled against an order that hospitals receiving federal funds could not maintain segregated facilities. Northern senators were also hostile toward Haynsworth because they knew that President Nixon wanted to add a conservative to the court and he specifically sought a Southerner for the court as part of his Southern strategy, which stemmed from the 1968 election. Finally, the Senate rejected Haynsworth by a roll-call vote of 55 to 45. Demonstrating a lack of faith in the president's choice, 17 Republicans—including Percy and members of the Senate leadership, such as Minority Leader Hugh Scott—had voted against Haynsworth.

After his vote against Haynsworth, Percy said, "I for one do not question Judge Haynsworth's ability or his honesty . . . but I feel that honesty and ability are not enough. The times demand something more. Haynsworth does not meet the challenge of the times, a challenge that has placed our system on trial." He felt Haynsworth lacked sensitivity on civil rights and labor relations questions, and he continued, "Unfortunately the matter does not rest with that, for we must also weigh the accompanying insensitivity and seeming indifference to the appearance of propriety on Judge Haynsworth's part, a record that throws a dark cloud over his qualifications to serve on the Supreme Court." If Percy's comments do not seem sufficiently specific, they nevertheless sum up why many other senators did not vote to confirm Haynsworth.

The pressure prior to the tense roll-call vote was strong as the White House worked hard to bring reluctant senators around to Nixon's side. Ten of the 11 members of the Illinois Republican delegation to the House of Representatives called on Percy two days before the balloting and asked him to vote for Haynsworth.

Percy was criticized in Illinois for his vote against confirmation of Haynsworth. In order to see what effect his stand had on his popularity at home, Cook County Republicans took a poll, which showed 64 percent of those surveyed thought the senator did a good job, 15 percent were disappointed with his performance, and 21 percent had no opinion. The Republicans did not measure Nixon's popularity; but early in his administration, and particularly during his first year, the president looked good in public-opinion polls. In July, 1969, 62 percent of the people in a Louis Harris poll approved of Nixon's conduct in office.

Nixon would not abandon his attempt to have a Southerner named to the court. Within two months of his defeat on the Haynsworth nomination, he offered the name of Judge G. Harrold Carswell of Tallahassee, Florida, a member of the U.S. Court of Appeals for the Fifth District, for the Supreme Court. After the nomination of Carswell, and early in the discussion of his suitability, Nixon and his advisers thought that the Senate surely did not have the staying power for two showdowns over presidential nominations. They were wrong. The questions about Carswell involved his position on civil rights and his lack of brilliance on the courts where he had served. The legal profession was allied against Carswell. Also reflected in the final vote were some Senate grievances against the White House. On April 8, 1970, the final tally showed 45 senators for confirmation of Carswell and 51 against; Percy was among the latter. When the smoke had cleared after the Senate rejection of Carswell, even the president's aides admitted that the judge's credentials did not compare favorably with Haynsworth's.

Percy recalled later that one of the persons most upset by his Carswell vote was John D. Ehrlichman, the president's chief domestic counselor. Apparently, Nixon understood the basic reasons for Percy's vote, or at least Percy thought so. At a meeting with the president in the fall of 1970, Percy and Nixon discussed the senator's vote. Percy recalled, "He had expressed to me his personal understanding on the Carswell vote and said, 'I'd like to have had your vote, but I can understand that you have to vote your conscience and your judgment because you are a United States senator—I know, I was one.'" Percy remembers saying that he wished the president's staff members understood the separation of powers as well as Nixon did.

Vice-President Spiro T. Agnew accused the Senate of being taken in by "the biggest snow job in history" on Carswell. In a speech at the University of Illinois, in Urbana, Percy called the Agnew accusations "completely false." He added, "For me to have voted aye for Carswell would have gone against everything, all I have worked for for many years. I simply could not do it." Percy did not commit himself on Carswell until the last minute. He spent the night before the vote analyzing the judge's reversal record. He had also consulted several law-school faculty members in an attempt to assess Carswell's legal abilities. Later, when Nixon nominated Judge Harry A. Blackmun of Minnesota, a member of the U.S. Court of Appeals for the Eighth Circuit, to the court, Percy said, "The Senate is not to be rushed. It will give the [Blackmun] nomination the same consideration the others had." Without much hesitation he voted for Blackmun's confirmation. He had done the same with Chief Justice Warren E. Burger before Haynsworth and Carswell. The votes by Percy against the latter two were the extent of his opposition to Nixon's court nominations. More than a year later Percy announced his support of the nominations of Lewis F. Powell, Jr., and William H. Rehnquist to the court, although some of the same persons who had criticized the civil rights positions of Haynsworth and Carswell also criticized Rehnquist's attitude.

Percy's votes on Haynsworth and Carswell were only two examples of issues during 1969 and 1970 that earned him an anti-Nixon reputation. The debate that seemed to set the stage for the major executive-legislative conflict in those years centered on the Safeguard antiballistic missile system, more commonly known as ABM. In the early days of the Nixon administration, ABM headed the priority list. It played a major role in the United States's overall diplomatic relations with Russia, which included limited-arms talks. Nixon felt a strong defense posture provided a base for discussions with Russia and China. The president knew that the Senate vote on ABM would be close, and his staff applied pressure on those senators, including Percy, who were considered to be potential swing votes.

Nixon aides made it clear to Percy that a vote against ABM would cost him dearly. Percy said, "They had literally blackmailed me on my ABM vote to try to force me to vote for a system that I felt was a terrible waste of money—a technical monstrosity—and subsequent events have proved how correct I was." The price for Percy's vote was the National Home Ownership Foundation, which was the watchdog agency for the federal housing program Percy had worked hard to pass a year before in Congress. "I was told clearly and unequivocally this would cost me and it did.... There are ways the great power of the White House can be used to express great displeasure." The National Home Ownership Foundation was never activated, although the law authorizing it had been passed. Percy said he was astounded that the White House would "take it out of the hides of the poor." A final blow to Percy came later when he learned he would have been named president of the foundation's board. Percy believes that absence of a watchdog agency has permitted fraud to proliferate in federal housing programs.

The debate on ABM, and the concurrent pressure from the White House, took from March until August. Percy had been opposed to ABM from the beginning. When Nixon made the plan public in March, 1969, Percy said on a television show, "For 25 years now we have always been building more arms in the name of peace. Each escalation has always called for another counterescalation." In August, prior to the voting on two amendments that would have crippled the ABM proposal, Percy announced that an opinion poll of his constituents showed them "almost evenly divided" in their opinion of the ABM system.

On August 6, 1969, the Senate voted on the two key amendments. One amendment, proposed by Senator Margaret Chase Smith of Maine, would have rejected any spending of funds on the ABM. It was defeated when Vice-President Agnew symbolically cast the tie-breaking vote that defeated the measure. The other amendment, called the Cooper-Hart, would have given partial approval to an ABM system. The Cooper-Hart amendment provided funds for research and development of an antiballistic missile system but not for the proposed Safeguard system. It failed 49 to 51, with Mrs. Smith voting against the amendment because it was too much of a compromise for her. Of the 43 Republicans in the Senate, Percy and 12 others voted for the Cooper-Hart amendment. Joining Percy were George D. Aiken, Edward W. Brooke, Clifford P. Case, Marlow W. Cook and John Sherman Cooper of Kentucky, Charles E. Goodell, Mark O. Hatfield, Jacob K. Javits, Charles McC. Mathias, Jr., James B. Pearson, William B. Saxbe of Ohio, and Richard S. Schweiker. Thirty Republicans supported Nixon's Safeguard program and so voted against the Cooper-Hart amendment. Ultimately, on November 6, 1969, ABM funding was authorized by Congress.

The other administration issue of 1969 and 1970 that brought out Percy's opposition most sharply was the costly supersonic-transport (SST) subsidy program. It came after Haynsworth, Carswell, and ABM and added another item to the list kept by those individuals who felt that by 1970 Percy had virtually abandoned the president. Percy said he would vote a "resounding no" when the proposal to increase the funding for the SST came before the Senate. He had voted for the initial financing of the program, but now would have none of SST. He said he had made a "mistake last year" in voting for the program: "If the bankers won't finance the SST, why should we stick the taxpayer with the cost. We don't have enough money to even keep our nation's largest railroads solvent." The SST-funding proposal came before Congress at a relatively bad time for the nation economically, and the Congress simply did nothing about it in the 1970 fall lame-duck session. The Nixon staff resurrected the idea at the beginning of the 92nd Congress, and on March 25, 1971, the Senate voted to deny more funding for the SST. Percy was among those senators who cast a negative vote. The House had also voted to discontinue funding. Finally, by mid-August, 1971, Congress passed an appropriation to finance the phasing out of the SST program.

Not all major administration bills received Percy's negative vote. In 1970, for example, Percy criticized the administration's omnibus crime bill for the District of Columbia because it contained a controversial no-knock provision, which permitted forcible surprise entry by police once a bench warrant had been issued. Percy noted that "many Americans seem willing for the first time in 200 years to sacrifice basic constitutional freedoms because of their fear for their own survival." He also said that such provisions as no-knock are "a response only to the frantic cry for self-protection and survival and do not raise or react to the question of ultimate morality. When we permit the law to be nothing more than an expression of outrage or . . . hysteria, we infringe upon liberty and promote injustice. I am unwilling to sacrifice freedom and justice to reach this goal."

That comment must have raised some eyebrows in the Nixon administration. The District of Columbia crime bill was the direct result of the Republicans' "return to law and order" pledge, which had been a prominent feature of their 1968 election campaign. Attorney John Mitchell took personal charge of the crime bill. He believed that the people who elected Richard Nixon—the "silent majority"—wanted such provisions as no-knock to protect them from lawlessness.

After several amendments and alterations Percy voted for the crime bill, which passed Congress and became law. When reminded that he had branded the no-knock provision as repressive and dangerous, Percy offered an explanation: "I believe the process that ultimately led me to change my mind is instructive for us all. I think it is representative of the difficult choices that one faces in weighing the rights of an individual and the rights of our society as a whole." He reported that the original House version of the crime bill would have been easy to vote against, but the compromise that came from the conference committee "swept away most of its noxious features." Still, the final bill did not entirely satisfy the senator. He said it was a choice between getting a crime bill with one distasteful provision and not getting a crime bill at all.

In a report issued by the Senate Government Operations Committee in November, 1973, Percy called for repeal of the no-knock provision in the law and for an amendment that would allow victims of drug raids to sue the federal government. His statements came after individual rights were abused during drug raids across the nation. Percy's comment contained no mention of his previous switch of positions on no-knock. Percy observed, "A climate has developed where, on occasion, doors are kicked in, residents are terrorized, property is destroyed, lives are irreparably scarred, and for the sake of administrative convenience, questions and answers are dealt with later. Too often, I fear, 'later' really means 'never.'" Percy introduced repeal legislation in 1974, with further comments about individual rights: "If allowed to spread, a callous disregard for the rights of some citizens in the name of law and order could set off severe public backlash against the concept of law enforcement." The Senate approved repeal of the provision in the summer of 1974, and later in the year President Ford signed the measure.

Also in 1974 Percy, as ranking Republican on the Government Operations Committee, called for a General Accounting Office investigation to determine how many government investigative units there are and how they are funded. Percy expressed fear of the proliferating federal units that do investigative and intelligence work. "We find ourselves threatened by the specter of a 'watchdog' government breeding a nation of snoopers," he said.

The first Nixon administration was faced with the emotional and highly publicized issues of the Supreme Court nominations, ABM, and SST. It was a time of testing, and Percy failed the test because he could not support the president on these matters. Ignored by the White House and the public were the dozens of times Percy had supported Nixon proposals, such as the omnibus crime bill, and had tried to work with the president's aides. But Percy's constituents were upset by his lack of support for the president on major issues, and by 1971 his popularity in Illinois had slipped dramatically.

In foreign affairs Percy and Nixon were divided on how to handle Vietnam, but despite the chasm between them on the war, Percy remained a public supporter of the Nixon foreign policy. During the 1972 election campaign Percy openly criticized the bombing of North Vietnam, but he added that Nixon had been "a great president for foreign affairs." Throughout the Watergate period, Percy remained one of the few Republicans who had any kind words for Nixon in most public appearances. In an interview during that time, Percy called the Nixon foreign policy "extraordinarily perceptive, creative, innovative, bold. I think it will have a mark on history for a long time to come." Percy did not extend that commentary to Nixon's domestic programs.

Nixon played the nation's most frustrating issue, the Vietnam war, cautiously during the 1968 election campaign against Hubert H. Humphrey, the Democratic nominee. The war belonged to the Democrats and Lyndon Johnson. By election time Johnson had escalated the U.S. commitment in Vietnam from a few military advisers to about 560,000 troops. Nixon did not need a definitive position during the campaign, and he sidestepped any specific declarations. He told the American people that he had a plan for ending the war, but in fact it was not until he took office that work began on a plan. In any case, the strategy worked, and Nixon made it through the campaign without being pressed for a clear position on the war.

Even when the president and his advisers had formulated a Vietnam plan, Nixon refused to reveal the details. He hoped to continue the Paris peace talks, hold secret talks when feasible, and withdraw U.S. troops from South Vietnam as soon as the South Vietnamese army could assume a greater role in front-line fighting. While the president outlined this Vietnamization program, he held fast to a hard line with North Vietnam in the Paris peace talks and elsewhere and left the impression publicly that he would not be played for a sucker.

On numerous occasions in the four years before the war ended for American troops, Percy said he supported the president in his overall effort to have South Vietnam assume a greater role in the fighting and in his determination to bring U.S. troops home. After the 1968 election, in anticipation of learning Nixon's secret plan to end the war, Percy joined other members of Congress in an informal moratorium on criticism of the new president's Vietnam program. During this lull in debate, Nixon and his aides hammered out the details of a withdrawal announcement. Meanwhile the moratorium became shakier as time progressed. In April, 1969, Percy, without implying any criticism of the administration's Vietnam policy, expressed his view that at least 50,000 American troops should be withdrawn from South Vietnam in that year. "Anything else than that would not do the job" of convincing the South Vietnamese that they should not place "total reliance on our security forces." With rumors from Washington that a Nixon withdrawal plan could be expected at any time, Percy said, "The trend is now very apparent [that] the Nixon administration seeks to place renewed emphasis on the South Vietnamese themselves." As time neared for Nixon to announce his program, other dovish senators also began to call for reduction of troop totals.

At midyear, 1969, Nixon announced his withdrawal program after a meeting with South Vietnam's president, Nguyen Van Thieu. Percy showed his support of the Nixon plan by organizing a demonstration of solidarity among fellow Senate critics of Vietnam just prior to Nixon's departure on an Asian tour in July. Percy organized the effort after meetings with Henry Kissinger, the president's national security adviser at the time. The demonstration of support was for the benefit of the North Vietnamese. As Percy said on the floor of the Senate, "There is nothing to be gained by prolonging the conflict." He added, "Nixon does not intend a unilateral American withdrawal from Vietnam, and Hanoi and the National Liberation Front must be aware that a majority of the American people support this position." Percy said he had polled students on 10 Illinois campuses, and the students "overwhelmingly supported the position of the administration" as opposed to pursuing military victory or unilateral withdrawal.

While Percy wanted withdrawal from Vietnam, he would not join those senators who, during the years of 1969 to 1971, wanted to establish a definite withdrawal date. Percy felt that the president should establish his own date, but he knew that Nixon probably would not do so publicly. An early attempt in Congress to set a withdrawal date came in late 1969. Senator Charles Goodell of New York proposed the end of 1970 as the date for withdrawal. Percy feared that such a date might lead to a hasty pullout, which would not be in the best interest of the United

States, and he opposed the Goodell suggestion. In an August, 1970, letter to Illinois editors, Percy said, "I strongly believe that a political settlement in Vietnam is vastly preferable to a legislated, fixed-time withdrawal, because it would end the war, not just end American participation in the war." But in February, 1971, Percy joined his Senate colleague from Illinois, Adlai E. Stevenson, in urging Nixon to declare a definite schedule· for withdrawal of all American troops from South Vietnam. Percy said a firm timetable "probably will be the only way we can bring about useful and meaningful negotiations." This was a departure from his original position of total opposition to a final deadline, but he did not offer a deadline of his own, and by the end of the war in 1973, he was calling for a fixed withdrawal date. Percy was one of the last Republicans who opposed the war to support a specific withdrawal date.

During this period Percy supported the president on broad Vietnam policy on the one hand while picking at him about specifics on the other. When Vietnam fighting reached a lull in the fall of 1969, Percy asked Nixon to end the "bombing and shelling of South Vietnam and suspend ground offensive operations as long as the enemy takes no advantage of the situation." Percy also saw the lull as an opportunity to curtail hostilities in a trade-off with North Vietnam. The president did not see the situation in the same way, though his aides treated the suggestion politely. Percy wanted to give Nixon as much negotiating room as possible, but when he saw the president veer from a basic line of Vietnamization and withdrawal, he spoke out, as he did in a television interview in February, 1971, when he said: "Our avowed purpose is to get out of Vietnam—and Indochina—and to protect our forces as we withdraw. We can argue about the tactics being used, but that is our avowed intent and purpose as prescribed by the President and endorsed by Congress."

In April, 1970, Nixon announced what became known as the Cambodia incursion. The president said that he had sent South Vietnamese and American forces on missions into Cambodia to seek out North Vietnamese troop sanctuaries. He said, "I shall meet my responsibility as Commander in Chief of our Armed Forces to take the action necessary to defend the security of our American men." Angry members of Congress accused the president of taking extraconstitutional action without having consulted Congress.

Nixon's decision to invade Cambodia touched off sparks on campuses across the nation. Protest meetings and marches were organized. On May 4, at a demonstration on the Kent State University campus, four students were shot and killed. The nation was outraged by the shootings, and Percy, obviously upset and disturbed by what had happened, addressed the Senate on May 6. He called the shootings a "tragic mistake of national significance, bringing grief and sorrow to the families involved as well as to all Americans." Percy said, "All Americans must stop their provocations of each other." He appealed for moderation and tolerance on the part of students and the federal government. The promise to "bring us together" must not be just a slogan, he said; "it must be a motto that guides our every action, every day." The Commission on Campus Unrest, appointed by the president, stated later that protest among university students was a reaction to "a . . . profound crisis in the nation as a whole."

A more direct Percy reaction to the Cambodian invasion came in a "sense of the Senate" resolution on May 14. The resolution, which was approved by the Senate, attempted to focus on the historical dilemma of whether a president could commit U.S. troops to battle without the approval of Congress. In part the resolution said, "It is declared to be the sense of the Senate that the President should not utilize the armed forces of the United States in interventions abroad for any combat activity without the express consent of the Congress." The only exception would be if the nation had to respond to a direct attack, the resolution said. Although the resolution did not bind Nixon, it could not have pleased him at a time when he badly needed Senate support of his Cambodian invasion.

Percy did not stop his criticism of President Nixon and the Cambodian affair. On June 15 he addressed the Stanford University graduating class, which included his son Roger. Percy's speech focused on dissent in American society and the responsibility of the government to "renew and rebuild itself." He outlined four steps for the renewal:

1. "Admit this war was a tragic error without military or moral justification" and end American involvement in Indochina.

2. "Vow that the U.S. no longer has any desire to play policeman to the whole world or inflict American values on their cultures."

3. "Commit full energies to nation-building at home—reversing urban decay, improving housing, education, health and welfare services."

4. "Seek out those issues on which there is consensus and marshal all of the forces in a common effort to solve problems." He cited pollution as an example of a problem that presents "no philosophical or partisan barrier to a united approach now."

By this time Nixon was not taking advice from anyone in Congress, and particularly not from someone as outspoken in his criticism as Percy had been. Any possibility of Nixon and Percy finding common ground on the war issue seemed to vanish by the summer of 1970.

The pendulum of support-opposition swung again in the fall of 1970, a few months after the Cambodian operation was announced. In October, Nixon had proposed a five-point peace plan, which included a cease-fire in Indochina. Percy submitted to the Senate a resolution, supported by his colleagues and adopted, praising Nixon's peace plan. Percy said the idea was "fair and equitable and lays the basis for ending the fighting and moving toward a just settlement of the Indochina war." Just a month before, Percy and 13 other senators from both parties had sent a letter to the president urging that the United States propose a cease-fire at the Paris peace talks. Percy followed the resolution with a trip abroad at the request of Kissinger and William P. Rogers, the secretary of state. His objective was to persuade the heads of state in the eight countries he visited to pressure Hanoi for settlement of the war. Percy took copies of the Senate resolution—"The only time we [Percy and Nixon] ever agreed on anything on Vietnam"—to the national leaders to show the Senate's support of Nixon's peace plan. Nixon specifically asked Percy to talk with Mrs. Indira Gandhi, prime minister of India, with whom Percy was personally acquainted. When he returned from his trip, Percy reported to Nixon.

While Nixon was trying to bring the war to a close without losing his bargaining power with the North Vietnamese, Percy voted for proposals that reasserted the Senate's role in making war policy. He voted for the Cooper-Church amendment to prohibit American military activities in Cambodia after July 1, 1970. The amendment did not have much impact on immediate policy because Nixon had already announced his intention of ending the invasion and pulling troops back by July. The significance of the vote was that Congress was asserting itself in making war policy. When the McGovern-Hatfield amendment to the 1971 defense-appropriations bill appeared in the Senate, Percy opposed it. The bill, which failed when only 39 senators supported it, would have cut off funds for the war after January 1, 1971, unless Congress officially declared war. Percy still could not be pushed to support the imposition of a deadline on Nixon regardless of the congressional issue involved. Nevertheless, he took the opportunity to urge Congress on to more involvement in Vietnam policy. He said after the McGovern-Hatfield amendment failed: "The Vietnam war is the worst single mistake the United States has ever made. . . . The Congress must share with the President the responsibility for bringing it to an early end." The key, he inferred, was to get Congress and the president together, not to encourage each to seek its own way.

During the 1972 election year, Percy—particularly upset by the bombing of North Vietnam, which he had opposed since the Johnson administration—lapsed uncharacteristically into mild profanity to make his point: "We should be out of Vietnam by now. North Vietnam is not going to give the prisoners of war back until we do get out. That bombing isn't worth two hoots in hell."

However, even during the bombing of North Vietnam, which was resumed later in 1972, Percy remained convinced that the administration was trying to end the conflict. He traveled to Vietnam and conferred with Secretary of State Rogers; Ellsworth Bunker, American ambassador to Vietnam; and Henry Kissinger before offering his support to the Nixon strategy. At the same time he told colleagues and reporters that Nixon had to end the conflict by late January, 1973, or else face a cutoff of funds.

At a Republican Senate caucus early in 1973, Percy introduced a resolution supporting "the efforts of the President to end the tragic conflict in Indochina now through negotiated settlement." The resolution passed, 16 to 10, on a show of hands but was not viewed as a true reflection of sentiment. Several senators had left before the vote, and there was little debate on the resolution. When the withdrawal of U.S. troops from Vietnam occurred in 1973, Percy was joyous and later often reminded persons of Nixon's accomplishment in ending the conflict for U.S. soldiers.

American involvement in the Vietnam conflict, which had so bitterly divided the nation, left its mark on Congress. The House and Senate passed legislation in 1973 restricting the war-making powers of the president. Nixon vetoed the compromise bill, but Congress overrode his veto, making it law.

On the Vietnam war issue Percy and Nixon responded to different pressures. At the time of their disagreements on Vietnam from 1969 to 1973, they had each made separate commitments to a long list of issues, all of which made their arms-length relationship predictable. Vietnam was a piece of that picture, but not the total. As president, Nixon faced many political considerations in keeping together his uneasy constituency while at the same time bringing the war to a close. Percy, on the other hand, had only a state constituency to be concerned with and his own future to chart. Complaints from Illinois, and particularly Nixon partisans, did not sway him. However, Percy was not totally opposed to Nixon's war policy. But he parted company with the president over specific aspects of Nixon's handling of the Vietnam situation. On most of the other major issues during this same period, Percy frequently followed the Republican congressional party line, but on a handful of issues, which also had great public exposure, Percy's position ran counter to the administration's. This pattern of selectivity helped build and establish the Percy reputation for independence.

Despite evidence to the contrary, Percy seldom would admit that any problems existed between him and President Nixon. Percy reminded questioners that he had sponsored some administration legislation and told them that relations could not be better. One of the proposals that Percy had sponsored for the president was the administration's plan for reorganization of the executive branch. Percy introduced the package to the Senate Government Operations Committee in 1972. By then Percy had become ranking Republican member of the committee. He believed the reorganization would make the executive more responsive to the legislative branch. The administration's proposal did not get far and eventually got lost among the problems of Watergate and the shuffling of people in and out of the White House. Percy was chief sponsor of the executive's revenue-sharing bills in 1972, a program approved by Congress. He also cosponsored the administration's environmental package that year. In the Watergate period, when the administration's domestic programs almost came to a standstill, Percy did not sponsor or cosponsor any major legislative proposals.

The relationship between Percy and Nixon ultimately put the Illinois senator under the gun with his constituents, his Senate colleagues, the White House staff, and the media, which seemed to delight at any indication of a rift between the two men. After Percy's anti-administration votes in 1970 and 1971, some Illinois newspapers with strong Republican heritages called for the senator to change parties if he could not be more supportive of Nixon programs.

Although the reaction of the media was annoying, Percy's difficulties with Nixon's staff were more serious. President Nixon's aides had utter disdain for Congress, and their attitudes made even the most pro-Nixon senators and congressmen recoil. The president's staff selected Percy for particular attention, although they also directed sabotage efforts at other senators, such as Charles Mathias and Jacob Javits, who often voted against the president. The loyalty test applied even to those considered more in step with Nixon. When Senator Robert J. Dole of Kansas crossed Nixon on an issue or two, the White House abandoned him and publicly embarrassed him by removing him from his position as chairman of the Republican National Committee.

In 1970 Nixon had used his influence in key Senate contests and had won a few and lost a few. With the help of Vice-President Agnew, Nixon had purged one liberal senator, Charles Goodell of New York. The administration threw its weight into the New York Senate race behind James L. Buckley and deliberately sank the incumbent Goodell. Percy campaigned as hard for Goodell as he had for other Republicans in 1970. The administration obviously hoped the lesson in New York would deter other renegade Republicans who strayed from the Nixon line. After the election Nixon commented that he expected more support from Percy in the future. The inference seemed clear; if Percy did not stay in line, someone else might have administration support in 1972 to challenge Percy in an Illinois Republican primary. The Nixon attitude and the purge of Goodell may have been the catalysts for Percy's independence drive in the 1972 election. In a speech during the 1972 campaign, Percy said to a gathering of Illinois AFL-CIO members, "I think you know one thing: There isn't any political machine, there isn't any business interest, there isn't any labor lobby or any other lobby that controls my vote. Nobody owns me."

Maybe it was the quality of competition in the 1972 Senate race that gave Percy an opportunity to stress his independence of any lobby, and particularly of President Nixon. Roman Pucinski, an effective Chicago Democrat but an inept statewide campaigner, never mounted much of an offensive against Percy. Percy's well-financed advertising campaign emphasized an appeal to independents and Democrats. A Percy slogan proclaimed, "He is his own man," and a campaign brochure offered a testimonial from Senator Birch Bayh, a Democrat from Indiana: "Your vote was one of the handful which helped write a new chapter in profiles in courage." Senator Bayh was referring to Percy's 1970 vote that helped defeat the nomination of Judge Carswell.

After the 1972 election, published reports surfaced in Washington that the tentative handholding between the president and Percy had ended. Until that time there were frequent public reconcilations, and the two obviously tried to make it through the election campaign without an open breach. Percy acknowledged that there were Percy-haters in the White House, although he quickly noted his supporters were there too. But by now it had become obvious that Percy's support for any proposal was its kiss of death in the White House. One such proposal, which affected his home state, was the plan to build a second metropolitan airport in rural Waterloo, Illinois, across the Mississippi River from St. Louis. The measure had been sent by the Department of Transportation to the desk of John D. Ehrlichman, the president's chief domestic adviser, late in 1972 for his consideration and decision. Obviously the matter came to his attention because of its political implications. Many people in St. Louis who had contributed large amounts to the 1972 Nixon campaign were publicly opposed to the Illinois site, and they began to pressure the president's aides. Supporters of the Illinois site urged Percy to press for the program, but Percy and his staff moved cautiously. They knew that Percy's active endorsement most certainly would have doomed the project. However, the plan got lost in the events of Watergate early in 1973 and Ehrlichman's subsequent departure from Washington. Further attempts by Percy to force a decision met with little success, although the proposal was sent back to the Department of Transportation for further consideration.

Through much of the first Nixon term the White House forces against Percy were led by H. R. Haldeman, Nixon's chief of staff, and Ehrlichman. In commenting on his troubles with the pair, known as the "German mafia," in 1973, Percy said, "Historically, the Republican umbrella has been broad enough to shelter an invigorating variety of opinions. Unhappily, however, some of the President's recently departed advisers [Haldeman and Ehrlichman] seemed determined to check the free flow of ideas within our party. Their concept of a 'good' Republican was a rubber stamp incarnate."

The most intense activity against Percy occurred in the first two years of the Nixon administration. Documents revealed during the investigation of the president's aides by the Senate Watergate committee in 1973 told of efforts to organize a letter-telegram-telephone campaign against Percy and two other senators, Charles Goodell of New York and Charles

Mathias of Maryland. The idea behind the plot was to discredit the three by protesting their "anti-Nixon activities." The White House persons involved included Haldeman, Jeb Stuart Magruder, and Lyn Nofziger, a Nixon aide who had formerly served California's Ronald Reagan. These same persons were involved in letter-telegram campaigns against the media, particularly the television networks and the *Washington Post* and the *New York Times*. Part of the campaign against Percy included getting editorials favorable to Nixon and opposed to Percy into the Copley group of newspapers in Aurora, Joliet, Wheaton, Elgin, and Springfield. Under the guidance of James Copley, who died in 1973, the papers seldom swerved from allegiance to Nixon.

In a memo to Haldeman, Magruder noted that "on Percy, we have a group in Illinois and in other parts of the country who are sending telegrams and letters to him, particularly on the war but also on all issues that he seemed to disagree with the President." Most of the memos were written in the first two years of the Nixon administration. As another memo stated: "This program needs to be subtle and worked out well so that [the senators] receive these items from their home districts as well as other points around the country." The zeal with which the plans were laid out is evident in the tone of one memo from Haldeman. He called for the campaign to criticize the senators "on their consistent opposition to the President on everything he is trying to do for the country." Haldeman and Magruder both became central figures in the Watergate scandals.

Earlier in 1973 Percy learned that he and 10 other Republicans had been on a Haldeman "blacklist" in 1969. The blacklist was not the famous "political enemies list" revealed in the testimony by John W. Dean III, Nixon's legal counsel, at the Watergate hearings. Columnist Jack Anderson, who made the blacklist public, said the 11 were to be punished by being denied White House invitations, patronage, and campaign help. Percy said he was not surprised to learn of the blacklist and could care less if he were not on the White House's social-acceptability list. His children were also dropped from White House invitation lists.

Haldeman and Ehrlichman believed Percy played to the media and used the media to attack Nixon. Perhaps they saw Percy as more of a potential national personality than other senators, and that is why they often focused on him. Their dislike of Percy bordered on loathing. After the 1972 elections, during which there appeared to be a truce between the Percy and Nixon camps, Washington press reports claimed that White House staffers were out to end the chances of Percy being nominated in 1976 even before Percy could get his campaign effort into gear. While there was some displeasure with Percy's ideological positions, his tactics in the Senate, and his romance with the media, what Haldeman and Ehrlichman really disliked was Percy's personal style. As far as these two were concerned, the perfect administration man wore subdued suits, spoke only when spoken to, carried the baggage when it became necessary, and deferred to the chief at all times. Percy did not fit that mold, or any other. Percy said, "They felt because he [Nixon] was a Republican and I was a Republican senator, therefore I should rubber stamp and approve whatever they felt they wanted, whether it's ABM or Carswell or Vietnam." Furthermore, they felt that Percy socialized too much. He spoke too quickly in front of microphones. His enemies in the White House viewed him as shallow and opportunistic. The ultimate insult that Nixon staffers could muster was to refer to Percy as "shell and hollow," an obvious twist on Bell & Howell. True believers in the White House saw Percy as a phony.

A former cabinet member in the Nixon administration said, "They had some strange ideas about loyalty. You could support them on four things in a row, but if you took the wrong direction on the fifth, they did not like it one bit." He remembers that the White House attitude toward senators often reflected who the senators had been seen talking to or socializing with. The same former cabinet officer recalls discussing Percy's vote on Carswell with Peter Flanigan, then a presidential aide. When the cabinet officer said that there ought to be some consideration given Percy for having studied the matter carefully before arriving at his decision, Flanigan told him that he obviously did not understand the meaning of loyalty.

Other attempts to discredit Percy were made. There had been rumors for some years that in 1969 Nixon's communications director, Herbert Klein, had attempted to plant stories with the *Chicago Tribune* regarding Percy's attitudes about the war. The *Tribune*, Percy's harshest newspaper critic in Illinois, has on several occasions during Percy's political career jumped on the senator for his anti-Nixon activities and statements. The White House hoped the stories would hurt Percy's image in the nation's heartland. Concrete evidence to support this rumor surfaced during investigations of the Senate Watergate committee in the fall of 1973, when a committee member, Lowell P. Weicker, Jr., presented a White House memorandum from Nixon to Klein. In the memorandum, dated October 3, 1969, Nixon asked Klein to contact the *Tribune* and suggest that it come down hard on Percy for "his ties with the peace group." Editors of the *Tribune* denied any contact with Klein on the subject and said that any disagreements the paper had with Percy were not prompted by the White House. A spokesman in Percy's office said the senator had no contact with "peace groups" at the time of the memo and suggested that the White House had deliberately used derogatory words to identity a group of senators who were pressing for a reduction of U.S. forces in South Vietnam. This document confirmed Percy's suspicions, held since 1970, that the White House was leaking information "that was designed to embarrass or weaken me in Illinois."

The harassment by Nixon's aides got so bad in 1970 that Percy sought a chance to talk to Nixon about the problem. The opportunity arose during a meeting held officially for Percy to inform the president about his visit to the heads of state in eight nations. Percy remembers that Nixon seemed impatient and inattentive during the report, which Percy presented with Henry Kissinger present. When Percy got up to leave, Nixon indicated a desire to talk about politics. He told Percy that he needed him in 1972 when they both would be up for reelection. Percy agreed it would be nice to work together but that it would be difficult because Nixon's staff seemed bent on the senator's destruction. Nixon asked Percy for examples of intimidation and Percy responded with a story of Nixon staff harassment during Senate consideration of the antiballistic missile. "When I finished that example," Percy said, "I looked to see whether he was aware of it. Here was an overt attempt by his staff, but I had no indication of whether he knew about that or not." Nixon asked for another example, and Percy told of his suspicions that the Nixon staff had planted stories in the *Chicago Tribune*. "They chose my own home state newspaper," Percy said, "and you're trying to chop me up." Percy added that he felt the newspaper should resent being used by Nixon's staff, particularly if there was a motive and a purpose to the plant. Percy related other examples, and Nixon listened, never giving any indication that he knew of the efforts or that he found them unreasonable. The conversation, according to Percy, turned hot a time or two, and Kissinger left before it ended.

After Percy told Nixon of the problem he felt a little better, but he still had mixed feelings: "I had difficulty overcoming a feeling of resentment because of the attempted intimidation of me as a United States senator to find some means by which my judgment could be influenced not by facts on a decision, but by other factors that would reach me or get to me."

Percy believes the obvious attempts to intimidate him ended with the Nixon conversation, although his relationship with the Nixon staff members turned colder. He still did not get far with them when it came to Percy-sponsored programs. The White House aides, especially Haldeman and Ehrlichman according to Percy, "didn't understand the Constitution and didn't apparently believe in it," particularly as it applied to the separation of powers. There has been some speculation that Percy might have been more successful in passing legislation, getting projects for Illinois, and improving his image if he had gone along more with Nixon and his staff members. Percy doubts it. He said, "There's no way you can be cozy with them without subordinating your principles to it, because the way to get cozy with them would have been to go along with them on the questions of principle that I simply couldn't." The votes that were crucial to Haldeman and Ehrlichman were the ones that Percy could not, on principle, go along with. On Carswell, for example, Percy said, "We realized when we voted against him that this is one of those litmus tests that we had flunked. In their judgment there's just no way to get along unless you go along."

Did the White House staff pursue this feud with Percy on its own, or did orders come from the president? Obviously, in the case of the Klein order to contact the *Chicago Tribune*, Nixon directed the activity. Beyond that incident the answer is not entirely clear. However, the White House under Haldeman and Ehrlichman seldom did anything that did not have the president's stamp of approval. They had license to speak for the president and often did. Therefore, it must be concluded that the activity against Percy was condoned by Nixon, and even occasionally ordered by him.

After Nixon became president, he and Percy met on several occasions to discuss everything from politics, such as at the White House session in 1970, to the problems of the aged and questions of international diplomacy. Often these discussions took place on airplane trips between Washington and Chicago.

On one plane trip in June, 1973, Percy and Nixon discussed Prime Minister Edward Gough Whitlam of Australia, an outspoken critic of American involvement in Vietnam and particularly the incursion into Cambodia in 1970. Apparently Whitlam's comments had infuriated Nixon. On a visit to Australia in 1971 Percy had talked with Whitlam, then leader of the opposition party, and knew that Whitlam's criticism of U.S. involvement in Southeast Asia had been greeted with enthusiasm by the Australian people. In 1973 Whitlam had informed Percy and other U.S. officials that he would be visiting Mexico and Canada and would like to stop off in Washington for a talk with Nixon. Percy believes that until he and Nixon discussed the situation on the plane, Nixon had no intention of meeting with Whitlam. Percy told Nixon that American-Australian relations were at stake and that a rebuff to Whitlam would only anger the Australian people. Percy also said that Whitlam had not been any more critical of American war activities "than millions of Americans." Percy hoped Nixon would invite Whitlam to Washington for a breakfast, dinner, or luncheon. He told Nixon, "You cannot—having spent a week with [Leonid] Brezhnev—say you don't have an hour for an ally." Nixon said on the plane that he would meet with Whitlam, and later in the day the president announced his intentions. The meeting occurred a month later.

On another plane trip in 1973, after both Nixon and Percy had spoken at a national conference on the aging in Chicago, the two discussed problems of the elderly. Percy had just completed a series of hearings on nursing homes, so he talked at length on the subject. After the discussion Percy remembers that Nixon issued a series of executive orders implementing legislation to aid elderly citizens that Percy had been working on for more than a year. Percy believes that his conversation with Nixon raised concerns for the elderly to a higher priority on the White House agenda.

Sometimes the Percy-Nixon discussions happened during periods of great disagreement, and they often appeared, as publicly reported, to be reconciliation gatherings. Percy remembers most of them as cordial discussions, often only on a single subject, with little small talk. Meetings of the two without another person in attendance were rare. Although he enjoyed some access to the president, there was one occasion when the president ignored a plea for a meeting. That was in 1972 when the administration and Percy were locked in combat over consumer agency legislation. Percy sought a presidential session to thrash out a compromise, but the White House did not respond.

Percy's increased stature on the national scene and his willingness to comment on topics of national interest set the stage for his role as critic on the most cataclysmic issue to arise in Washington during the Percy tenure, and one of the most significant in the history of the United States. In a word—Watergate. It started as a break-in, became a cover-up scandal, and ended with the resignation of a president.

It would be hard to find a public official in the nation not directly connected with the litigation or investigations of Watergate who spoke as frequently on the subject as Percy. Most Democrats said nothing, preferring to let Watergate revelations speak for themselves. Most other Republicans avoided commenting on the incidents as they occurred, choosing to defend the president when possible and occasionally accusing the Democrats of conducting a partisan witch-hunt. If senators and representatives were not awed by the prospect of having to be actual participants in the final, historic stages of Watergate, they were aware of the political ramifications, and silence became the surest course. But Percy, following no particular lead or advice from fellow Republicans, commented with frequency. Some senators grabbed single bigger headlines, but few could match the Percy record for sustained public discussion.

Percy had not participated in any Watergate or 1972 election campaign shenanigans. Also he had been only a minor target of the White House activists in the Watergate period. Operatives of the Committee to Reelect the President did stand watch at Percy's Washington office during the 1972 campaign. The surveillance on Percy, which was revealed in deliberations of the Senate committee investigating Watergate, amused Percy, but perhaps only because it did not amount to much. He said, "Strange thing was when Lowell Weicker discovered this he interviewed the fellow, who didn't understand why they did it, because he didn't recognize anyone or know anyone anyway. He thought it was rather a stupid assignment to stand out there for a couple of weeks.... He recognized no one. They were all constituents from Illinois." There were some reports of a Percy office being bugged, but an investigation proved there was nothing to them.

Percy first commented on Watergate before it became a national scandal. During his 1972 campaign for the Senate, Percy said he was satisfied that the Nixon administration was not involved in the bugging of the Democratic National Committee headquarters at the Watergate complex in Washington. On October 18, about four months after the Watergate break-in, he said a commission should have been appointed to investigate the bugging case as soon as it became public knowledge. As the Washington Post began to unearth the details of the labyrinthine plot to cover up the responsibility for the break-in, Percy again voiced confidence that President Nixon had no involvement in the incident. From then until the spring of 1973, Percy commented occasionally, but the rhetoric took no particular direction. That reflected the way in which the news regarding Watergate was unfolding. In those days the White House steadfastly refused to acknowledge any cover-up, and investigative news reports were still just barely scratching the surface. Newspapers worked overtime to shed light on the subject, but even the most aggressive papers were unable to provide continuity until Chief U.S. District Judge John J. Sirica made public a letter he had received in March, 1973, from James W. McCord, Jr., one of the Watergate burglars who were on trial. McCord revealed that perjury had been committed in the trial earlier in the year and that higher-ups were involved in the Watergate plot.

If there is a starting point for greater Percy comment on Watergate, it is April 30, 1973. On that day President Nixon announced the firing of John W. Dean, his legal counsel, and the resignations of H. R. Haldeman and John D. Ehrlichman, his chief of staff and domestic counselor respectively. That day also marked the first public acknowledgment by the White House that a cover-up existed. On national television early the following morning, and in subsequent public comments, Percy told of the insults and affronts he had endured at the hands of the president's men. Other senators joined in the criticism, at last feeling free to expose their relationships with the White House staff and no longer afraid of retaliation.

Hardly had the Senate convened at noon on May 1, the day after Nixon's announcement, than Percy brought to the floor a "sense of the Senate" resolution requesting President Nixon to appoint a special prosecutor, subject to Senate confirmation, to head the Watergate investigation. The resolution was submitted only a day after Nixon had nominated Secretary of Defense Elliot L. Richardson for the attorney general's job. Percy contended later that he had intended to bring the resolution anyway, but the president's nomination of Richardson, who would then take charge of the Watergate investigation, made it more timely. Percy had cleared the resolution with the Senate leadership the day before and had 18 cosponsors from both sides of the Senate aisle. Percy explained, "I believed that such an appointment would not only insure swift and impartial prosecution of the accused but would also convince the public that the executive branch was not investigating itself." The resolution passed on a voice vote with only five senators present. Later that afternoon Senator Carl T. Curtis of Nebraska asked the Senate to reconsider the resolution. Curtis and a few other senators objected that the resolution had not been cleared in committee and that senators had not been notified of its consideration on the floor. Part of the reaction by Curtis came because he was opposed to the subject of the resolution. Percy said that he gave written notice to all senators but that it might not have reached everyone in time. Percy consented to reconsideration with the understanding that a final vote would occur no later than May 8. That did not satisfy the senators, and they dropped the matter. There also was insufficient support for reconsideration. The episode left Percy somewhat chagrined, and it detracted some from his achievement. In the aftermath, Senator Adlai Stevenson of Illinois also criticized the resolution on substance. He argued that it did little more than attempt to stake a congressional claim on approving a special prosecutor. He wanted more specifics as to the authority of a prosecutor and White House assurances of the prosecutor's independence. Ultimately, procedure for selection of a special prosecutor did include more specifics, many of which were suggested by Stevenson.

On May 18 Archibald Cox was named special prosecutor with a directive to look into Watergate with prosecution of the accused as his goal. Thus, Percy made his point with the resolution and became one of the first Republican senators to pressure the president for a full disclosure of information.

The president resented Percy's resolution, viewing it as rude and unnecessary. Even his later admission that his first reaction to it was based on a mistaken assumption that Percy had not supported Richardson's appointment never explained the outburst that made headlines. The *Chicago Tribune* quoted Nixon as saying, in a closed meeting of his cabinet, that Percy would never be president "as long as I have anything to say about it." The outburst against Pery upset the senator's supporters because plans had been made to announce the formation of an exploratory committee to determine the extent of backing for Percy as the Republican presidential nominee in 1976. Up to that point Percy's strategy had been to attempt to neutralize Nixon's influence in advance of the 1976 convention so that early attempts by the senator's backers to round up convention support would not be impeded. It took a plane ride with Nixon in June and another meeting in the fall before the matter settled down and Nixon made public acknowledgment of his mistake on the facts. While Nixon in one way apologized for jumping to a conclusion, he never retracted the remark about keeping Percy from the presidency.

Although there were aides who criticized the timing, the announcement of the formation of a committee to help Percy determine whether he should become a serious candidate for the presidency was made in June. The importance of the announcement so close to the breakthrough in the Watergate scandal—actually a little more than a month afterward— was that the two became irrevocably intermingled in the following months. One could hardly separate the man who spoke so often on the evils of Watergate from his goal of sitting in the White House.

On some occasions Percy's Watergate statements were random in nature and covered the same ground repeatedly, giving rise to criticism by media representatives that Percy had nothing new to say. These comments often came in the unstructured format of a press conference, where the subject of a question was predictable but not the thrust nor the answer. Percy occasionally took the reporters' bait and went beyond his previous statements, irritating his staff members and giving rise to some editorial criticism. On other occasions Percy used prepared statements to more carefully express his ideas on the full range of Watergate: missing tapes, impeachment, the office of the presidency, and political reforms. An example was the statement prepared for the Senate on June 25, 1973. In it, Percy said that the Senate and others should be vigorous in pursuit of the truth about Watergate and its associated questions but that they must be mindful of the separation-of-powers doctrine and resist the temptation to subpoena the president to appear before the Senate Water-gate committee. He cited the danger of attempting to put the president at the "beck and call of Congress. And the President cannot be subordinate to the Congress or the Judiciary any more than senators, congressmen, or judges can be subordinate to the President if we are to retain our constitutional system." He also warned Congress against asking or forcing the president to resign. At no place in the June 25 statement did Percy endorse the Nixon position on Watergate or reverse any of his criticisms. Still, the tone sounded to some extent like a sympathetic statement. A headline in the *Chicago Tribune* said, "Percy Defends Nixon's Handling of Watergate." Additional perspective on the statement must include the knowledge that on the day of the statement John Dean testified before the Senate Watergate committee and began to tell his story of Nixon's involvement. Until then no charges had been made linking the president directly with Watergate.

In comments specifically mentioning Nixon's actions, Percy hit particularly hard at the president's obligation to release all pertinent information on Watergate. On May 6, 1973, Percy said, "We [the nation] are strong enough to survive even the most chilling truths and wise enough to learn from them." Less than a month later in Galesburg, Illinois, Percy said, "The President can secure the nation's trust if only he now will trust the nation with the whole truth." He also called Watergate "a pervasive, unprecedented pattern of misconduct, impropriety, and deceit."

The pattern of Percy's comments on full disclosure parallels attempts by various agencies, committees, and individuals to get the complete White House record of tapes, once their existence was revealed. At the Senate Watergate hearings in July, 1973, it was learned that Nixon's Oval Office conversations had been recorded since 1971. Later that month, Special Prosecutor Cox subpoenaed the tapes.

By the fall of 1973, Nixon's refusal to release the tapes had become a major issue. When Cox announced he would begin a court fight to obtain them, he was fired. After an impeachment-inquiry resolution was introduced in the House, on October 23, 1973, Nixon surrendered certain tapes and documents to Judge Sirica.

On October 27, 1973, in the wake of the firing of Cox and the related resignation of Attorney General Richardson, Percy prepared a resolution to create an office of special Watergate prosecutor. This went beyond the resolution he submitted in May. The new prosecutor, Percy said, would be appointed by Nixon, subject to congressional confirmation, but could not be dismissed by the president. Under Percy's plan the president would have been required to file with Congress a notice of dismissal, which could have become effective only if neither the House nor the Senate voted it down. The plan also stipulated that the president could relieve the special prosecutor of his duties only for neglect of duty, malfeasance in office, or violation of the statute that had created his office. Percy criticized Nixon's declaration that the Watergate investigation would move ahead with the appointment of Henry Petersen of the Department of Justice. Percy said that Nixon's course eliminated congressional involvement. The resolution was offered, but the appointment of the special prosecutor was settled between Nixon and Congress later without resorting to the Percy resolution. On November 1, 1973, Leon Jaworski was appointed special prosecutor.

Although the Percy proposal got bypassed, some persons had viewed it as an ideal arrangement. Washington columnist Charles Bartlett said, "The great virtue of the alternative proposed by Sen. Charles Percy is that it has roots in the precedent set in the process of unraveling the Teapot Dome scandal. Percy wants the president to pick a special prosecutor who will be subject to confirmation by the Senate. The only diversion from the Teapot Dome precedent is that President Coolidge named two men, a Republican and a Democrat, to serve as special counsel." Bartlett concluded, "The innovation of the Percy proposal is an effort to protect the special prosecutor against precipitous discharge by the President."

Following a White House statement that several subpoenaed tapes never existed, Percy on November 6 again called on Nixon to put everything on the table. Later that month he announced that Nixon planned to meet with congressional members to discuss Watergate. "I think this is the beginning of full and total disclosure," he said optimistically. "Anything related to the possibility of criminal activity should and must be revealed. I think the President is prepared to do this now." For a week in December, during what Nixon called "Operation Candor," members of Congress met with Nixon at the White House in a series of highly publicized meetings. Mixed reports came from the sessions, but few of those attending claimed that Nixon had cleared up any of the Watergate questions.

In February, 1974, when Nixon failed to provide the specific tapes and documents demanded by Jaworski, Percy said that Nixon's refusal broke a personal pledge made to him by Alexander M. Haig, Nixon's new chief of staff. According to Percy, at the "candor" meeting he attended in the White House, Haig made an "absolute commitment" to Percy that the president would submit whatever information was required. Percy said that Haig had assured him he was speaking for the president, who happened to be standing a few feet away in conversation with others.

White House refusal to release tapes and documents to Jaworski in defiance of a court order, Percy said, would constitute a "high crime" that "ensures impeachment." At a Chicago press conference shortly afterward Percy came dangerously close to calling for the president's resignation, so close in fact that the Chicago Tribune headlined that Percy had issued such a call. Later, the paper admitted that the headline had drawn the wrong conclusion from Percy's remarks. When pressure for Nixon's resignation increased later in the year and several large newspapers—including the Tribune—called for the president's resignation or impeachment, Percy only noted that Nixon was a "vastly weakened President" from the landslide victor of 1972. He said it was becoming "increasingly difficult for Nixon to govern," but he urged Nixon to continue to be active in foreign affairs.

Percy would not listen to any excuses for not making the tapes available. The White House repeatedly stated that certain tapes could not be presented to Jaworski because of national-security questions. Percy discarded that reason with all the rest: "I have personally said to General Haig that the cloak of national security will not wash any longer; the people will not believe it; the Congress does not believe it; I do not believe it." He said if the White House did not trust the special prosecutor then it ought to get a new one. But if that happens, Percy said, national security should not be the reason because "no one believes that any longer."

Meanwhile the House Judiciary Committee began its hearings on the president's impeachment. In a March 10 national television appearance, Percy commented on how Nixon's refusal to provide the tapes could lead to impeachment. He said if Jaworski took the tape request to the Supreme Court and "if the President then refused to abide by an order of the Supreme Court, in my judgment that is an impeachable offense, and I would vote for impeachment because no man, be he President or otherwise, in this country can place himself above the law."

It seemed inevitable that Percy's comments on Watergate would evoke a response from Nixon. On March 15, 1974, the president appeared in Chicago before a group of sympathetic partisans. During the question and answer session that followed Nixon's prepared remarks, James Bell, a state senator from Joliet, Illinois, said, "In my district you are thought of belovedly by thousands of people, and I think you ought to hear that." Nixon responded, "Perhaps you ought to tell your U.S. senator that." After an audience response of laughter and applause, Nixon added, "Let me be sure that no one misunderstood my remarks about Senator Percy. He obviously has the right that anybody has to be a candidate for the nomination of President of the United States. He has great ability, as I've often pointed out." Percy took the jab resolutely. Nixon made it "in good gamesmanship," Percy countered. "It was a humorous comment." Percy had declined an invitation to be with Nixon at the meeting, indicating he had a previous commitment.

In mid-April both the House committee and Jaworski subpoenaed additional tapes. The White House, through Haig and Nixon's chief legal counsel, James D. St. Clair, repeated the president's contention that the tapes already released to Sirica covered all the relevant information needed for the prosecutor's investigations. This did not satisfy Percy. In a television interview on April 22, 1974, Percy said that the failure to hand over the tapes to the prosecutor and the House committee appeared to be "impeding justice. I continue to see reluctance, a dragging of feet, almost what might be considered a hindrance of justice."

On April 30, in lieu of the tapes demanded by the investigators, Nixon released edited transcripts of his Watergate conversations. After the transcripts were made public, Haig said, "The President has now put out for public assessment what we consider to be all of the relevant information on the Watergate story."

Pursuing the pledge Haig made to him in 1973, Percy had begun a correspondence with Haig on the question of Jaworski's request for additional tapes. Percy now brought Jaworski into his correspondence with Haig, and at one point in May made public a letter he received from the special prosecutor which replied to the White House contentions. In it

Jaworski said, "The special prosecutor should determine what documents and recordings are important for matters within its jurisdiction. The White House is not privy to the scope or results of our investigations and, therefore, is in no position to judge what material is required for the pursuit of those investigations and the prosecution of any trials." Jaworski said the White House cooperation "cannot be measured by the volume of materials produced. One must look at each request on its merits." One of Percy's motives in publishing the letter was to reaffirm his position. He said, "I urge the White House to reverse its present position and spare us unnecessary and risky confrontations. We should allow those who are duly constituted, and vested with the authority, to decide what is relevant and necessary."

In presenting the correspondence, Percy acknowledged in brief some of the editorial criticism he had received for speaking so frequently on Nixon and Watergate. The criticism had focused on the possibility that he might some day sit in judgment of the president in a Senate trial. Percy said, "I do not prejudge the matters now under investigation. I recognize that ... I may be called upon to sit as a juror in judgment of these critical matters. However, it is not improper, and indeed I believe it is essential, to point out my deep concern about the manner in which the White House is responding to the special prosecutor and to the House Judiciary Committee." Nixon should turn over the actual tapes and not just transcripts of specific conversations, Percy said. As to whether this route constituted an impeachable offense because it was not in compliance with the subpoenas, Percy's comment was that "the House is the supreme and sole authority to try impeachment. It's the responsibility of the House to determine what they require."

Most senators avoided speculation about impeachment while the House hearings were going on. Through much of that time, opinion polls showed there was greater public sentiment for a presidential resignation than for impeachment and a trial. Some in Congress worried that impeachment would bring the nation a burdensome set of woes. Speaker of the House Carl Albert was one who expressed that concern. But not Percy, who said, "I think this is a very strong country with the most literate electorate in the world and best informed. We have gone through all kinds of stress and strain in this country, and we can take it."

As the House committee hearings were drawing to a close, Percy grew pessimistic: "I have the ominous feeling we will have a trial in the Senate." Percy and most of the other members of the Senate were prepared for that possibility as events now moved rapidly in that direction. On July 24, the Supreme Court ruled that all subpoenaed tapes must be turned over to Judge Sirica; a few days later the House Judiciary Committee voted to recommend impeachment.

The final Watergate bombshell exploded on August 5, when Nixon released tapes of conversations that had taken place in the White House on June 23, 1972. They were so devastating in their indictment of Nixon that many of the president's staunchest supporters deserted him. Capitol Hill activity in those days centered on attempts by some members of Congress to pressure Nixon into resigning. Percy kept quiet during most of this time, as did other Republican senators considered to be longtime critics of Nixon. Only when the resignation came—on August 9, 1974—did Percy appear on television and comment about Nixon. He deplored the deceit but preferred to look ahead to other problems, such as how legal matters involving Nixon would be handled. Percy felt that the constitutional intent in situations such as Watergate was met by the resignation, although he felt the nation could have survived an impeachment and trial. Percy said, "The end was accomplished through the use of the impeachment process, even though that process was not completed."

In his comments on the effects of Watergate on the presidency, Percy called for a restructuring: "Watergate really was a result of an overreaction of the President to try to get away from the morass that he got into as President, and then he tried to isolate himself." Percy said that the presidency is too much for one man, and the restructuring could begin by eliminating some of the more ceremonial functions of the office. He noted that many foreign nations have a president for receiving and entertaining diplomats and performing other ceremonial work and prime ministers to run their countries. In the United States the president must fill too many roles, Percy said. The president is president, prime minister, chairman of his own political party, and often has to serve as secretary of state. "There has to be a restructuring of the job to make it more manageable," Percy concluded.

As Watergate became a national obsession, it was obvious to Republicans and Democrats that the Republican party could be in for some rough times in the off-year congressional elections of 1974. The resignation took much of the pressure off Republicans in advance of the elections, but it nevertheless was a difficult year for the party. Amid hints of potential Democratic landslides, Republicans tried to restore grass-roots confidence in the party's ability to shake off Watergate and avoid responsibility for it. Percy joined those who said the party should not be blamed for criminal and unethical acts in the White House and pointed out that the 1972 presidential campaign was run by a committee set up outside the regular party apparatus.

One of Percy's more extensive references to the responsibilities of the party came in a speech on February 8, 1974, at the Lincoln Day dinner of the United Republican Fund of Illinois. He called on Republicans not to become apologists for the offenses of Watergate. He said the acts are far removed from the traditional values and the "principles and beliefs of the

Republican party." Later in his remarks Percy called for a response from the party to Watergate. He said that the GOP should "devise and enact long overdue reforms in the areas of campaign financing and public disclosure by officeholders." He asked for a commitment from the party to the rule of law and a pledge that those who committed illegal acts be dealt with justly but firmly. Percy wanted the party to "reaffirm our profound wariness of 'big brother' intervention in our daily lives, whether it comes in the form of wiretapping our phones or permitting army intelligence to keep files on private citizens." Finally, he called for an end to secrecy and duplicity in government, which he said produced first Vietnam and then Watergate.

In other speeches Percy returned to a favorite theme: broaden the membership of the party. In a speech at Burlingame, California, he first called for the party to disassociate itself from Watergate and then open its doors to a diverse membership in order to avoid losses at election time. "We must be the party of the open door," he said. "We must be much broader based. We want the bankers, sure, but we want their depositors too. There's a lot more of them. We want the doctors, yes. But we want their patients too."

Congress responded to Watergate by wrestling again with laws governing campaign financing, a subject frequently before the body. Disclosure of contributions for congressional and presidential campaigns was required by law beginning April 7, 1972, but loopholes remained as evidenced by the fund-raising activities of the Committee to Reelect the President, which was heavily involved in Watergate. In a speech at the National Press Club on May 30, 1973, Percy discussed ridding society of the "stains of Watergate" and suggested several reforms that Congress should undertake. He called for "a strict limit on all campaign spending, not just media expenditures; a blanket prohibition on all but token cash contributions; a limit on the amount a single individual can contribute to insure that ambassadorships are removed from the auction block; the elimination of dummy fund-raising committees; effective enforcement machinery; and creation of a blue-ribbon commission to investigate every aspect of our election laws."

Percy talked for months about strict election-law reforms along the lines of his May 30 speech. When resolutions were submitted to the Senate late in 1973 and again in early 1974 for public financing of federal campaigns, Percy voted for the measures and spoke for their passage on the Senate floor. In 1974 the Senate approved a public-financing plan and sent it to the House. It became law later in the year. In the meantime Percy continued his bombardment against the evils of big money. In February, 1974, Percy said that "unquestionably" big money is a corrupting influence in politics. He said by 1972 "the nation had become so cynical about politics and politicians, in fact, that spying and break-ins were widely assumed to be commonplace facets of campaign strategy. I for one do not believe they are politically commonplace at all." He said that elections should be won or lost on the merits of the candidates and that no financial contributor should be allowed to place himself in a position to extract special treatment. Accompanying these comments were pledges by Percy to make full financial disclosure if he became an active presidential candidate in 1976.

In subsequent speeches Percy recognized a degree of hopelessness in the effort for election reform without an accompanying improvement in governmental behavior. "Government has long been viewed as foolish, bureaucratic, and hopelessly extravagant," he said. "But only recently has it became an object of national contempt." He added to election reform the need to end "duplicity and secrecy" in government and called for those in political life to seek the people's trust again: "I don't know if we can reverse these trends.... We have got to revamp communications between candidate and voter, government and the governed. It is time, quite simply, to trust the people with the truth."

To inferences that Watergate had not taught Congress any lessons, Percy responded with the example of the exploratory committee for his presidential campaign. On national television in April, 1974, he said, "We've learned a great deal. Not a penny has been contributed or can be contributed to my campaign for the exploratory committee that is in cash—not a single penny.... We limit the amount that any individual or any group can give. We report fully every single penny that has been collected, and we report fully on every single expenditure.... I think we learned a great deal about getting away from these suitcases full of cash that got us into the excesses of that [1972] campaign."

Percy will not be remembered as the person who blew the whistle on Watergate or the person who finally persuaded a reluctant president to release White House tapes or to resign. He was not a member of the Senate Watergate investigating committee and so had no vote. In one sense Percy used Watergate to widen the gap between him and the president and also as part of his political strategy. It gave Percy exposure on a national scale and established him as a spokesman on the conduct of government and the presidency during the time when his presidential aspirations were high. Washington columnist Clayton Fritchey, who writes for the *Los Angeles Times* Syndicate, may have recognized accurately Percy's role in Watergate. Months before the resignation, Fritchey said that "he [Percy] is the only one who has had the nerve to stand up to the President and criticize him personally for the Watergate scandals."

The relationship between Nixon and Percy paralleled some of the nation's most tumultuous times. Nixon inexorably was involved in the events because the president had to deal with them. Percy, on the other hand, voluntarily involved himself. As a result, the record of their confrontations, and public statements on all varieties of issues reflect their feelings toward each other, personally and professionally. On a personal basis the relationship was a roller-coaster ride, which left observers never quite sure of the footing at any one time. Professionally, they often seemed headed in the same direction, with similar goals for the nation and the party. This cooperation never reached lockstep, as Percy increasingly developed positions and actions independent of the administration. Still, neither could do totally without the other, and that often tempered judgments and actions and kept the relationship from completely falling apart.

If Percy feels some relief after all that happened to Nixon, it is because of his total disassociation from Watergate and the knowledge that after 1968 he kept his distance from Nixon and his followers. That gives Percy some right to a final comment on Nixon's plight, which stands also as a postscript on their association:

"The unanimous evidence of wrongdoing had grown so compelling... that his departure from office was inevitable. It is important to remember that the Nixon presidency was brought down by the President's own words and actions."

CHAPTER XI

PERCY, FORD, AND THE FUTURE

All political campaigns have a certain smell—an aroma of victory or apprehension or élan or, heaven forbid, defeat. For 18 months or more the Charles H. Percy campaign for the Republican party's presidential nomination smelled of determination. It did not have the vibrance that was associated with the Kennedys' campaigns, the blind zeal connected with Goldwater's, or the cocksureness identified with Lyndon Johnson's. It had a style of its own, as campaigns should. There was security in the knowledge that, regardless of the odds, everything would turn out satisfactorily. The odds against Percy's campaign effort succeeding were great because his standing in the national surveys never looked particularly good against the more familiar names in the Republican party. Still, the drive of the candidate, his enthusiasm, and the spirit of the hunt kept the campaign alive.

Percy's campaign resembled the McGovern effort of 1970 and 1971 in its early start and dedication, but there was more money as well as more organization from the beginning. Some observers likened the campaign goals to those of Goldwater when he won control of the party in 1963 and 1964, but Percy's campaign plan was designed for an extended effort. Charles Percy had no intention of being labeled another Harold Stassen, William Scranton, George Romney, or even Nelson Rockefeller. He prepared for the long haul and never denied being a candidate.

That was the picture until the Percy campaign had the props knocked from under it in August, 1974, by the ascendancy of Gerald R. Ford to the presidency.

Percy's landslide election of 1972, in which he received the largest plurality of votes given any candidate for the Senate in the history of Illinois, made him a serious candidate for his party's presidential nomination. Before that victory, seeking the presidential nomination had been just an idea, even though a strong one, with many of the senator's followers, especially those who had worked with him since his first days in the Senate. Percy always had been considered a candidate for higher office. By 1972 he looked ready for the presidential race. Still young at 53 (57 in 1976), Percy had steered clear of Nixon and Watergate, had maintained a moderately dovish position on the Vietnam war, and had not aligned himself with any particular faction in his party or in Congress. Some supporters saw this nonalignment as more of a liability than an asset because it made his power base elusive. In spite of his record and his overwhelming victory in 1972—a reflection of his popularity with Illinois voters—Percy was still viewed with skepticism by some Republican leaders in his own state.

Before making any determinations on whether or not to seek the presidency, Percy hired a Washington consulting firm to study political trends and the delegate-selection system that would be used in the 1976 primary and convention process. The firm—Bailey, Deardourff & Eyre—concluded in a six-volume study that if Percy conducted a four-year effort he had a strong chance at the nomination. An analysis of the candidates in the field at the time helped Percy confirm that conclusion. Vice-President Spiro T. Agnew held the front-runner position. He benefited from President Nixon's enormous popularity, which had resulted in their landslide election victory in 1972. Many Republicans agreed that Agnew could have the 1976 nomination for the asking. Other possible candidates included Democrat-turned-Republican John B. Connally of Texas, the standbys Ronald Reagan and Nelson Rockefeller, and a small list of dark horses. Winning the party's nomination looked like an uphill battle for Percy, although no one in the field actually had it locked up.

Percy was ready by early 1973 to take his first major step toward seeking the presidential nomination. In February he organized an exploratory committee, which was to commission research through the Bailey firm. The exploratory committee's existence was officially announced in June, 1973, with the avowed purpose of helping Percy decide whether to run in 1976. Percy said he would make his final decision after the 1974 congressional elections. Few were fooled. For all intents and purposes, the decision to go had been made. Thomas J. Houser, the chairman of the exploratory committee, and other Percy advisers thought the early announcement—almost three years before the 1976 national convention—was premature and potentially injurious to the campaign. But by this time Percy, recognizing that the atmosphere of Watergate had put a premium on doing business without any hint of secrecy, wanted his candidacy in the open.

When Percy's campaign began to pick up some momentum late in 1973 and early in 1974, two possible rivals for the nomination were out of contention. Agnew had been convicted of income tax evasion. Percy called the Agnew case a "tragedy for the nation, for the Agnew family, and for the former vice-president himself." Connally lost ground steadily because of investigations into his political activities. The selection of Ford as vice-president had also dealt a blow to Connally's chances.

One of the first steps in the campaign was to raise money. Old friends and one relative made the first contributions. Arthur C. Nielsen, Jr., of Winnetka, Illinois, who was the exploratory committee's treasurer and the 1974 finance chairman for the Percy drive, donated $5,000. The president of A. C. Nielsen, Inc., the media-rating service, Nielsen had been a friend for years. Two other longtime friends from Illinois, William B. Graham of Kenilworth and Richard Duchossois of Flossmoor, each contributed $5,000. Involved in many fund-raising ventures for Percy, Duchossois has always been high on Percy's list of contributors to his election campaigns. Sharon Percy Rockefeller gave $3,000. Percy himself donated $5,000, but Houser said that "he [Percy] does not have access or control of the funds."

Before the end of 1973, the first major request for funds had been made. Included in the mailing was a letter signed by Milton S. Eisenhower, brother of the former president. Eisenhower wrote of Percy: "We need a leader the people believe in. Senator Percy is that man. He is an independent man ... whose only 'special interest' is America." Eisenhower and Percy had been friends since the 1950s.

During the exploratory process, a total of $230,000 was raised, and $190,000 was expended. The rules for donating to the campaign were that no cash would be accepted, every dollar raised would be reported publicly, and donations from individuals could not exceed $5,000. Percy said he intended to finance his preconvention campaign principally through contributions in the $15 to $100 range. Houser could not imagine raising the millions necessary for a campaign through such small contributions. Aides estimated that it would cost as much as $15 million to win the nomination.

In addition to raising money, Percy's strategy for the presidential drive in 1973 called for putting together a small organization and arranging an expanded travel schedule for 1974. Percy spoke in 15 states during 1973, a heavy schedule for a U.S. senator. In 1974 he planned to revisit these states and to make trips to another 16 states. Many of these visits were to have occurred during the fall congressional campaigns. Percy also planned to spend 30 days in Illinois working for state and local candidates. Some of the state visits were canceled after the Nixon resignation. However, Percy did campaign frequently for Illinois candidates.

Out of Percy's travels came some indications that conservative opposition toward him was softening. One writer reported from California after a Percy swing through that traditionally Republican country: "Now there are signs that some of the antagonism and animosity against Percy is thinning. A few conservatives are even saying that Charles Percy is nominatable as well as electable." The writer credited the Percy "I am my own man" theme with the improvement and added that "Watergate has given Percy a new image." Other trips west brought a mixture of good and fair reports. Aides felt good about a trip to Hawaii because Percy apparently impressed the businessmen he met. In Oregon, one aide gave Percy's performance a "B minus."

In the early stages of his campaign, Percy stepped up his public comments on national issues, which most of the time involved events relating to Watergate. He appeared frequently on nationally televised interview programs in an attempt to get increased exposure for his ideas. At this time Percy was the only openly declared candidate on the campaign trail. Other potential candidates, particularly Reagan and Rockefeller, needed less publicity because they did not have as far to go as Percy did to win voter acceptance.

Percy and his advisers knew they were running without the support of the regular Republican party leadership and many of its workers. They planned to work around the party faithful as much as possible by cultivating the governors and establishing separate organizations of volunteers in each state. They also decided to publicly announce Percy's strategy for entering primaries much earlier than had been done in most campaigns in recent history, in order to get a reading from politicians and persons in the states affected, as much as for any other reason. Percy later said that these plans, although they seemed firm, might be altered if conditions changed.

The first primary Percy intended to enter was the one in Illinois, which is held in March after the major presidential-preference primaries in New Hampshire and Florida. The actual date is always subject to change by the Illinois legislature. Most political observers felt that Percy's decision to avoid the New Hampshire and Florida primaries was a wise move because the constituencies in those states would not have been kind to him. By not entering these primaries, the senator would not risk getting knocked around by other candidates and would conserve badly needed funds. If he were to win in Illinois, he would then have entered the primaries in the adjacent states of Wisconsin and Indiana and then moved on to Ohio. If Percy also won these three primaries, he would go west. He envisioned a showdown on the West Coast, where nomination battles have been won and lost: Kennedy won in 1960, and Rockefeller lost in 1964, as did Humphrey in 1972.

Shortly before the Nixon resignation in 1974, many of Percy's operatives in Illinois feared that Percy would not have a chance in the state primary against Ronald Reagan, a nationally known and more-conservative opponent. H. G. ("Skinny") Taylor, who sampled Downstate waters for Percy, did not think the senator would do well in the delegate-selection election, which was held at the same time as the presidential-preference vote, unless he made up ground with grass-roots politicians. Taylor did not expect Percy to make the effort. Working Illinois out of Chicago, Houser, while less pessimistic, also recognized that Percy would have problems unless he could enlist the support of major Republican leaders in the state. Earlier in the year Percy had appointed Richard B. Ogilvie, the former governor, to solicit funds from professional groups. Percy supporters banked heavily on Attorney General William J. Scott to neutralize conservatives by at least quietly declaring for Percy. But even with this backing, the strategists still worried about a primary showdown in Percy's own state with someone as conservative as Reagan.

One of the senator's strategies was to keep the campaign as open as possible. The headline of a Percy story in one state newspaper was "Run Early, Run Clean." That meant the disclosure of all funds raised by the exploratory committee and a pledge by Percy that he would reveal his personal finances if he became a "full-fledged" candidate. In response to the public's concerns about financial abuses by politicians, Percy had decided to limit individual donations to $5,000 and to encourage much smaller donations. As part of his policy of openness, Percy and his aides met in April, 1974, with senators and representatives and their congressional aides to explain his bid for the nomination and outline as much of his strategy as possible. Percy never made any secret of his quest, although he left the final decision open.

Congressional support came slowly for several reasons. It was too early for most congressmen, even those who were friends of Percy or who were philosophically in step with him, to commit themselves for 1976. Some of them still held hopes of being considered for the nomination if a deadlock occurred.

Another part of the senator's campaign strategy concerned the promotion of a Democratic opponent for Percy. He and his aides flatly declared that they expected the Democratic nominee to be Senator Edward Kennedy of Massachusetts. They wanted to promote Kennedy as the Democrats' choice because of information gathered by the Louis Harris polling organization throughout much of 1973. Harris ran surveys to determine if certain Republicans could beat Kennedy. The Republicans were Percy, Agnew, Connally, Reagan, Rockefeller, Senator Howard H. Baker, Jr., of Tennessee, and Ford. The results showed that Percy, Baker, and Ford would defeat Kennedy. Percy's margin over Kennedy was 46 to 44 percent, Ford's was 48 to 44 percent, and Baker's was 45 to 44 percent. As much as a year after Harris released the data, Percy still used it in his mailings. It constituted part of his main pitch to Republicans: "I can win in 1976." Houser said, "We're going to make the Republican party decide what it wants: a winner or someone who can't win but they feel comfortable with." In a Peoria, Illinois, appearance, Percy said his chances depended on "whether the Republican party wants to win elections or not." Kennedy's withdrawal as a presidential candidate in the fall of 1974 put an end to Percy's strategy of promoting the candidacy of the Massachusetts senator.

Throughout most of 1974 public-opinion surveys showed Percy lagging behind other Republicans in the eyes of party members. One of the last national polls taken before Nixon's resignation revealed that most of the major contenders—Reagan, Ford, Rockefeller—were well ahead of the pack, and the pack included Percy. His standing among Republicans made many persons compare the Percy effort to that of George McGovern, who trailed in the public-opinion polls until almost the last few primaries of 1972.

All during his campaign for the nomination, Percy looked for issues that would increase his visibility and broaden his appeal. In addition to Watergate, the economic problems of the nation seemed a possible topic. Aides had urged him to seek an issue with consumer appeal, and the economic situation served the purpose. His aides had also pleaded with him to choose specific subjects on which to comment rather than spreading himself thin by making statements on a large number of issues. By the end of his presidential effort, Percy had still not hit on a theme that could have been carried all the way through the primaries to the convention. In one comment to a reporter, Percy tried to express his concerns for the issues of a campaign: "I share with all a faith in free enterprise and business, a strong national defense. I think our skills in business should be applied to government to make it run more efficiently and at less cost. I also think there are certain human values that we must not forget. We have an obligation to our poor, disabled, and elderly to assure that they too can live in comfort." Percy had always been interested in all of these subjects. During the campaign there never was any inkling of new programs or issues that Percy expected to explore and elevate to importance in the minds of the public.

Only days before the resignation of Richard Nixon, all those who had been initial contributors to the exploratory effort received a mailing that requested more funds and announced that a major drive soon would be started. But the money would not be needed.

After the inauguration of Gerald R. Ford, Percy wrote a final letter on the campaign to his supporters. In it, he applied the logic of the moment: "From everything I see, he [President Ford] likes his job and undeniably has the option to submit himself and his programs to the Republican party for its decision as to whether he should bear the standard in 1976. And there is every reason for him to expect approval and the nomination if he wants it." For the moment this was all that Percy could say.

Although Percy's 18-month campaign did not get far enough to make any major mistakes or achieve any outstanding coups, it may still hold some lessons for future candidates. The organizational effort, the planning and the strategy, could stand as a primer for most future candidates for a presidential nomination, and especially for moderates or liberals in the Republican party.

From the beginning Percy and his strategists realized that the chances of obtaining the nomination were slim and depended on many unpredictable events. They recognized that a moderate would always be the underdog, and if a moderate were to have any chance, he would have to start early and work hard for several years, always mindful that the effort might come apart at any time. No other way existed for someone in Percy's position in the party to achieve the nomination, and that is likely to remain the plight of those with a moderate philosophy or with minimum grass-roots party support. Percy could live with this underdog role because he had been there before, in 1964 and 1966, and had shown he could survive the consequences. Future candidates may not have that much confidence in their own ability or in the fates.

Percy's aborted presidential effort left Illinois Republican party politics in a muddle. Illinois Republicans saw victory in 1976 more surely in their grasp with Percy heading the national ticket, or at the very least it would generate more voter interest in the Republican ticket. After the disastrous 1974 congressional elections, the party needed a boost. Without a Percy at the top of the ticket—in fact, neither of the two U.S. Senate seats are up for election in 1976—and with incumbent Democrats in key state positions, some "sure things" probably will be reassessed before commitment time. Attorney General William J. Scott decided that 1976 is not the year to seek the governorship. So the door is wide open for someone who has not had much statewide exposure.

The absence of Percy's name on the ballot in either the primary or the general elections of 1976 would mean that Illinois Republican candidates have more of an uphill battle against well-entrenched Democratic incumbents, such as Governor Daniel Walker. Making the task more difficult than normal are the Republican defeats in the 1974 general election and the Chicago city election in 1975. Illinois Republicans have learned over the years that, while they have their quarrels with Percy, they like to have the senator's name on the ballot whenever possible.

No greater struggle faced Charles Percy in the first few months of Gerald Ford's presidency than learning how to adjust to and live with the Ford style and friendships. Percy's relationship to Ford and the administration's policies in the period leading up to the 1976 presidential contest could have grave implications for the senator.

Ford's background in Congress and his friendships with those Illinois congressmen who do not look kindly upon Percy and the moderate wing of the Republican party presented a special challenge to the senator. One of Ford's longtime associates in Congress, Leslie Arends, who retired in 1974, had the new president's ear during the first months of his tenure. If Percy's name came up in any discussions, Arends would not have chosen Percy's positive side to express to Ford. There were others among Ford's congressional friends who might also have spun some yarns that would not be to Percy's advantage. Robert Michel of Peoria and Edward Derwinski of Chicago's Southwest Side are philosophical comrades of Ford and often ideological antagonists of Percy.

Tempering the opinions of Percy's political adversaries are those among Ford's associates—such as John Anderson, a moderate congressman from Illinois—who have a good relationship with the senator. Included in this group is Donald Rumsfeld, who was appointed White House administrator by President Ford. Percy and Rumsfeld are considered friendly even though the latter, while a U.S. representative from Illinois, had a conservative voting record. However, both legislators in their turn fought for congressional reforms. Having Rumsfeld in the inner circles of the White House could be a mixed blessing for Percy.

The relationship between Percy and Rumsfeld may depend on whether the latter has political ambitions in Illinois, as is frequently rumored. While Rumsfeld was ambassador to NATO, he was briefly considered as a possible challenger of Adlai Stevenson in 1974. Most of the speculation involving Rumsfeld and Illinois politics centers on whether he will seek the governorship in 1976. The field is by no means wide open to Rumsfeld, but with Republican fortunes in the state diminished, any recognizable national figure would have an advantage. Rumsfeld would need Percy's blessing to enter the Illinois picture in 1976 or 1978, and that necessity could keep the two men on reasonably good terms at least until the time for such decisions arose.

Rumsfeld's luring of Illinoisans and other midwesterners to the Ford administration could strengthen Percy too. One of the most notable appointments was that of Edward H. Levi, former president of the University of Chicago, as attorney general. Percy called Levi "one of the most qualified persons who could be nominated to serve this government." Rumsfeld was credited with persuading Ford to nominate the Illinoisan. Another addition to Ford's staff was Robert A. Goldwin, a former University of Chicago professor who had worked with Percy as an intellectual advisor early in the senator's political career. Goldwin was appointed special consultant to the president.

When Gerald Ford was vice-president, and consequently a potential candidate for the presidency, Percy called on him and several of the other possible candidates before launching his own campaign full throttle. After his visit with Ford, Percy said, "I have had a talk with Jerry Ford. He's an outstanding, marvelous man, a good friend for a quarter of a century. He thinks the committee—the exploratory committee—should be carried on. He said it's good for the country and good for the party."

One of President Ford's first tasks was to select a vice-president. The appearance of Percy's name on early lists of possible candidates was designed to make the senator feel good but did not reflect Ford's personal preferences. When the narrowing process started and Rockefeller seemed increasingly to be the front-runner for the vice-presidential nomination, Percy clearly had no chance. There were any number of reasons at the time, but none more powerful than the fact that Percy was unacceptable to some elements of the party, and Ford needed maximum party acceptance. Some gossip columnists said that Percy's chances were nil because of an incident that occurred during Senate hearings into Ford's background after he was nominated as vice-president by Nixon. John Childers, an aide to Percy, had heard a rumor that Ford might have accepted a political contribution from milk-industry representatives in Illinois. At this time the milk industry was under suspicion because of revelations concerning large sums of money donated to political campaigns allegedly in return for future favors. Percy told Childers to report the information to the Senate Rules Committee, which conducted the Ford inquiry. The committee determined later that no milk-industry gifts had been made to Ford. Although the rumor persisted that the episode had angered Ford, most observers agreed that it would not have been held against the senator if he had truly been a prime candidate for the vice-presidency. In Illinois, the senator's supporters called the selection of Percy for this post improbable because it would have created a vacancy in the Senate and his replacement would have to be named by the Democratic governor, Daniel Walker. And Ford needed all the Republican help in the Senate he could muster.

In the first year of Ford's administration, a series of crises involving energy, the economy, and questions of national leadership kept the president's standing low in public-opinion polls. His presentation of a budget early in 1975 that projected at least a $52 billion deficit for the year ending July 1, 1976, caused widespread political speculation. Commentators and columnists said that Ford had sealed his political doom with continued forecasts of high unemployment and economic doldrums. Conservatives in the Republican party openly criticized Ford and threatened a third-party movement. Still, Ford insisted he would be a candidate in 1976. Percy refrained from any public comment at the time, although others in Congress began talking of alternatives to Ford in 1976.

Percy's first major disagreement with a Ford decision did not focus any singular attention on the senator. The issue involved was Ford's decision to grant Nixon a pardon. Percy was out of the country when the announcement was made, but when he returned several days afterward, he issued a statement that repeated much of what had been said several times by others. He called the pardon "an honest mistake in judgment." The Ford decision, Percy said, "reinforced the cynicism of millions of Americans who believe the legal system is heavily weighted in favor of the rich and powerful." He said that the nation's judicial system had been undermined by the pardon and that "serious questions" about the system's effectiveness had been raised.

Later Percy provided observers with further evidence that he would not blindly accept administration programs. Less than two months after Ford's presidency began, Percy helped sponsor a bill that would have reversed a White House decision to permit Nixon to maintain ownership of the infamous White House tapes. The bill began in the Government Operations Committee, of which Percy is ranking Republican member. Percy's stand in this minor dispute was an indication to everyone that he expected to take each issue on its own merits rather than obediently fall into step with the Ford administration.

Percy's determination to maintain his independence did not hurt his new standing in the White House. After years of being a social and political outcast with the Nixon administration, the Illinoisan benefited from the more-open atmosphere of the Ford presidency and its friendliness toward congressional members, regardless of past misunderstandings. Although Percy declared that his social status in the White House meant little to him—"I don't need my ego massaged"—aides agreed that Percy responded positively to the overtures of President and Mrs. Ford. Before the economic summit in the fall of 1974, Ford invited Percy to the working meeting that laid the groundwork for the summit. No such invitation would have been extended to Percy during the Nixon years. Percy said that he had been a dinner guest more often in the first six months of Ford's administration than in the six years of the Nixon administration.

Percy had not been to a state dinner at the White House in several years, and so he was pleased when, early in December, 1974, Ford asked the Percys to a formal affair for Helmut Schmidt, chancellor of West Germany. Percy is reported to have searched most of the tables in the dining room for his place card only to discover to his delight that his hosts had seated him at the president's table between Katherine Graham, publisher of the *Washington Post*, and Mrs. Ford. A close aide to Percy called this seating arrangement "a nice gesture."

Although Percy pursued some courses that differed from those of the administration, and gave every indication of continuing to do so, he still felt he could work with the Ford people. "I couldn't work with Nixon, but I think I can get on with Ford," he said after several months of the new presidency. "There is no question of Ford's decency, honesty, and openness," Percy added. "But he's not getting a grip on things and not getting results." Percy singled out the Ford style of leadership for some specific criticism, saying, "You can't go on forever acting like a minority leader." The senator, cordial to the president publicly and complimentary when possible, questioned whether Ford was up to all the pressures and challenges of the presidency.

In his public statements, Percy has carefully qualified his withdrawal from consideration as a presidential candidate in 1976. He has said he will support Ford if the president does an exemplary job. The implication is that Percy might become a candidate again if he concludes that Ford is not measuring up to expectations. However, should Ford decide to cozy up to Ronald Reagan and the other more-conservative forces in the party, Percy might still challenge him for the nomination whether or not he has "proved himself to be an outstanding president." Other politicians seem to be waiting to see if Ford can sustain enough party support to win the nomination in 1976.

Because Ford took some unpredictable actions in his early months as president, his withdrawal from contention can never entirely be discounted even though his open declaration has been made. Thus, Percy and other potential candidates are forced to play a waiting game. They are not even sure what they are waiting for. Although at least technically Percy could declare his candidacy for the presidency at any time before the 1976 national convention, practically speaking he would need primary campaign exposure well before that and an accumulation of delegate votes. Percy hinted at a probable deadline for a declaration of his candidacy when he acknowledged that "I've never had any plan other than to go in Illinois first. We could wait until a week before the primary to declare."

In his political career Percy has been primarily concerned with current problems and their solutions. He has not developed any detailed plans for the foreign policies and domestic activities of the next decade. His role has been that of a contemporary man, with roots in past actions and programs. Thus, it is necessary to explore his public statements and his actions to see the future through his political eyes.

Percy has been concerned with foreign affairs for a great part of his working life. His general interest in foreign travel, the activities of other nations, foreign trade, and the intricacies of diplomacy, war, and international power plays is the nearest thing to a constant factor in his public life. Thus, it is possible to predict that foreign affairs will continue to be an area of utmost interest to Percy.

Percy believes the underpinning of a durable foreign policy "is a strong defense." He has held this view since his work on the Committee on Program and Progress report in 1959. He has said that the report was "probably the strongest imprint I've had on anything political." On the subject of defense, the document said that the free world must "maintain a great military force as far into the future as we can foresee.... We must be ready with a variety of weapons and forces. No single weapon and no single service, by itself, can effectively deter aggression. The temptation to put too many eggs in one basket must be strongly resisted." That statement seemed to allude to the atomic bomb and said in general language that other conventional weapons and armies would be necessary on a continuing basis.

In the Senate, Percy has voted for the maintenance of military strength and the cautious development of new weapons systems. He has given his overall support to most of the military procurement proposals in Congress but has taken issue with selected items, such as the funding of the Safeguard antiballistic missile system. In 1970 Congress passed one of the more controversial military procurement bills, which authorized funds for a limited ABM system, the C-5A cargo plane, the MIRV missile program, and more ships, submarines, and F-14 and F-15 fighters. Percy made some minor alterations in the bill, and these amendments were approved. He proposed the encouragement of longer tours of duty for military personnel and a direct cut of 25 percent in expenditures for most personnel rotation. His other proposal prohibited disposal, except in emergencies, of chemical or biological warfare agents that had not been detoxified. Percy voted for the final Senate version of the bill and the ultimate conference committee plan, which was opposed by Mark O. Hatfield, J. William Fulbright, Charles E. Goodell, and other Senate antimilitarists.

Percy has made a study of the research and development function of the Department of Defense and its effect on procurement proposals. The thrust of his comments has been to improve the efficiency of research and development as a means of maintaining defense strength and cutting costs.

For the short-term future, Percy sees military expenditures continuing to take a sizable chunk out of the federal budget: "I do not foresee the possibility of reducing the military budget by any large amounts. We might cut some overseas bases and even some domestic bases, but sometimes it takes more money to pay for the consequences of closing down a base than it does to keep one going." Percy believes that serious efforts will be made to keep the military budget from increasing. He feels that sufficient federal funds will be found to keep necessary social programs going if the economy can begin to expand at a more normal rate in the future and the military budget can be held constant. Percy notes that a large percentage of the military budget on the short term will be devoted to maintaining a voluntary army. He favors continuing that kind of military expenditure because of the soundness of the volunteer program.

In Washington most of Percy's longtime feelings about foreign matters are well known, and many date back 20 years or more to the days when, as a businessman, he occasionally testified before Congress. Percy favors unrestricted trade with all foreign nations and opposes protective tariffs.

He supports such overseas alliances as NATO, although he feels that European nations should pay a larger share of the amount needed to support the organization. He has voted against Senate efforts to reduce the U.S. military commitments in Europe. He has pointed out that European nations should pay more of the costs of maintaining U.S. military installations because American-financed aircraft runways and buildings in these countries "are not things that are ever going to be shipped back to the United States."

At few points in his Senate career has Percy taken major exception to foreign affairs policies. However, he has criticized the way Nixon was conducting the Indochina war and some of Ford's actions during the final collapse of South Vietnam. Each year Percy has supported the Senate's foreign aid authorizations even though the Congress as a whole is turning from foreign aid programs. He backed Nixon's doctrine of providing military aid to foreign nations without getting involved in their military operations. One revealing comment shows how Percy feels about the link between defense and diplomacy. When Percy voted for the foreign military assistance bill in 1971, he said, "It would be foolhardy for us to reduce this program, to gut the Nixon doctrine of enabling other countries to defend themselves." However, after a 1972 trip to the Far East, Percy worried that giving aid to countries run by dictators might involve more than just dispensing money or supplies: "If the United States continues to provide massive military assistance to such governments, there is a feeling that a very real danger exists that the United States will share the blame of authoritarian regimes and will invite grass-roots antagonism for its role." Percy did not propose an end to this support but counseled that "American military involvement with such regimes must be kept at such a level that the United States is not perceived as the sponsor or protector of undemocratic governmental processes."

Percy's dedication to the Nixon-Kissinger-Ford foreign policy has been stronger than almost any tie Percy has made in his years in Congress. In a television appearance on March 10, 1974, during a period of flaming oratory against Watergate, Percy called the Nixon-Kissinger policy "brilliant, creative, innovative." Percy probably would have used the same person—Henry Kissinger—to carry out foreign policy if he had been president during the Nixon period, he has said. During the period when his 1976 presidential hopes were highest, Percy said, "If I were elected President, I would not foresee major changes in that policy at all." In Percy's mind, "that policy" included reduction of nuclear weapons and a close relationship with Europe. He favored a continued détente with Russia and increasingly friendly relations with China—"I had publicly taken the position we can't leave 800 million people in an outlaw situation." Percy wanted the United States to take maximum advantage of fast-growing Communist markets in Eastern Europe and elsewhere instead of letting Western Europe and Japan serve them almost exclusively. He opposed any thought that the United States should refuse to sell goods because a country might be run by Communists.

Percy said Nixon and Kissinger went far beyond his hopes in reaching a tentative accord in the Middle East during 1973. Further evidence that Percy supported Nixon's foreign policy is shown in the voting records tabulated by Congressional Quarterly, which selected issues that represented key Nixon proposals. In 1969, for example, Percy voted with Nixon foreign policy issues 79 percent of the time and against only 5 percent.

Percy's admiration for Kissinger has been virtually unlimited. He worked with Kissinger during the 1950s when they served together on a study project of foreign and domestic issues for the Rockefeller Brothers Fund. Others who served on the project included Dean Rusk, who would be appointed secretary of state for Presidents Kennedy and Johnson; Chester Bowles, who became a foreign affairs adviser to President Kennedy; and John Gardner, who is now chairman of the citizens' lobby Common Cause. Both Percy and Kissinger have kept in close contact and often appear at the same Washington social events.

Kissinger formed the backbone of the foreign affairs establishment of the 1970s in Washington, and Percy became a willing member of the group. The secretary of state had asked Percy to work in the Senate for support of his foreign policy, and Percy responded to such requests even during the Vietnam war. Kissinger, for his part, kept Percy high on the list of senators to be provided with confidential information about diplomatic ventures.

After Ford became president, Percy began to question the development of the administration's foreign policy as practiced and executed by Kissinger, but the criticism has not included Kissinger personally: "The problem of the Kissinger approach [which is basically a one-man operation] is that all individuals are mortal. We eventually must reach a point where it ends, for whatever reason." What carries on in the absence of the individual is a strong foreign policy structure not based on a personality cult, Percy has said. He added that although Kissinger's special kind of diplomacy is satisfactory in emergencies, what we will soon need is "a foreign affairs structure that can outlast an individual." Percy felt that Ford should have taken time in the early months of his administration to form broader and longer-lasting foreign affairs policies. He called the state-department policies of 1974 a "mishmash." Percy particularly was critical of Ford's failure to fill key administration jobs dealing with economic affairs in foreign policy.

Despite Percy's reservations about the Kissinger policy of individual diplomacy, the senator supported his work. In early 1975 Percy's Senate colleague from Illinois, Adlai Stevenson, used harsh words to criticize Kissinger's handling of foreign affairs. Percy attributed the Democratic senator's remarks to "politics" and dismissed the whole incident as a personal quarrel between two public figures. Percy nevertheless was upset because Stevenson had chosen to berate Kissinger on the eve of critical negotiations by the secretary of state in the Middle East. Unswerving in his public commitment to Kissinger's efforts in this part of the world, Percy said of him: "He is the one person today who has the chance to put the pieces of this mosaic together. I have to believe in him."

During the early months of the Ford administration, Percy served as a member of the U.S. delegation to the United Nations. The three-month delegate term is rotated among members of Congress. Because the time spent at the UN is short, the impact of U.S. senators on its policy is almost nonexistent. Many of the senators view the episode only as a break in the Washington routine. Percy seemed dedicated to making his tenure something other than just an interlude. He took full advantage of the opportunity and the exposure the position afforded to comment on a range of international questions. Carefully avoiding lengthy statements that might conflict with Kissinger's diplomatic efforts, Percy branched out into other areas in an attempt to establish some points that might be used in the future shaping of a detailed foreign affairs program.

In October, 1974, Percy called on the General Assembly's Social Affairs Committee to provide more jobs for women: "It would be the essence of hypocrisy if the UN Conference for International Women's Year were convened in 1975 without prior action within the United Nations to put its own house in order." Secretary General Kurt Waldheim countered by saying he would encourage a more equitable hiring balance but would not set quotas for men and women.

In the same month, Percy introduced a resolution at the UN calling on all participants in armed conflicts to provide information on persons who have been killed or who have been listed as missing in action. The effort was consistent with Percy's efforts to help American families whose relatives were prisoners of war or were missing in action.

Early in his three-month term, Percy presented a major speech at the UN on the many pressing economic problems of the world but did not outline any major strategies for solving them. In the course of the speech, Percy called for a lowering in the price of international crude oil and the development of alternate sources of energy; asked the UN to help encourage overpopulated countries to develop plans that would eliminate unrestrained population growth; and suggested that the world's food problem could be solved by an international system of nationally held food reserves and increased investments in research, fertilizer production, and development-assistance programs.

During his brief tenure as a UN delegate, Percy observed the continuing saga of Third World animosity toward the larger and more affluent member nations, such as the United States. To make their sting felt, a large number of Third World nations supported the request of Yasir Arafat, leader of the Palestinian Liberation Organization (PLO), to speak at a meeting of the General Assembly. With more than 100 of the 138 member nations counted as Third World representatives, there was not much the minority could do. Percy said later, "They used those numbers to gallop roughshod over the legitimate views of the minority."

Arafat's appearance in the fall of 1974 created a storm of protest in the United States, especially among sympathizers of the Israeli cause. The official U.S. policy was that Arafat should not have been accorded the privileges of UN membership or even recognition as a chief spokesman of the Palestinians. What disturbed the United States and the other large powers was not so much Arafat's appearance and his call for a Palestinian state, but the overt support and interaction of the Third World membership with the PLO leader in the UN forum. At least for the time that he spoke, Arafat stood as a symbol of the Third World struggle against the interests of the nations that had run the UN for most of its history.

Percy's public statements supported U.S. policy toward Arafat's presence in the UN. After the PLO leader's appearance, Percy said in an article written for United Press International: "Arafat couched his demand—the displacement of Israel by a Palestinian state—in gentle terms. But as he raised his arms to acknowledge the applause, the gun holster at his belt was clearly and symbolically visible." The fact that Arafat carried a weapon during his speech seemed to back up those pro-Israel supporters who cried that Arafat was little more than a terrorist butcher who had come to call on the UN.

Percy did not agree with those in Congress who viewed the antagonism of the Third World nations toward the United States as a betrayal. He called for a "new détente" between the developed and developing nations and rejected suggestions that the United States withdraw from UN membership or, at least, withdraw its financial aid: "Americans must suppress the tendency, when the UN tide runs against us, to threaten to pick up our marbles and go home.... American dollars are important but probably no longer crucial to the UN, which already is turning increasingly to the new-rich oil nations for support." Percy also recognized the obligation of rich member nations to help less-fortunate ones: "Clearly, the richer nations have a special responsibility to help narrow that economic gap.... More crucial than U.S. dollars is the need for continued aggressive and enthusiastic American participation in the political, economic, and social issues that confront the world community." But the effort is not one-sided, Percy said. He challenged the Third World "to demonstrate that it understands the value of U.S. participation—and the fragility of our enthusiasm."

Three months after his UN tour ended, Percy had not forgotten the experience. He called upon the Senate Foreign Relations Committee to review U.S. involvement in the world organization: "Criticism of the United Nations has probably never been greater than it is now in the United States.... There are still those who would prefer to see the U.N. suffer the same fate as the League of Nations." Percy said he was not one of them. He added that U.S. participation in the UN had not been studied by the Senate committee in 20 years.

Percy's ventures into foreign affairs occasionally have gained him a quick headline in the United States and in a foreign nation or two. On a world tour in 1967, Percy came under gunfire in Vietnam and editorial fire in the United States. Percy visited Vietnam in 1972 during the Christmas bombing of North Vietnam and issued statements that angered U.S. officials and resulted in published criticism of the senator. None of those reactions compared with those generated early in 1975 after Percy's 23-day Middle Eastern tour, in which he visited 13 nations on business for the Foreign Relations Committee. The trip itself did not really differ from those made by other members of Congress. The impact of this junket occurred after Percy's return to the United States.

Percy had gotten off to a rocky start in his political relationship with American Jews. During the campaign for the Illinois governorship in 1964, stories were circulated that Percy lived in a community where no Jews were allowed. His residence at the time was in Kenilworth. During his Senate years Percy worked hard to establish himself as a friend of the Jews, and particularly a friend of Israel. Eventually, Jews in Illinois turned out in large numbers to vote for Percy, many of them breaking traditional Democratic party ties to do so. As a senator, his statements on the survival of Israel and the U.S. military and economic relationships with that country were infrequent and noncontroversial but supportive. From year to year he and as many as 70 other senators formed a bloc of votes sympathetic to granting aid for Israel. Depending on the situation, the Senate generally granted the administration's requests to provide military aid to Israel so that the balance of power in the Middle East could be maintained.

In 1975, less than a month after the UN session ended, Percy began his tour of the Middle East. Although he had an opportunity to visit with Arafat, Percy declined because he recognized the political danger of such a meeting in view of the furor caused by Arafat's 1974 UN speech and because he was concerned about having fruitful talks in Israel later in the trip. During the trip Percy's public statements, reported by the U.S. wire services, should have given some hint of the impact the talks with Arab leaders were having on his attitude about the future of the Middle East. At first the Arab newspapers reported that Percy's comments were much like those made by dozens of other visiting U.S. legislators. But later, when the drift of Percy's position became clear, the Arab press cheered loudly.

After concluding a four-day stay in Egypt, Percy said, "No one wants another war, but I fear that unless there is a breakthrough soon on the negotiating front, time, tensions, and events may conspire to ignite another major conflict." In Jerusalem, Percy raised doubts about the seemingly unswerving support for Israel in Congress. Replying to a question about the reaction to a potential preemptive strike at the Arabs by Israel, such as in the 1967 war, Percy said, "I feel assured the American support for Israel in the past will not be available in the present or in the future, and Israel will have to stand alone." Percy also commented on a $2.2 billion aid request by Israel. He said that support "will not be easy for us because it would increase our national debt, add to inflation, unbalance our budget further." Another key to Percy's change of attitude came in his comment from Jerusalem that Israel should go along with Henry Kissinger's proposal that they make greater territorial concessions.

As his tour ended, Percy said, "Every Arab country now recognizes that Israel is here to stay." He said the Palestinians "have a legitimate right to a homeland of their own" and urged Israel to recognize this. Percy said it was "inevitable that the Palestinians will negotiate with Israel."

Even though the comments Percy made during his Middle Eastern tour seemed to show a change in his pro-Israel stand, the bombshell for Jews did not come until a few days after the senator returned to the United States. At a breakfast meeting with reporters in Washington, Percy said that the time seemed right for a negotiated settlement in the Middle East. He asked Israel to meet with the PLO and to pull back to its pre-June, 1967, borders. Percy finished by saying that American support could not be counted on if Israel launched a preemptive strike against the Arabs. No other U.S. official had publicly called for such major Israeli concessions. Officially, Kissinger had simply stated that a prelude to settlement was more negotiation, although he reportedly also put pressure on Israel to yield on some points.

The uproar in the Jewish community of Chicago and Jewish organizations throughout the United States that followed Percy's statements was predictable, but the senator seemed to be shocked and surprised by its intensity. A specific comment Percy made about Arafat and later repeated several times was strongly criticized. He said, "I'm convinced that Arafat is, relatively speaking, a moderate." Later, in a face-to-face confrontation in Chicago with Jewish leaders, Percy said that his statement referred to Arafat's philosophical leanings relative to other Arabs. He voiced a fear that, if Arafat did not survive as head of the Palestinian movement, other more-extreme leaders would surface.

While calling on the Israelis to make concessions, Percy also addressed the Arabs on what their contributions to a negotiated settlement should be, but his points were lost in the onslaught of criticism that erupted. Percy said that the Arabs must acknowledge Israel's right to exist, provide formal diplomatic recognition of Israel, give Israel free use of the Suez Canal, and enter into economic and cultural contracts with Israel.

Percy acknowledged that he lost substantial Jewish support. He joked that one columnist had noted there were 650,000 Jews in Illinois and 35 Arabs. "It will take a long time to overcome the damaged relationships," he said. Most of Percy's Senate and congressional colleagues were silent. The silence reflected general agreement with what Percy had said and recognition that Congress would be taking a harder look at Israeli requests for aid. Almost immediately after Percy's trip, Kissinger made one of his frequent trips to the Middle East, and most of the subjects raised by Percy were on the secretary of state's agenda. Kissinger denied that he had put Percy up to any of his comments. Percy did talk with Kissinger after he made his statements, and there was some speculation that during Percy's trip Kissinger had received cables from him. However, the secretary of state hardly could have been surprised by Percy's remarks. Joseph A. Farrell, Percy's administrative assistant, acknowledged that the senator's statements had amazed some of his Washington staff members. They may have been surprised that Percy decided to express his views so quickly and without benefit of staff debate. One of Percy's friends said he suspected that the senator had not consulted his staff because he did not want to be talked out of his conclusions. The White House remained silent throughout the entire episode.

Sensing that some persons might have thought that his tour through the Middle East had too much influence on his attitudes, Percy later tried to place the events in a larger context: "I had been casting about for months for the single most important thing this country could do to restore confidence in itself and others. I decided it was to settle the Mideast situation. If we put our whole prestige behind the effort, I thought it could have great effect on our morale as well as our standing in the world. Obviously, too, it would remove the threat of another oil embargo." Percy also saw a role for himself in bringing Congress together in a bipartisan effort to achieve peace: "After congressional action on Turkey, Greece, and the Russian trade matter, I thought Congress needed some unity, and the Mideast was a good place to pull together."

Percy related his efforts in the Middle East and his concentration on foreign affairs in 1975 to his recognition of the nation's biggest problem: "It is an ingrown pessimism, a loss of confidence in ourselves and our leaders. It involves our role in the world: how to dominate the world scene after really losing a war in Southeast Asia." Percy related this pessimistic national attitude to the weakening of U.S. influence in the UN and the collapse of the Russian trade deal early in 1975: "From Springfield to Chicago to Washington, the Watergate aftermath included a loss of confidence based on morality in politics and a drift in leadership. We needed a few spectaculars."

The vehicle through which Percy's future activity in foreign affairs will undoubtedly be channeled is the Senate Foreign Relations Committee. What role the committee—of which he became a member in 1972—will play and how much influence it will have in forming U.S. foreign policy depends greatly on its chairman. Under J. William Fulbright, who lost his Senate seat in 1974, the committee actively tried to influence foreign affairs but seldom in concert with any administration. Under Fulbright's successor, Alabama's John J. Sparkman, the committee's direction is less predictable. It will continue to be a forum for debate but may lack force with the administration and the public. Many observers expect Sparkman to be less dynamic and forceful than Fulbright. Early indications are that Sparkman runs a more-open committee than Fulbright did. Standing in line to succeed Sparkman is Idaho's Frank Church, who was reelected in 1974.

For Percy and other members of the committee, international travel and study are fringe benefits. Since joining the committee, Percy has traveled annually, often during congressional recesses. His trips have taken him to all corners of the world, but mainly to Europe and the Far East.

As a foreign affairs activist in the Senate, he has developed an expertise in the rhetoric of foreign affairs, which according to time-honored tradition must be hard-nosed in order not to betray a softness toward those who someday may be diplomatic or military foes of the United States. One example involving Percy occurred on a trip to England in July, 1974. Writing in the *London Evening Standard*, Percy replied to statements by a U.S. professor that Americans accept the idea of being overtaken by the Soviet Union in international influence: "There is no chance for the USSR to overtake the U.S.A. in the next 10 years other than in the fields where they are already supreme such as the ballet—not economically or militarily or politically or in the fields of management and labor relations, space, ecology, medicine, computer technology, science, humanities, civil liberties, or what have you." Percy's laundry list indicated that American society still had an advantage over anything Russia could offer. In what amounted to some flag-waving for the benefit of Londoners, Percy added: "In peaceful competition they shall neither bury us nor surpass us in 10 years or 20.... Just let them attack Great Britain and see what the U.S. and NATO forces would do." Such communications showed that Percy's political views had their roots in the cold war days of the 1950s. However, changes in U.S. policy since that time have somewhat tempered his stand.

Further evidence of Percy's growing activity in matters of concern to the Foreign Relations Committee occurred in 1975 before Communist forces overran the capital of Cambodia. A clamor for increased emergency aid to help that nation was begun by some congressmen and particularly by President Ford. Sentiment in Congress, however, was running against further assistance to that country. The compromise-aid package that the committee finally voted to the floor of the Senate was fashioned by Percy, and it was he who cast the deciding vote in the committee.

After the fall of Cambodia, the Foreign Relations Committee considered a proposal to provide South Vietnam with military aid, an action Percy firmly opposed. But while the debate was still going on, South Vietnam was taken over by the Communists.

It is difficult to predict what new ideas Percy might thrust upon the nation, Congress, or an administration as he gains increased seniority on the Foreign Relations Committee. To date, he has preferred to react to events rather than propose future policies. It also is not easy to foresee whom Percy might bring into an administration in the foreign affairs field, but with his experience in foreign matters stretching over a quarter of a century, he would not likely have trouble recruiting able people. One likely person is Peter G. Peterson, who followed Percy as president of Bell & Howell and worked at several jobs in the Nixon administration. One of those jobs was the newly created position of assistant to the president for international economic affairs, a post that should have been the ideal place from which to tackle the growing economic problems abroad. Many people in the foreign affairs field had hopes for the plan, but the job never was operational in the Nixon administration. Peterson did not get on with Nixon's White House group, and he was assigned to another government post. While Peterson could show up almost anywhere in a Percy administration, foreign affairs would certainly be a possibility. Peterson has continued his activities in international economic affairs as chairman of Lehman Brothers, a firm of investment bankers in New York.

Percy's long-range plans for domestic programs have not been extensive and do not provide much of a glimpse into what he feels are the nation's greatest long-term needs. The projects of continuing interest to the senator relate to problems as he visualizes them now rather than as they might exist in the future. High on his list of crusades is a comprehensive program of aid and relief for the elderly. Through his first eight years in the Senate, Congress has responded piecemeal to his plans on the subject, but the lack of action on his broadest proposals has not dampened his enthusiasm. Also a priority with Percy is the creation by Congress or the executive of productivity councils to measure the production of workers and relate it to the questions of wages and fringe benefits. He has proposed the idea several times without success.

Percy has identified some current needs that will necessitate action by Congress and the president in the short-term period until a new president is selected in 1976. The domestic production of food is one. He has said that the problem basically is how to feed ourselves and still sell agricultural products to the world. He would remove all trade restrictions and guaranteed prices and pull all acreage in the United States out of reserves and put it into production. Other general areas of future activity include "making the cities livable." In a discussion of federally subsidized housing, Percy said that high-rise buildings should be "totally abandoned." His answer would be to rejuvenate a federal housing program that builds scattered-site low-level housing and to encourage more home ownership.

Percy can be expected to maintain an interest in the economic problems of the nation, although he does not have a precise and detailed program for curing the nation's inflationary ills. During the last days of the Nixon administration, he suggested that the federal budget could be reduced by $10 billion. In an attempt to better balance the budget, President Ford proposed a surtax on income. At the same time, he announced a voluntary program of energy conservation that was aimed at making the United States independent of foreign oil interests. Percy belittled the effort in private. "The voluntary deal won't work," he said. "Project Independence by 1980 is a foregone flop if we continue to follow our present policies." He told officials in the Ford administration who dealt specifically with energy problems as they related to the economy that he thought a more drastic program of federal intervention was necessary. Percy said the public was prepared for a more severe program of energy conservation than the Ford administration had offered. But despite criticism, the president decided to stay with his voluntary energy-conservation program. So Percy announced a five-point energy conservation and economic program that he claimed would provide a 10 percent reduction of national oil consumption by the end of 1975. "For too many years Americans have been spoiled by cheap fuel and indulged themselves in the use of fuel-consuming vehicles, while people in foreign countries have been far more prudent," Percy said early in December, 1974. He then introduced five bills.

One bill called for a 10¢-a-gallon tax on gasoline in 1975, to be increased to 20¢ in 1976. The measure also included a tax credit for essential driving. At the time of the proposal, the Ford administration steadfastly opposed tax increases, but they ultimately made their way into administration and congressional proposals. The second bill proposed an auto-efficiency tax-incentive program that would have taxed "gas-guzzler" automobiles and offered a rebate to car buyers who sought cars that had proven high miles-per-gallon test scores. The idea was to place a premium on driving cars that were big and heavy and got less than 15 miles to a gallon. That proposal also surfaced later during congressional discussion of alternatives to the president's energy and economic programs. The third plan would have made state and local gasoline taxes nondeductible for federal income tax purposes. The fourth bill would have withheld federal highway funds from states that did not enforce the 55-mile-per-hour speed limit. This plan received strong support from Democratic task forces that later devised their own programs for conservation. The final bill would have abolished the Highway Trust Fund and used its funds to finance alternatives to vehicles as modes of transportation.

At the same time that Percy presented these five bills, he urged Congress to repeal the oil-depletion allowance for oil companies. The senator also proposed mandatory "no-drive" days to help conserve fuel.

These bills were proposed by Percy just a few days before Congress adjourned in December, and so debate or committee consideration was out of the question. He proposed them again when the 94th Congress convened in 1975, but by then, a whole new series of events had occurred. President Ford had abandoned his voluntary energy-conservation program and the surtax on income. He approved a tax-rebate bill and later raised the tax on imported oil. When his energy measures met with criticism from the Democratic-controlled Congress, Ford challenged the legislative branch to come up with its own program. The debate continued from that point, but it should be noted that many of the proposals Percy made in December were quickly included in the variety of programs that surfaced.

In still another economic proposal aimed at bringing more money into the federal treasury, Percy submitted bills in 1975 that would have raised taxes on liquor and tobacco. Percy said Americans should be "willing to pay more for the luxuries of life—the nonnecessities—in order to bring down inflationary forces on the necessities of life."

Percy feels he is prepared for deep involvement with the subject of the economy by virtue of his membership on the Joint Economic Committee and his background in business. He was prepared to make the economy the No. 1 issue of his campaign, and as long as the economy holds as many problems for the nation as it did in 1974, Percy expects to have plenty of opportunity for commentary, much of which would put him at odds with the Ford administration. It is improbable that Percy would consider it his role to suggest definitive economic policies in Congress. Those proposals more naturally come from the Senate and House Appropriations committees, the Senate Finance Committee, and the House Ways and Means Committee. The pattern Percy established in his first eight years in the Senate was to leave money-policy questions to the members and the chairmen of the four money committees and concentrate instead on public debate.

Much of Percy's public commentary and activity in the years from 1967 to 1975 related to the two critical national and international issues of the period, the war in Indochina and Watergate. As the economy and the survival of the nation in the international monetary system became critical issues after Watergate, Percy expanded his work in that area. The pattern remained the same: discussing the issues and suggesting broad outlines for possible programs. By 1975 Percy's approach to national and international affairs had been clearly established.

Charles Percy's future is no more easily charted than that of any able, mentally alert, physically sound, and opportunistic public servant. Being in the right place at the right time with the right issue could make all the difference. Although his campaign for the 1976 presidential nomination was discontinued when Gerald Ford became president, it could be reactivated at any time. Percy remains ready if Ford falters or Percy feels he must mount a campaign on principle. In the immediate wake of Ford's elevation to the presidency, those possibilities seemed remote, but persons who have survived politics at the national level in the 1970s know how rapidly the picture can change.

One factor that Percy must consider should he change his mind about seeking the presidency in 1976 is the ghost of Richard Nixon. The 1976 Republican National Convention will be the first in a quarter of a century in which Nixon has not had a key role. When Nixon resigned the presidency, he still retained a hard core of Republican support across the nation, which, in some national public-opinion polls, amounted to 25 percent of the electorate. The danger to Percy is that this sizable proportion of the population could be substantially represented at the Republican convention in the form of delegate votes. It would not take much to remind pro-Nixon delegates of Percy's opposition to the former president's programs and the senator's independence of the Nixon administration. Under what might now be considered bizarre circumstances, Richard Nixon could indeed make good on his word not to let Charles H. Percy become president if he could help it.

If Percy does not become a presidential or vice-presidential candidate, his energy and direction would be concentrated on his Senate career until the completion of his second term in 1978. In the past Percy has said that, barring a bid for higher office, he would be satisfied with running for reelection in 1978 and then retiring after completion of a third term. If that were to occur, Percy would finish his senatorial career at the age of 65, which is still considered the prime of life by many senators who have served well into their 70s or beyond.

Percy's reelection to a third Senate term cannot be viewed as automatic. In a primary, he would have to weather the usual threat of a Republican opponent backed by many Illinois party traditionalists, who will never give up trying to defeat him. A general-election challenge could come from any one of several Democrats who are becoming influential in the state. If Governor Daniel Walker seeks and is elected to a second term in 1976, he might decide to make a bid for Percy's Senate seat.

Looking beyond 1978, Percy would have to be considered a possibility for the Republican presidential nomination in 1980. At age 61, he would be considered not quite "too old" to seek the nomination. In the past Percy related to friends and associates that he had a plan for his life that included spending 25 years in private life, with Bell & Howell, and 25 years in public life. Counting from 1960 when Percy began to withdraw from his corporate endeavors, a third Senate term would fulfill his 25-year plan for public service. The same would be true if Percy were elected president in 1976 and served two terms.

If the thought of changing careers ever has crossed Percy's mind in recent years, he has not mentioned it publicly. He has said that he would relinquish his Senate seat only if he were bored or if there were someone "better to follow me." He has considered something as vague as "I'd change if there were a better opportunity to do something or some compelling personal reason." But he quickly adds that he is not bored. Percy's oldest daughter, Sharon, cannot imagine her father forsaking a continued career in elective public life even if a good opportunity did present itself.

A third Senate term could have a major advantage for Percy: seniority. In 1974 he moved up the seniority ladder when several Senate Republicans either retired or lost their bids for reelection. After eight years in the Senate, Percy remarked that more than half its membership had changed during his years in Washington. Many of the older senators who have blocked his proposals and spoken disparagingly of him would have left the political arena by 1978 and the years after. Percy could conceivably ascend to the position of Senate floor leader, but this possibility seems unlikely because of his style and his feelings, publicly expressed, about the job: "As I have observed, a leadership role necessitates a person's physical presence on the floor. It is not always productive listening to the rhetoric of a floor debate, and I find I can make more productive use of my time." It is possible that in time Percy could become the ranking Republican on the Senate Foreign Relations Committee, a role he would savor and gladly give up other Senate duties to hold.

Percy's relationship with politicians and party members in Illinois will remain a question no matter how successful he becomes in Washington. His independent appeal at the polls should serve him well in another Senate election, but it would have less impact in the 1976 state primary election because the presidential-preference vote is cast along party lines. Despite the unpredictability of individuals, Percy maintains solid support among those who contribute to election campaigns. This readily available source of funds makes it possible for Percy to mount a presidential campaign on relatively short notice. It is also a security blanket for Percy's political ventures in Illinois. When the senator was seeking funds for his presidential campaign, he appealed to the same individuals who had contributed to his Senate reelection, and they responded as they had in 1972. Three months after shutting down his campaign in 1974, Percy, through members of the exploratory committee, sent letters to persons who had contributed more than $100. They were asked what Percy should do about continuing the exploratory effort and what should be done with the small amount of money that remained. Fewer than 5 percent of the respondents said Percy should disband the committee and distribute the money. The remainder urged him to keep the committee intact and hold on to the campaign contributions; a few urged him to reactivate the committee immediately. These people, who would have been part of the nucleus of Percy's financial and voter support for the future, must have seen the potential for national leadership in his candidacy.

Illinois Republican leaders do not seem to see this same potential in Percy, either on a national or a state level. But, as a matter of fact, Percy is not interested in the role of state party leader. He does, however, need to keep himself visible in Illinois politics, and one way of doing so is to remain active in state party affairs. This will be easy for Percy to do until Republicans can fill the void in party leadership by electing a governor again. But Percy will step into the vacuum when necessary. After the Illinois Republicans suffered heavy losses in the 1974 elections, he called for the formation of a task force to revive the party. In explaining his lack of interest in the role of state party leader, Percy said: "No one can run a party from Washington. Dirksen couldn't do it, and I can't. All I wanted to do was provide some sense of direction and to help them find candidates for 1976. I was elected to be senator and not a political boss." The ideal state party leader is an elected governor, Percy said.

In the Senate, where Percy does desire to be recognized as a leader, he seems to have made some headway. He is recognized by his colleagues—Democrats and Republicans alike—as having a good staff, as being a hard worker, and as having the perseverance that is required in the legislative process. His instincts for timely legislation have been good and, in fact, have angered some senators because his legislative actions seemed too opportunistic. Percy has become more mature in his articulation of issues and thus has improved his public image. His leadership potential could receive more recognition in the future as longtime Senate residents are forced into retirement either by advancing age or by the voters. If moderates among Republicans gain strength in the Senate—Senators Jacob Javits, Richard Schweiker, and Charles Mathias were reelected in 1974—Percy could be a beneficiary. But those who hoped for a moderate surge in 1975 were jolted when Javits lost a bid for the chairmanship of the Republican caucus to conservative Carl Curtis.

It is not enough to have home-based voter strength, financial resources, acceptance in major portions of the party, and a handsome face. A senator's achievements must be visible and of lasting value. Try as he may, Percy has not been able to project the public image of a key legislator. The full measure of leadership recognition by the public and in Congress rests to some degree with an awareness of a legislator's accomplishments in improving the quality of the everyday lives of the people.

A story that has surfaced repeatedly throughout his career in public service is probably as accurate a mid-career perspective on the political future of Charles H. Percy as can be found.

In 1962 Percy visited with President John F. Kennedy in Washington. The two discussed mutual ambitions, and Kennedy is supposed to have asked Percy about his plans for the future. Percy replied, "One of the exciting things about the future, Mr. President, is that none of us can really prescribe what will happen to our lives."

NOTES ON SOURCES

A number of episodes in this book were based on information obtained in interviews of persons, many in public life, who wished to remain anonymous. If, in the judgment of the author, the request seemed justified, confidentiality was promised. The desire for anonymity was strongest among persons in Washington, D.C., where the author conducted several of the interviews on Percy's Senate career and his relationships with presidents and their aides. Most of the members of the Senate and House who were interviewed asked for and received a "no-quote" privilege. But the majority of the noncongressional individuals interviewed spoke for the record and without restrictions. Frequently those people who requested anonymity suggested other knowledgeable persons who did not ask for such privileges.

One of the more valuable sources of information on Percy's activities in Washington and on the background of congressional issues was Congressional Quarterly. Almost all the statistical information regarding congressional actions came from CQ publications.

In the following chapter-by-chapter notes, individual books are mentioned for their contributions on specific subjects. Some of these were used throughout as general sources. Two of the more helpful books on Percy's early political life—*Charles Percy: Strong New Voice from Illinois* by Martha Cleveland and *Charles Percy of Illinois* by David Murray—were written shortly after Percy was elected to the Senate in 1966. Supplementing these was *The Republican Establishment* by Stephen Hess and David S. Broder. The bibliography of Robert Howard's *Illinois: A History of the Prairie State*, one of the most complete single-volume histories of Illinois, as well as the text itself provided a substantial amount of information.

Clipping files from the newspaper library of the *Decatur* (Illinois) *Herald and Review* and numerous articles from Chicago daily newspapers supplied information that was used throughout the book. Also helpful were the author's personal observations of Illinois political activities, events in Washington, and national political conventions as well as the material gathered since 1968 for his newspaper column. Interviews with Percy from 1968 to the present provided specific information not available from other sources. Special sessions with the senator specifically relating to the book occurred in May, August, and November of 1974 and in February of 1975.

CHAPTER 1

Mrs. Vivian Jacobson's analysis of Percy occurred in 1974 in Chicago. Information on Percy's Depression recollections and his father's experiences during that time came from several sources, one of which is *Growing Old in the Country of the Young* by Charles Percy and Charles Mangel. Stories of Percy's money-making activities as a young man were confirmed by Percy and members of his family and staff. In a May, 1974, interview Percy recounted the story of the dinner at Joseph McNabb's house. The story of George Dickerson's business and its possible confusion with Bell &

Howell, which has appeared in a variety of publications, was confirmed by Percy. Information on Percy's management style and the reaction of Bell & Howell executives to his promotions came in part from an interview with William L. Johnson, who served as personnel manager of the company during this period.

CHAPTER II

During an interview Sharon Percy Rockefeller spoke of her father's efforts in rearing three small children and discussed her husband, John D. Rockefeller IV. Principal sources on the murder of Valerie Percy and subsequent events included interviews with Percy and Thomas J. Houser and stories, written by Arthur M. Petacque and Hugh F. Hough, that appeared in the *Chicago Sun-Times* in 1973. Percy's comments on the 1974 capital-punishment bill were found in the *Congressional Record*. Mrs. Loraine Percy expressed her feelings about financial privacy in a conversation with the author. Information from Arthur Anderson & Company appeared in Congressional Quarterly. In a May, 1974, interview Percy revealed the current estimate of his trust holdings. Travel details came from correspondence with Congressional Quarterly and from the *Congressional Record*. Percy related the "telephone-workman" story.

CHAPTER III

The *Chicago Tribune* printed the quote about Percy's piety. In a May, 1974, interview Percy discussed his religion and related much of the information about his wife. The quote about Percy's physical fitness came from correspondence with Peter G. Peterson. During a conversation A. A. Smyser, editor of the *Honolulu Star-Bulletin*, remarked on the impression he had of Percy during the senator's trip to the Islands. Percy's exchange with Marvin H. Pigg, president of the National Hearing Aid Society, was reported in wire-service dispatches and in Chicago newspapers. William C. Groninger, a Downstate reporter, wrote the author of his experiences in addressing Percy as "Chuck" and described the incident that showed how sensitive Percy was about his height. Especially helpful information on Percy's image and personality came from interviews with Thomas J. Houser, Milton Rakove, and H. G. ("Skinny") Taylor; this material was supplemented by data from the 1972 Ralph Nader election profile. Other sources for personal information about Percy were the *Chicago Tribune Magazine* and the now-defunct *Chicagoan* magazine. The author personally observed the incident involving Percy and Adlai E. Stevenson that occurred prior to the filming of their television show, "Your Senators Report," a series of short public-service programs that usually presented the two Illinois senators in a question-and-answer session with newsmen. The information on Mrs. Percy's attitude toward Roman Pucinski came from her and also from conversations with Percy staff members.

CHAPTER IV

The major sources of information on Percy's relationship with Dwight D. Eisenhower were the files at the Eisenhower Library in Abilene, Kansas. The bulk of pertinent correspondence is in the White House Central File and in the papers of such former White House aides as Sherman Adams. Background material on the selection of members for the Republican Committee on Program and Progress is also in the files as are the reports of committee meetings. Some data also came from the files of Bertha S. Adkins, under secretary of the Department of Health, Education, and Welfare. Percy's personal recollections supplemented the information from these sources and from the senator's December 17, 1970, Columbia University oral history project interview, a transcript of which is in the Eisenhower Library. Helpful books on the Eisenhower years, with portions pertinent to events in which Percy participated, include *Firsthand Report: The Inside Story of the Eisenhower Administration* by Sherman Adams; *Eisenhower: Portrait of the Hero* by Peter Lyon; *Eisenhower and the American Crusades* by Herbert Parmet; *The Republicans: A History of Their Party* by Malcolm C. Moos; and *Presidential Nominating Politics in 1952: The Middle West* (the 4th of 5 volumes) edited by Moos, Paul T. David, and Ralph M. Goldman.

Some information on the deliberations of the Republican Committee on Program and Progress came from a telephone interview and correspondence with Cornelius P. Cotter of the University of Wisconsin-Milwaukee, who served as executive director of the committee. His chapter in *Politics Without Power* (by Cotter and Bernard Hennessy) is rich in detail about the individuals involved and the work of the committee. Portions of *The Economics of the Political Parties* by Seymour Harris deal with the contradictions between the committee's report on economic policy and the programs of the Eisenhower administration.

Activities of the 1960 platform committee involving Percy were recalled by Karl Lamb, a professor at the University of California at Santa Cruz, who served as executive secretary for the subcommittee on civil rights. His recollections of Percy's handling of the platform committee after the Nixon-Rockefeller compromises in the Fourteen Point Compact of Fifth Avenue were especially keen. Other versions of Percy's involvement came from *Inside Politics: The National Conventions, 1960* edited by Paul Tillett; *The Making of the President, 1960* by Theodore H. White; and the Cleveland book on Percy. Some details on the Fourteen Point Compact of Fifth Avenue were found in each of these books and in *The Real Rockefeller* by Frank Gervasi and *Six Crises* by Richard M. Nixon. Comments by Percy were made during an interview.

CHAPTER V

The Shadow of Blooming Grove by Francis Russell gives a detailed description of the Illinois involvement in the Republican National Convention of 1920. Also helpful was *The Autobiography of William Allen White.* Voting patterns in Illinois from the Civil War through 1964 are discussed in *Midwest Politics* by John Fenton and in *Illinois* by Robert Howard. The information on Illinois Republicanism in the 1930s, 1940s, and 1950s came from a variety of sources, the most useful of which were Stephen Becker's *Marshall Field III*, Walter Trohan's "My Life with the Colonel" in the 1959 *Journal of the Illinois State Historical Society*, Thomas Littlewood's *Horner of Illinois*, and Frank Waldrop's *McCormick of Chicago.* Interviews with Illinois Republicans—namely, Attorney General William J. Scott, Milton Rakove, Thomas J. Houser, and U.S. Representative Philip M. Crane—provided valuable information. The *Illinois Blue Book* for several different years and the *Illinois Fact Book and Historical Almanac, 1673–1968* as well as Neil MacNeil's *Dirksen: Portrait of a Public Man* and Malcolm C. Moos's *The Republicans* filled in specific details.

Much of the information about the candidacy of Joseph Meek came from correspondence and other material found in the files of the Eisenhower Library in Abilene, Kansas, and from newspaper clippings. Specific events in the relationship between Eisenhower and Meek—for example, their meeting at the Illinois State Fair—were well covered by Chicago newspapers. The Illinois perspective on McCarthyism came from interviews with politicians and observers such as retired newspaperman David V. Felts, who was most helpful.

General information on Republican conservatism was found in *The Future of Conservatism* by M. Stanton Evans and in *The Emerging Republican Majority* by Kevin Phillips. The surveys conducted by Market Opinion Research in 1970 and 1973 and made available in part through the office of U.S. Representative John B.

Anderson of Illinois were used to compare political party identification in those years.

The U.S. census reports for 1970 and subsequent updated versions provided specific demographic information on congressional districts. Voting statistics came from compilations of election results in Illinois. Substantial sources for background information on Congress included the Ralph Nader 1972 election profile and the *Almanac of American Politics* by Michael Barone, Grant Ujifusa, and Grant Matthews. Congressmen Edward R. Madigan of the Illinois 21st District and Philip M. Crane of the 12th District were especially willing to discuss congressional activities. The story of Percy and Leslie C. Arends's common birth date was related by reporter Robert W. Sink. Other information on Arends came from the *Wall Street Journal* and Congressional Quarterly. The ratings of the political philosophies of selected public officials are published every year by various organizations.

The best sources for the history of Chicago newspapers were *Political Influence* by Edward C. Banfield, *In the Fullness of Time* by Paul H. Douglas, *McCormick of Chicago* by Frank Waldrop, and *Marshall Field III* by Stephen Becker. *Daley of Chicago* by William Gleason contributed to this section and to other discussions throughout the book of Chicago politics and the Republican party. Key interviews were with Thomas J. Houser; Richard Hainey, formerly of the Tribune Company; H. Richard Ciccone of the Associated Press in Chicago; H. G. ("Skinny") Taylor; and U.S. Representative Paul Simon of Illinois. Details of the Percy-George Tagge relationship came from William J. Scott and from Banfield's *Political Influence* and Neal Peirce's *The Megastates of America*.

CHAPTER VI

General background information on the politics of the mid-1960s appears in Neal Peirce's *The Megastates of America* and Kevin Phillips's *The Emerging Republican Majority*. Particularly valuable sources for the details of the 1964 gubernatorial campaign were the newspaper files of the *Decatur* (Illinois) *Herald* and *Review* and conversations in 1974 with Percy and Attorney General William J. Scott. Some information on the purge of the West Side bloc appeared in a September, 1964, *Time* magazine article on Percy. A number of sources provided a perspective on the 1964 Republican National Convention: *The Making of the President, 1964* by Theodore H. White gave an overview; and *The Vantage Point: Perspectives of the Presidency, 1963–1969* by Lyndon B. Johnson, *The Real Rockefeller* by Frank Gervasi, and *Barry Goldwater: Portrait of an Arizonan* by Edwin McDowell provided specific details. An academic account of the convention appears in *The National Election of 1964*, edited by Milton Cummings, which was also valuable for its thorough explanation of the actions of the moderates. Various articles from the *New York Times* describe party platform battles in detail.

Paul H. Douglas's personal financial statement for 1965 was reported in newspapers. Percy's efforts in the black areas of Chicago during the 1966 senatorial campaign are described in Douglas's *In the Fullness of Time*. This volume and *Dirksen* by Neil MacNeil contain information on the all-Asian conference. Percy's final comment on his contest with Douglas came from correspondence with the author in 1972.

Information on the preliminaries to the 1968 convention relating to the favorite-son and delegation-chairmanship discussions came from Associated Press dispatches and from articles in Lindsay-Schaub newspapers. Percy's recollections of his meeting with Richard M. Nixon varied significantly from the accounts of Milton S. Eisenhower. In his correspondence and in his book *The President Is Calling*, Eisenhower does not mention any specific conversation about Percy's immediate political ambitions. However, in a 1974 interview, Percy declared that his political future was a prime topic of discussion. Aside from Percy, Mrs. Rita Hauser and Thomas J. Houser were the main sources of information needed to piece together the story of Nixon's consideration of Percy for the vice-presidential nomination in 1968. Mrs. Hauser's involvement in the Nixon campaign made her version especially reliable. In *Catch the Falling Flag*, Richard Whalen discusses the vice-presidential story; and in *Before the Fall: An Inside View of the Pre-Watergate White House*, William Safire confirms that Percy was seriously considered for the vice-presidential nomination. *Nixon Agonistes* by Garry Wills describes the Percy-Nixon relationship at this time. Percy's statements about Nelson A. Rockefeller appeared in the *New York Times*. The issues of the 1968 pre-nomination campaign and the Republican National Convention are explained in *The Party's Over* by David S. Broder; *An American Melodrama* by Lewis Chester, Godfrey Hodgson, and Bruce Page; and *The Real Majority* by Richard M. Scammon and Ben J. Wattenberg. A basic work is *The Making of the President, 1968* by Theodore H. White.

The details of Percy's 1971 Washington party for Illinois Republicans came from interviews with H. G. ("Skinny") Taylor and Thomas J. Houser. Newspaper accounts and the author's personal observations and his interviews with Percy staff members were the sources for the information on the 1972 campaign. Common Cause Monitoring Project, Congressional Quarterly, and reports filed by Percy in compliance with the 1972 election law provided data on the contributions to Percy's 1972 campaign. Houser's explanation of his 1972 activities for the reelection of Nixon occurred in a 1973 interview.

CHAPTER VII

Percy discussed his views on free trade in a May, 1974, interview. The story of his involvement with the Fair Employment Practices Commission for Illinois came from the same interview and was confirmed in part by former speech writer Milton Rakove. State editors and politicians discussed the partisan background of Illinois newspapers that have a longtime association with Republican causes. Percy's 1970 defense of his Republicanism appeared in his correspondence with the author. In a telephone conversation Cornelius P. Cotter gave the author his perspective on the Republican Committee on Program and Progress.

Comments on Percy's stand on civil rights issues early in his career came from Rakove. *In the Fullness of Time* by Paul H. Douglas supplied additional information on Percy's mid-1960s civil rights actions. The stand Percy has taken in Congress on civil rights issues was reported by the Lindsay-Schaub newspapers in articles on the 1972 senatorial campaign. Also providing background information on Percy's position was the 1972 Ralph Nader election profile. The author personally observed and reported on the senator's activities at the 1972 Republican National Convention. The quotation on James L. Buckley's party affiliation was taken from a transcript of "Your Senators Report," the Percy and Adlai E. Stevenson television series.

CHAPTER VIII

Philip M. Crane, member of the U.S. House of Representatives from Illinois, discussed Congress in a 1974 interview. Data on new senators came from several interviews, including some with Adlai E. Stevenson. George Reedy's statement on Congress was made in Decatur, Illinois, in 1974. Some information on Percy's 1967 Vietnam trip came from a conversation with Kenneth V. Schmid of Chicago, who accompanied Percy. Peter G. Peterson commented in an interview on Percy's early tendency to cover too many issues rather than focusing on just a few. Of particular aid in providing background information on the Senate was *Who Runs Congress?* (a Ralph Nader Congress Project) by Mark J. Green, James M. Fallows, and David R. Zwick. Also adding perspective on Congress were reports by Common Cause and material found in *The Party's Over* by David S. Broder and in *Dirksen* by Neil MacNeil. Some of Percy's remarks on committee work appeared in the Ralph Nader 1972 election profile. Percy's colleagues were interviewed about his work style in the Senate. The senator's complaint about working on the Appropriations Committee was made at a 1971 meeting with Lindsay-Schaub newspaper editors. The *Congressional Record* provided some data on congressional proposals to open up committee meetings.

The 1974 statements by Barry M. Goldwater on Percy's presidential chances were taken from several wire-service dispatches. Percy's Washington staff discussed the senator's role in the passage of the Drug Abuse Office and Treatment Act, and their information was confirmed by Congressional Quarterly. George D. Aiken, former senator from Vermont, commented on Percy's Senate activities in a 1974 interview, which particularly emphasized Percy's May, 1973, resolution to appoint a special Watergate prosecutor. Percy spoke about the Springer dam project in conversations with the author. William L. Springer's perspective on congressional relationships was taken from his letter to the author. In an article he wrote for the Lindsay-Schaub newspapers in 1966, Percy told how he best could represent Illinois in Congress. Senator Adlai Stevenson's comments on federal programs for Illinois were made in public statements and private correspondence. Percy explained his 1972 vote on revenue sharing in a telephone conversation. Stevenson's attitude on revenue sharing has been recorded in studies by the President's Advisory Commission on Intergovernmental Relations.

Richard B. Ogilvie provided background information on Percy's efforts to get an increase in federal welfare funding for Illinois. The information on the allotment of money for Percy's Senate office operations came from correspondence with Joseph A. Farrell. News accounts and editorials related the problems that arose when Percy's supporters began to raise funds in 1967 to help the senator pay for the operation of his Washington office. Reporter Robert W. Sink filled in some background on Farrell from interview notes. During visits to Washington in 1972, 1973, and 1974, the author talked with congressional staff members. Viewpoints on Farrell from Percy supporters in Illinois were offered by Thomas J. Houser and H. G. ("Skinny") Taylor.

Percy's opinions on productivity councils were taken from articles by him and from the *Congressional Record*. The responses of labor and business to these councils were found in correspondence released by Percy. His exchange with Lester W. Brann, Jr., over the consumer protection agency also came from this correspondence and from the public statements of both men. Gerald R. Ford's comments on the "liberal" nature of the consumer-protection proposal appeared in an Associated Press dispatch. Accounts of Percy's 1971 tour with Senator George S. McGovern are discussed in *Growing Old in the Country of the Young* by Charles Percy and Charles Mangel. *Time* magazine, the *Washington Post*, and the financial pages of the *Chicago Tribune* and the *Chicago Sun-Times* carried reports of Percy's role in the Congressional Budget Act of 1974. Senator Stevenson discussed with the author the Senate attitude toward Nixon's 1972 impoundment of funds.

CHAPTER IX

The principal source of information on Everett M. Dirksen, particularly his personal relationships with colleagues and associates, was Neil MacNeil's *Dirksen*. The background information on early Illinois politics came mainly from *Illinois* by Robert Howard, *Horner of Illinois* by Thomas Littlewood, *Marshall Field III* by Stephen Becker, *The Republicans* by Malcolm C. Moos, and *In the Fullness of Time* by Paul H. Douglas. In interviews Thomas J. Houser, Peter G. Peterson, and George D. Aiken talked about Percy's senatorial relationship with Dirksen. *The Party's Over* by David

S. Broder discusses Dirksen's influence on party affairs in the early 1960s. Percy's recollection of the 1965 political agreement with Dirksen came from a May, 1974, interview. During a conversation with the author, Cornelius P. Cotter offered his observations of Harold Rainville in action during deliberations of the Republican Committee on Program and Progress. Some specifics on the relationship of Dirksen and Lyndon B. Johnson were found in the former president's memoir *The Vantage Point*. Dirksen's statements on the Vietnam war are chronicled in the *New York Times* and the *Washington Post*. Some of Dirksen's attitudes on Congress and public service are described in *Who Runs Congress?* (a Ralph Nader Congress Project) by Mark J. Green, James M. Fallows, and David R. Zwick. Percy's statement after Dirksen's death is from material in the Library of Congress.

Much of the material on Adlai E. Stevenson came from personal discussions with the Democratic senator. Percy commented on his relationship with Stevenson in interviews held in May and August of 1974 and in February of 1975. Some of their positions on Vietnam issues came from transcripts of their television appearances. A study by the *Chicago Sun-Times* provided information on Percy's judicial appointments.

CHAPTER X

In a May, 1974, interview Percy recalled the reactions of Richard M. Nixon and members of the administration to his vote against G. Harrold Carswell. Percy spoke in the same interview about how his negative vote on ABM cost him the assignment to the National Home Ownership Foundation board. In a letter to the Lindsay-Schaub newspapers, Percy explained his decision to vote for the District of Columbia crime bill that contained the no-knock provision. The early years of Nixon's administration are described in *Nixon in the White House: The Frustration of Power* by Rowland Evans and Robert D. Novak and *Nixon Agonistes* by Garry Wills. Of particular assistance in understanding Nixon's pre-presidential years was *The Resurrection of Richard Nixon* by Jules Witcover. Percy's positions on Vietnam as well as Nixon's statements and policies on U.S. involvement with the Saigon government came from *New York Times* files, David Halberstam's *The Best and the Brightest*, and Theodore H. White's *The Making of the President, 1972*. The source of Percy's comment on a timetable for withdrawal was a letter to the Lindsay-Schaub newspapers. Quotations on withdrawal and U.S. intentions in Vietnam were taken from transcripts of television programs. A special perspective on the Cambodian incursion and Nixon and the campus riots of 1970 is included in *The Imperial Presidency* by Arthur Schlesinger, Jr., and *A New Road for America: Major Policy Statements, March 1970 to October 1971*. Percy's remark on the 1972 bombing of North Vietnam was made to the author.

Specific details about Percy's difficulty with Nixon's staff are confirmed in *An American Life: One Man's Road to Watergate* by Jeb Stuart Magruder. He offers details of the letter-telegram campaign against Percy. Other information on this incident is included in the documents of the Senate Watergate investigating committee. In an interview Percy spoke at length about his conversation with Nixon in 1970. Peter G. Peterson, in a conversation with the author, confirmed some of the information on Percy's trouble with Nixon staff members.

Some background on Watergate came from *All the President's Men* by Bob Woodward and Carl Bernstein. Printed news reports provided key dates. The surveillance of Percy during the Watergate period was brought out during an interview. The author witnessed some of the activity that occurred early in May, 1973, involving Percy's Senate resolution. Senator Adlai E. Stevenson's reaction came during a conversation with the author. Nixon's remark about Percy on March 15, 1974, in Chicago, was taken from Chicago newspapers. Selections from the correspondence between Percy and Leon Jaworski were published in the *Congressional Record*.

CHAPTER XI

Thomas J. Houser's feeling about the premature announcement of the exploratory committee was expressed in a 1974 interview. Data on initial donations to the committee came from a June, 1973, report to the secretary of the Senate. The committee's income and expense figures are for the period up to the resignation of Richard M. Nixon. Details of the campaign strategy are from the Bailey report (firm of Bailey, Deardourff & Eyre) and from conversations with Percy and Houser. The report from California about Percy's campaign progress appeared in the *Chicago Tribune*. Percy and Houser explained the Illinois strategy. Wire services and the *Washington Star-News* reported the April, 1974, meetings with congressmen and aides. Harris poll figures pitting Republicans against Senator Edward Kennedy were used by Percy in a mailing to exploratory-committee contributors. The national poll taken just before Nixon's resignation was by Gallup.

The milk-industry story regarding a Percy aide and Ford is in *Jerry Ford Up Close* by Bud Vestal and *Gerald Ford and the Future of the Presidency* by J. F. terHorst. Percy's press secretary, Thomas Flaherty, related the story of the senator's invitation to a White House state dinner.

In an interview Percy commented about a strong defense and about the military budget. A document prepared by Percy's staff critiqued the research and development function of the Department of Defense. *Kissinger* by Marvin and Bernard Kalb gives details of the 1950s study group for the Rockefeller Brothers Fund. Percy's comments on Henry Kissinger's brand of diplomacy were made in November, 1974. The senator talked about Adlai E. Stevenson's criticism of Kissinger in February, 1975. In a story he wrote for United Press International, Percy referred to the attitudes of Third World countries in the United Nations. Percy wrote in 1972 of U.S. policies in the Far East in a report for the Foreign Relations Committee entitled "Economic and Political Developments in the Far East." Some general foreign affairs background was offered by Alex Seith of Chicago, a former president of the Chicago Council on Foreign Relations.

Accounts of Percy's 1975 trip to the Middle East are principally from Chicago and Washington newspapers, with Percy supplementing the facts in an interview. Adding valuable details via telephone conversations and correspondence was Mrs. Vivian Jacobson of Chicago. Also helping with background material were Joseph A. Farrell and Thomas Flaherty of Percy's staff.

Peter G. Peterson's troubles with Nixon are explained in several books, including *Before the Fall* by William Safire. Details of Percy's proposal for energy conservation are from statements issued by his office and from bills prepared for Congress.

The story of the 1962 conversation between Percy and John F. Kennedy, which occurred in Washington, came from *The Republican Establishment* by Stephen Hess and David S. Broder.

INDEX

249